COMING BACK TO JAIL

COMING BACK TO JAIL

WOMEN, TRAUMA, AND CRIMINALIZATION

ELIZABETH COMACK

FERNWOOD PUBLISHING
HALIFAX & WINNIPEG

Editing: Robert Clarke
Cover image: Judith Baldwin
Cover design: Jesse Warkentin
Printed and bound in Canada

Published by Fernwood Publishing
32 Oceanvista Lane, Black Point, Nova Scotia, B0J 1B0
and 748 Broadway Avenue, Winnipeg, Manitoba, R3G 0X3
www.fernwoodpublishing.ca

Fernwood Publishing Company Limited gratefully acknowledges the financial support
of the Government of Canada, the Manitoba Department of Culture, Heritage and
Tourism under the Manitoba Publishers Marketing Assistance Program and the
Province of Manitoba, through the Book Publishing Tax Credit, for our publishing
program. We are pleased to work in partnership with the Province of Nova Scotia
to develop and promote our creative industries for the benefit of all Nova Scotians.
We acknowledge the support of the Canada Council for the Arts, which last year
invested $153 million to bring the arts to Canadians throughout the country.

Library and Archives Canada Cataloguing in Publication

Comack, Elizabeth, 1952-, author
Coming back to jail : women, trauma and criminalization / Elizabeth Comack.

Includes bibliographical references and index.
ISBN 978-1-77363-010-6 (softcover)

1. Women prisoners--Canada--Case studies. 2. Imprisonment--Psychological
aspects--Case studies. 3. Post-traumatic stress disorder--Case studies. 4. Justice,
Administration of--Canada--Case studies. I. Title.

HV9507.C62 2018   365'.6082   C2017-907900-X

CONTENTS

ACKNOWLEDGEMENTS

Writing this book has been far from an individual enterprise. Despite all of the time I have spent alone in front of my computer, searching for relevant sources or struggling with words, many more people have had a hand in bringing this book into being.

First and foremost are the forty-two women who were willing to take a risk and trust me with their life stories. Several of the women commented that they were motivated by a desire to help other women who found themselves in similar situations. My hope is that in sharing their stories, and in my efforts to make comprehensible what has happened to them, I have done justice to their trust and their motivation.

Gaining access to prisoners is often a difficult undertaking. In my case, that access was made possible by the willingness of several individuals to accommodate my request to meet with the women, and I thank them for their support. Trevor Markesteyn (Chief Correctional Psychologist at Manitoba Justice), Margo Lee (Women's Correctional Centre Superintendent), and Bridget Kozyra (WCC Assistant Superintendent) were instrumental in facilitating my access to the Centre. Theresa Barrault (WCC Program Coordinator) helped in organizing my meetings with the women who had expressed an interest in participating in the study.

The research that underpins this book was made possible by a grant from the Social Sciences and Humanities Research Council of Canada (SSHRC) to the Manitoba Research Alliance (MRA) for our project "Partnering for Change: Community-Based Solutions for Aboriginal and Inner-city Poverty." I am indebted to my colleagues at the MRA for their support of the study on which this book is based. The book itself has been published with the help of a grant from the Federation for the Humanities and Social

Sciences through the Awards to Scholarly Publications Program (ASPP), using funds provided by the SSHRC.

I also had the benefit of input from a number of colleagues. Jim Silver, Laureen Snider, Debra Parkes, Shoshana Pollack, Gayle MacDonald, and Diane Crocker took time from their busy schedules to read either all or portions of the text and provide me with thoughtful feedback. It goes without saying, though, that any errors or omissions that remain in the book are my own doing.

Kathy Jaworski had the arduous task of transcribing the forty-two interviews. The women's stories were not easy to hear, and I appreciate the difficult time that Kathy spent alone at her computer in completing that task.

As a university professor I have had the privilege of working with a host of bright and talented students over the years. One of those students, Cerah Dubé, put her skills to work in assisting with the reference check and compiling the index for the book.

My words do not always come across as clearly as I would like them to. As I tell my students, writing is a practice, something that we have to work at continually. My writing practice has benefited enormously over the years from my association with Robert Clarke, whom I like to refer to as "my copy editor." As with previous projects, Robert put his skills to work in making *Coming Back to Jail* more readable, and I thank him profusely.

The impetus for this book emerged from one of my previous books, *Women in Trouble* (1996) — and my "soul sister," Judith Baldwin, created the cover art for that book. Since then Judith has moved from drawing to working with fabric. I am forever indebted to Judith for the amazing artwork that she produced for the cover of *Coming Back to Jail*.

And then there's the folks at Fernwood Publishing. My work as an academic committed to realizing social justice has been incredibly enriched by my association with this independent Canadian book publisher that produces "critical books for critical thinkers." Errol Sharpe, Beverley Rach, Candida Hadley, Nancy Malek, Heather Fillmore, Debbie Mathers, Curran Faris, and James Patterson are all to be commended for the heavy lifting they do in bringing books from an idea to print and making sure those books get to their readers. As always, special mention is due to my publisher, Wayne Antony. I worked closely with Wayne in producing *Women in Trouble* in the 1990s. Since that time I have come to rely heavily on his critical mind and keen sensibilities in pretty much everything that I write — and to the point where anything of merit that I've managed to accomplish in this life is pretty much because of him. "Thanks" doesn't seem to quite cut it, but you should know by now how important you are to me, Wayne.

Doing research and writing a book that focuses on trauma are challenging endeavours, especially when trauma is also happening in your own life. Unlike many of the women featured on the pages of this book, I have been blessed with a strong support system to help me through traumatic times. On that score, thanks are due in particular to my "little sister," Aly. You are truly a wise woman and I am grateful for your presence in my life. I am also eternally hopeful that girls and women will not encounter the kinds of trauma that the women at the heart of this book have had to endure. As this book goes into production, I am blessed by the arrival of my first grandchild, Joni Elizabeth. May the future look brighter for your generation.

Elizabeth Comack
November, 2017

CHAPTER ONE

WOMEN IN TROUBLE

S arah and I had last met over two decades ago. In 1992 she was incarcerated at the Portage Correctional Institution (PCI), which at the time was
Manitoba's primary custodial facility for women. I was visiting the Portage
jail to conduct interviews with the women being held there — and in particular to explore the connections between the women's histories of abuse
and their conflicts with the law. In all, twenty-four women — including
Sarah — agreed to meet with me and share their life stories. The interviews
formed the basis of a book published in 1996. Taking my lead from a sug-
gestion made by one of the women, I called the book *Women in Trouble*.

Women in Trouble endeavoured to bring together two important social
issues: male violence against women and the invisibility of incarcerated
women in correctional policies and practice. In the early 1990s, largely
as a result of feminist politics and research, Canadians were beginning
to acknowledge the widespread and pervasive presence of male violence
against women. The Violence Against Women Survey (VAWS) — the first
national survey of its kind — showed that one-half of Canadian women had
experienced at least one incident of physical or sexual violence since the age
of sixteen; one in four women had experienced physical or sexual violence
at the hands of a male partner (Statistics Canada 1993).

While the high incidence of violence was becoming established, little was
known about the full impact of that violence on women's everyday lives.
That was especially the case for women who ended up in prison. As Ellen
Adelberg and Claudia Currie (1987) so aptly put it, incarcerated women
were deemed to be "too few to count." Their numbers paled in comparison
to the number of men who ended up behind bars — a condition that ostensibly provided the rationale for designing prisons with men only in mind
and thereby perpetuating the invisibility of criminalized women.

Studies such as the VAWS had documented the nature and extent of the abuse encountered by Canadian women; and we were also beginning to learn about how abuse invaded the lives of women in conflict with the law. The Canadian Task Force on Federally Sentenced Women, for example, found that of 191 women interviewed, over two-thirds (68 percent) said they had been physically abused as children or adults; half of them (53 percent) reported being sexually abused at some stage in their lives. Among Indigenous women the figures were considerably higher: 90 percent (35) said they had been physically abused during their lives, usually regularly over long periods, and 61 percent (24) sexually abused (Shaw et al. 1991: vii, 31). A study conducted by the Native Women's Association of Canada (Sugar and Fox 1989: 6) found that "27 of the 39 women (69%) interviewed described experiences of violence: rape, regular sexual abuse, the witnessing of a murder, watching our mothers repeatedly beaten, beatings in juvenile detention centres at the hands of staff and other children." Of these 39 women, 34 (87 percent) had been victims of assaults as adults (p. 7).

My own analysis of the responses of 727 women admitted to the Portage Correctional Institution between January 1988 and May 1993 indicated that the incidence of abuse reported by the women was pervasive (Comack 1993). Some 78 percent (565) of the women reported having been sexually and/or physically abused in their lifetimes. Indigenous women were more likely to report abuse experiences than were non-Indigenous women (81 percent versus 71 percent). Similar to results found in other studies on violence against women, the abusers were overwhelmingly male and likely to be a person known to the victim; the aggression was likely to be repeated over a period of several years.

Drawing on the narratives of twenty-four of the women at the Portage jail, *Women in Trouble* sought to expose the impact of abuse on the lives of criminalized women and, in the process, consider how the women's law violations were intricately connected to those abuse experiences. In doing this, I drew on Liz Kelly's (1988) work to explore the coping, resisting, and surviving strategies that the women adopted to deal with abuse encountered as children and as adults.

Coping refers to "the actions taken to avoid or control distress" (Kelly 1988: 160). How a woman defines her experience, and the context in which it occurs, will determine how she copes with abuse. In addition, her options will depend on the resources available to her at the time and subsequently. These options include her own inner resources and those of her social network as circumscribed not only by her gender but also by her age, race, and class. While women's coping responses are "active, constructive adaptations to experiences of abuse" (Kelly 1988: 160), not all of those responses will have positive outcomes for the girl or woman who adopts them. Too often, coping strategies take the form of "damage control techniques" (Sleeth and Barnsley 1989: 171) — including turning to drugs and alcohol to alleviate pain (Comack 1996: 42).

While coping implies a long-term process, *resisting* — "to oppose actively, to fight, to refuse to cooperate with or submit" (Kelly 1988: 161) — suggests a more immediate opposition to abuse. Resisting denies the abuser certain forms of power. The "extent and form of women's resistance" to particular assaults depend on the circumstances of the events and "on the resources that they feel they can draw on at the time" (p. 162). Moreover, the use of resistance also depends upon past experiences of abuse, especially in terms of the cumulative impact of those experiences on her current perceptions of the situation. In resisting her abuser, a woman may at the same time also be dealing with her memories of past experiences of abuse (Comack 1996: 42).

Surviving means "continuing to exist after the life threatening experience that is part of many experiences of sexual violence. It is the positive outcome of coping and/or resistance" (Kelly 1988: 162). Physical survival is one thing; emotional survival is another. Emotional survival becomes "the extent to which women are able to reconstruct their lives" in order to limit the "overwhelming and continuing" harm of the abuse (p. 163). All of the women I interviewed for *Women in Trouble* had physically survived experiences of abuse. Whether they had survived emotionally and psychologically was less than certain. For many of them, surviving was a process — and their struggles to contend with the effects of abuse experiences were often compounded and complicated by the continuing abuse in their lives.

The concepts of coping, resisting, and surviving reflect the strategies that women adopt to deal with experiences of abuse, thereby affording insights into the impact of the abuse on their lives. But to draw out the connections between abuse history and women's law violations, I used the concepts in a different way: to describe the particular ways in which women's law violations become part of coping with, resisting, and surviving abuse.

Sometimes a woman's law violations are part of her struggle to cope with the abuse and its effects. Merideth, for example, had a long history of abuse, beginning with her father sexually assaulting her as a young child and extending to several later violent relationships with men. She was imprisoned for bouncing cheques. She told me she was writing the cheques to purchase "new things to keep her mind off the abuse."

I've never had any kind of conflict with the law. [long pause] When I started dealing with all these different things, then I started having problems. And then I took it out in the form of fraud. (Cited in Comack 1996: 86)

Sometimes the connections are direct, as in the case of women sent to prison for physically resisting their abusers. Janice, for instance, was serving a sentence for manslaughter.

I was at a party, and this guy, older guy, came on to me. He tried telling me, "Why don't you go to bed with me. I'm getting some money, you know." And I said, "No." And then he started hitting me. And then he raped me. And then [pause] I lost it. I just, I went, I got very angry and I snapped. And I started hitting him. I threw a coffee table on top of his head and then I stabbed him. (Cited in Comack 1996: 96)

Sometimes the connections are even more entangled, as in the case of women who end up on the street, where abuse and law violation become enmeshed in their everyday struggle to survive. Brenda described her life on the street:

Street life is a, it's a power game, you know? Street life? You have to show you're tough. You have to beat up this broad or you have to shank this person, or, you know, you're always carrying guns, you always have blow on you, you always have drugs on you, and you're always working the streets with the pimps and the bikers, you know? That alone, it has so much fucking abuse, it has more abuse than what you were brought up with! … I find living on the street I went through more abuse than I did at home. (Cited in Comack 1996: 105–6)

Women in Trouble also featured the "prisoning" of women, a term that I created to connote the process of imprisonment and to place the focus on the women's experiences of that process. In that regard, one of the revelations to emerge from speaking with the women at Portage was that so many of them had to go to prison to gain access to the resources they needed to resolve their troubles, including someone to talk to about their abuse experiences so that they could begin to heal.

A TIME OF OPTIMISM

When I was working on *Women in Trouble* there was cause for optimism that meaningful change was in the offing. Given the expressed commitment by the Canadian state to the ideals of social citizenship (what came to be called the "Keynesian welfare state") — that all citizens had a right to a basic standard of living, with the state accepting responsibility for the provision of social welfare for its citizenry — the prospects seemed bright for attending to issues such as violence against women and women's treatment by the criminal justice system. This optimism had been made all the more possible with the entrenchment of the Canadian Charter of Rights and Freedoms in 1982, especially the invoking of section 15 (the equality section) in 1985, which prohibited discrimination on the basis of sex. In a climate that appeared to be favourable to hearing women's issues, feminists and women's advocates lobbied throughout the 1980s and 1990s to bring about a number of changes.

The feminist movement had been making gains in addressing the issue of violence against women. In particular, wife abuse was transformed from a private trouble to a public issue meriting state response. Consequently, the number of shelters for women encountering violence in their homes increased dramatically through the 1980s. In 1973 the first five shelters in all of Canada were opened; by the end of the 1980s there were four hundred (Goodhand 2017; Alberta Council of Women's Shelters 2009). With a directive from the Attorney General in 1983 to treat violence in the home in the same way as violence occurring in public spaces, police services across the country began implementing mandatory charging policies in cases involving domestic violence. The increasing number of domestic violence charges led to the establishment of specialized family violence courts across the country (Ursel, Tutty, and Lemaistre 2008). The criminal justice system was recognizing violence against women in other ways. In 1990 the Supreme Court rendered its decision in *R v. Lavallee*, giving legal recognition to the Battered Woman Syndrome as a mitigating factor in cases of women charged with killing their abusive partners (Comack 1993; McIntyre 1993; Sheehy 2014).

At the same time, a basic momentum occurred in the area of corrections. The Task Force on Federally Sentenced Women issued its groundbreaking report, *Creating Choices*, in 1990. The task force called for a transformation in women's corrections, including the closure of the federal Prison for Women (P4W) in Kingston, ON, and the construction of four new regional facilities spread across the country as well as Okimaw Ohci, an Aboriginal healing lodge in Maple Creek, SK. *Creating Choices* took a decidedly "women-centred" approach. Arguing that criminalized women were "high needs/low risk" and therefore required very different treatment than their male counterparts, *Creating Choices* opened the way for the advent of "gender-responsive programming" aimed at providing resources that would address women's specific needs. As Barbara Bloom, a U.S. advocate of gender-responsive programming, argued: "In order to design effective treatment programs that match female offenders' needs, it is important to consider [their] demographics and history ... as well as how various life factors impact on their patterns of offending" (Bloom 1999: 22). Key among those demographics and factors were histories of physical and sexual abuse.

Pressure for change was also building at the provincial level. In Manitoba, the 1991 Aboriginal Justice Inquiry (AJI) report included a chapter on the imprisonment of Aboriginal women in the province (Hamilton and Sinclair 1991: ch. 9). Among its many recommendations the AJI report deemed the Portage Correctional Institution to be an "inappropriate facility" and called for its closure (p. 501). Built in 1893 to house male prisoners, the PCI was considered long past its prime. While the AJI report was shelved by the Conservative provincial government in the ensuing years, the election of an NDP government in 1999 led to the establishment of the Aboriginal Justice Implementation Commission (AJIC). Issued in 2001, the AJIC report focused on the provision of services in the community; the commissioners explicitly avoided a focus on "improving" correctional services. However, one recommendation they did follow up on was the push to close the PCI. The report recommended that a new facility be built, with adequate treatment, training, and cultural supports (AJIC 2001).

Also in 2001 the Elizabeth Fry Society of Manitoba, with the support of a number of Aboriginal and women's organizations, launched a human rights complaint of systemic discrimination against women prisoners in Manitoba. The basis of the complaint was that the services provided to men and women in the province were not equal. The Manitoba Human Rights Commission, responding in November 2004, found merit in the complaint, citing differences with respect to available programming, visits with family and children, access to recreational facilities, and space devoted to mental health treatment. The commission also found evidence that Aboriginal women were treated differently than Aboriginal men. Aboriginal men, for instance, had access to a sweat lodge; Aboriginal women had no programming specific to their needs (Lafreniere, Fontaine, and Comack 2005).

While the Manitoba Justice Minister had announced in July 2002 that the PCI would be closed and a new facility constructed, it was not until December 2004 that he appointed a three-person consultation committee to hear recommendations from the community as to how to proceed. The committee held consultations in Portage la Prairie, Winnipeg, and Thompson, and submitted its report to the government in March 2005. The report made thirteen recommendations, including the construction of a facility that could provide a wide range of services both culturally appropriate and based on a women-centred approach; a healing lodge for Aboriginal women serving provincial and federal sentences; and transitional housing for women in the community. The government finally released the report in April 2006 and announced that a new women's facility would be constructed in the Rural Municipality of Headingley, just outside of the province's main urban centre, Winnipeg (Government of Manitoba 2006).

The Women's Correctional Centre (WCC), which took six years to construct at a cost of $79.5 million (Government of Manitoba 2012), opened in February 2012. With an official capacity of 196 beds and 120,000 square feet of space, this new "state of the art" facility was touted as providing the resources and space to provide women with rehabilitative programming and access to medical and dental care. It had a large kitchen that would double as a training facility for learning life skills and food and culinary skills. In addition to providing "more intimate spaces" for women in a number of subunits, the WCC included a special unit designed for up to twenty-five women serving federal sentences, which meant that women sentenced to two years or more would no longer need to be transferred out of province. As one reporter who toured the facility described it, "If a jail can be cheery, this one may be it. The new facility is bathed in natural light. Each cell has a window, and even interior rooms receive an abundance of natural light either from skylights or indirectly, such as from atop a dividing wall" (Kusch 2012).

Given the passage of time and the opening of this new correctional centre, I began wondering about whether or not things had really changed since the writing of *Women in Trouble*. Are experiences of abuse continuing to have an impact on women's lives? Were the connections I had found between women's histories of abuse and their law violations continuing to prevail? How were the women finding the experience of imprisonment in this "new and improved" facility? Are criminalized women now afforded access to the resources they need to resolve their troubles? In short, are women still in trouble?

To address these questions, in the spring of 2014 I set about to interview women incarcerated at the WCC. I was initially hoping to meet with twenty-four women — the same number interviewed for *Women in Trouble* — but after visiting each of the units in the prison and explaining my intentions, I found forty-two women expressing a willingness to participate in my study (for more information about the research process, see Appendix). As it turned out, one of the women I interviewed happened to be Sarah.

SARAH'S STORY

When I had first met Sarah back in 1992, she was twenty-eight years old and the mother of eight children ranging in age from one to twelve. When I interviewed her that first time, Sarah's recollections of her childhood were centred mainly on her relationship with her mother, who, she said, "drank a lot." Sarah, although not the oldest child, was largely responsible for caring for her younger siblings. That included sleeping during the day "just so I could stay up all night" to watch over them while the adults in the household were drinking.

As Sarah recalled, "Anything could have happened. Like, you know, a fight or something would happen. God, I've seen a person get shot, and one get stabbed." Sarah did not just witness violence. She disclosed that she was subject to several sexual assaults as a child, including being molested by her mom's boyfriend. Sadly, her mother did not come to her aid in dealing with those experiences. As Sarah recalled during our first meeting: "I never did get help for anything that happened to me. I never told anybody." Still, she said, her mother "always knew" about it. Sarah ended up "always thinking myself dirty and worthless and — I don't know, I was never doing anything right." But, she said, her mother "didn't do anything, and I was too scared."

To cope with her unsettled home life, Sarah began running away and left home for good at the age of thirteen. As she put it, "I got into drinking and running. I just took off from home and never came back. I've always supported myself right 'til I met my kids' father."

Sarah was fourteen when she met her common-law partner, the father of her eight children. At first, they "used to get along just great" but then, according to Sarah, "he'd get jealous" when she was talking to other men. "He'd be lookin' at me with the corner of his eye, you know? And all of a sudden he'd go BAM! Right in my face. For no reason." Sarah said that she "got so used to the routine" that she knew what to expect. She never told anyone about the abuse. "I don't know why. I guess not to get him in trouble." She also never used to fight back, until one time when she was pregnant with her fourth child. Sarah had been trying to sleep, but her partner wouldn't let her. So she smashed a beer bottle and stabbed him in the face, and then went back to sleep.

When she awoke several hours later she was covered in his blood. An ambulance was called. Sarah grabbed a belt and "started goin' crazy on him again" and smashing things in her apartment. Sarah recalled: "Everybody thought I'd went crazy on them. And I wasn't even drinking!" In trying to make sense of her actions, Sarah talked about how "the abuse was always there." On that occasion, in discovering her anger, Sarah had found an outlet for relieving the stress and tension that had been building as a result of her partner's abuse: "I guess I needed it after I'd — I didn't feel guilty anymore."

When I spoke to her in 1992 Sarah was on remand for a robbery charge. It was her first time in the Portage Correctional Institution. She had ended her relationship with her common-law partner a year previously. Sarah had been drinking regularly and lost custody of her children as a result. When that happened, she began using cocaine. For the past year she had been shooting up as many as ten times a day and drinking regularly. When I asked her where she got the money to support her habit, she replied: "Rob people. I was so, I could do anything when it comes to coke. I could rip off my best friend, you know? I could do anything, just for the money, just to get it."

"COMING BACK TO JAIL"

So there we were, in the summer of 2014, sitting down for another interview. This time Sarah and I met in a small classroom adjacent to one of the units at the Women's Correctional Centre. We started our meeting by going over the notes I had taken from the first time we met, some twenty-two years previously. While the transcripts of the interviews had long since been shredded, I had kept my notebook that recorded the main points and themes of each of the twenty-four *Women in Trouble* interviews. After going through those notes I asked her, "So what have you been doing since then?" Sarah replied with a chuckle: "Coming back to jail."

After our first meeting in 1992, Sarah had ended up serving "about nine months" at Portage on the robbery charge. While her stay at the PCI was the only time she spent there, she was incarcerated regularly in the Winnipeg Remand Centre. As she put it, "I was a Remand lifer." She eventually ended up serving a five-year sentence at the Edmonton Institution for Women and Okimaw Ohci Healing Lodge in Maple Creek, SK. When we met at the WCC in 2014 Sarah was serving a two-year sentence for assaulting her common-law partner.

On her release from the PCI Sarah had been resolved not to take up the relationship with her common-law partner again. She met another man and became pregnant with her ninth child. But he too became "very abusive, very controlling," so she walked away from that relationship and had the baby on her own. Sarah lost the baby to Child and Family Services (CFS) the day the little girl was born. She had also lost custody of her other children to CFS. (Three of her children were adopted out. They have since made contact with her.)

To deal with that loss, Sarah turned to drugs and alcohol:

> When I lost my kids, I figured I just gave up. Gave up on everything. Never figured — 'cause I always heard that I was never a good enough mother, you know, so it kind of hurt. And, yeah, and I just lived on drugs and alcohol, like, always. Drugs and alcohol was my thing. That was the only way I knew how to cope.

Sarah eventually regained custody of her children from CFS. "Once they got back I just gave up all the drugs, but I was still a binger on weekends. During the weekdays I stayed sober for them. Weekends they were usually at grandma's, you know what I mean, and it was my time, I guess. I just drank." I asked Sarah whether it had been hard to give up the drugs: "No. Because I think my kids were a big part of my life that was missing for me, that I think that being alone all the time and the only world that I knew was just my kids, you know. So to give up the drugs and have my kids back was the best thing ever [chuckles]."

Over that time, though, Sarah's anger had been building, and to the point where she described herself as "a really angry person." Complicating matters, Sarah didn't stay away from drugs for long. She met a man who supplied her with crack cocaine, which only exacerbated her anger. "It's an awful drug. It made me suspicious of everybody. My anger was even worse, ten times worse. So that's why I can't go back to crack. I've been off it for how many years now, almost, what, five years — no, longer than that, way longer than that."

Sarah's anger led to a series of assault charges, including one incident in which she was charged with aggravated assault, forcible confinement, and uttering threats. A woman she had met several years previously had come to her house for a visit. The woman got into an altercation with one of Sarah's daughters. Seeing the woman on top of her daughter, Sarah said that she "just flipped. I just lost it." The police came to the house the next day and laid the charges. In combination with other outstanding assault charges, Sarah ended up serving a five-year federal sentence starting in 2007.

Sarah has since come to believe that her anger stems from the sexual abuse she encountered in her childhood: "That's why I built so much anger. From keeping all those secrets and not talking to anybody and not letting anybody in my life, letting them know. If I let them in my life they're going to judge me. I was so scared of that." As she had done in our first interview, Sarah also talked about the lack of support from her mother in dealing with the abuse. But her understanding of her mother's situation was now different. "I blamed my mom for a lot of stuff, you know, but now I come to realize that she was only a child herself, so her behaviour, what she taught us, is what she knew herself, so it wasn't her fault, you know what I mean?" Sarah's mother had also been sexually abused as a child:

> She told me she's been raped by her uncles and everything like that, you know, and never done anything. So I figured it was okay for me to be touched by everybody else and not say nothing because, you know what, I'd be a rat, I'd be a troublemaker. And that always stuck to me as a little kid, right. So but, you know, when you get older, how to cope with that is you live with all the shame, and the resentment and everything like that. And that was all building up, deep down inside me.

Sarah had more than her childhood experiences to contend with. Abuse was a continuing feature of her life. "For the longest time I tried to find a partner, and every partner I found was so damn abusive towards me, you know. Whereas I finally started turning around and abusing them. I started hurting them, like, big time." While she had been in other relationships, her common-law partner continued to be a presence in her life. "I'm with somebody, he makes sure he ruins that relationship. You know what I mean? He goes, 'No, no,' he goes, 'She's mine. We have kids.' And it's still that control. Whereas, and in a way I got so used to it, I think. You know what I mean?"

Her most recent sentence is "because I finally fought back with that guy, my kids' dad. That's why I'm here. I had beat him up so bad." Sarah saw her situation as unfair. As she told her common-law partner: "I says, 'I'm in jail this time. You know what? You should have been in jail…. You should have been doing this time. 'Cause I don't charge you. You beat the shit out of me for weeks and all of a sudden I fight back and then I'm in jail.'"

WOMEN IN TROUBLE — STILL

Clearly, abuse has been a defining feature of Sarah's life. She not only survived the sexual abuse she experienced as a child but also encountered abuse at the hands of her male partners. Turning to drugs and alcohol was a coping strategy, a way of dealing both with the loss of her children to CFS and her anger and the sense of shame prompted by her experiences of being sexually abused in childhood. As Sarah commented, "coming back to jail" has also been a defining feature of her life. In terms of the abuse-law violation connections, Sarah's most recent charges appear to be directly connected to the ongoing abusive relationship with the father of eight of her children.

Experiences of abuse were also prominent in the stories told by the other women I spoke to at the WCC — of encountering physical and sexual abuse as children and teenagers, and abuse from their male partners. Given a predominance of young ages — thirty (71 percent) of the forty-two women were between the ages of eighteen and thirty — the majority of these women represent the next generation, the children of the original *Women in Trouble* cohort. Similar to the accounts of the women in the original cohort, their stories tell of unsettled childhoods, of being taken into care at a young age, of ending up on the streets as teenagers, of pregnancy and motherhood at early ages, of losing their children to the custody of Child and Family Services. Moreover, like Sarah, many of them had coming back to jail as a defining feature of their lives. Overall, thirty (71 percent) of the forty-two women had previous experiences of incarceration; twelve (40 percent) of those women had been held in custody as youth. As one of the women commented, "I grew up in the Youth Centre."

It would appear, therefore, that women are still in trouble. They are encountering a variety of problems, conflicts, and dilemmas in their lives, all of which are bringing them into conflict with the law. Yet in the past two decades since *Women in Trouble* was released, both the socio-political terrain and the theorizing and research on criminalized women have shifted quite noticeably — creating in turn significant changes in how we understand the factors that bring women into conflict with the law and their treatment by the criminal justice system.

THE SHIFTING SOCIO-POLITICAL TERRAIN

The optimism for substantive social change that many of us were feeling in the early 1990s gradually eroded with the harsh impacts of capitalist globalization, economic restructuring, and welfare state retrenchment on everyday lives.

Over the following decades, the increasingly international or global nature of corporate capitalism led to significant transformations within particular nation-states, including Canada. Corporate restructuring and downsizing — designed to keep up with these new forms of global production relations and financial systems — led to heightened levels of profit accumulation, inequality, and immiseration. While there are some 1.3 million corporations in Canada, sixty Canadian-based firms account for 60 percent of all corporate profit. In 1950 the average profit of a firm within the top sixty was 234 times larger than that of an average firm in the corporate universe. By 2007 that number had risen to 14,278 — a sixty-fold increase in six decades (Brennan 2012). Canada's CEO Elite 100 — the 100 highest-paid CEOs of companies listed in the TSX Index (only two of whom are women) — had an average annual compensation of $8.96 million in 2014. In contrast, Canadians working full-time, full-year earned $48,636 in 2014, which means that Canada's CEO Elite 100 make 184 times more than Canadians earning the average wage (Mackenzie 2016). This wage gap has been growing. In 1998 the highest-paid 100 Canadian CEOs earned 105 times more than the average wage (Mackenzie 2012).

Meanwhile, more and more Canadians have become reliant on food banks in order to get by. The first Canadian food bank opened in Edmonton, AB, in 1981. By 2008 the country had over seven hundred food banks. According to Hunger Count 2016, an annual survey of food banks and emergency food programs carried out by Food Banks Canada, during one month in 2016, 863,492 Canadians used a food bank, a 28 percent increase since 2008. Some 36 percent of food-bank users are children (Food Banks Canada 2016).

While the gap between rich and poor widened, under the sway of globalization the state's expressed commitment to social welfare was undermined. In its place, neo-liberalism became the new wisdom of governing. Premised on the values of individualism, freedom of choice, market dominance, and minimal state involvement in the economy, neo-liberalism marks a dramatic shift in emphasis from collective or social values towards notions of family and individual responsibility. Subjecting the economy to market forces and cutting back on social welfare meant that increasing numbers of people — individuals and families — were left to fend for themselves, without the benefit of a social safety net. Instead of formulating policies and targeting spending on programs that would meet the social needs of the members of society (education, health care, pensions, social assistance), governments now focus on enhancing economic efficiency and international competitiveness. With the "privatization" of responsibility, individuals and families are left to look after themselves. Under neo-liberalism, the market-based, self-reliance, and privatizing ideals of the new order replace the ideals of social citizenship. As Janine Brodie (1995: 57) explains it:

> The rights and securities guaranteed to all citizens of the Keynesian welfare state are no longer rights, universal, or secure. The new ideal of the common good rests on market-oriented values such as self-reliance, efficiency, and competition. The new good citizen is one that recognizes the limits and liabilities of state provision and embraces her or his obligation to work longer and harder in order to become more self-reliant.

In this era of restructuring, the government talk of the need for deficit reduction was translated into cutbacks to social programs, and gains made by the women's movement in the previous decade came under serious attack. As one example, during its time in office from 1995 to 2002 the Conservative government in Ontario under the leadership of Premier Mike Harris implemented a series of drastic changes to the provision of social assistance. Poor women were most vulnerable to these changes. Welfare benefits underwent significant cuts, recipients (including mothers with young children) were expected to undertake employment activities (known as "workfare"), and those deemed to be "undeserving" of state support were ferreted out by means of increased surveillance (including welfare snitch lines). Anyone found guilty of welfare fraud was subject to a lifetime ban from receipt of social assistance (a law subsequently appealed in 2003) and to vilification and life-threatening sanctions — as in the starkly revealed case of Kimberly Rogers, who died while under house arrest for welfare fraud (Mosher 2014; Chunn and Gavigan 2014). These changes amounted to a dramatic shift away from the principle of citizens' entitlement to government support to meet basic needs — towards an emphasis on the "responsibilization" of individuals through engendering self-reliance and independence. As Laureen Snider (2014: 282) states, "The goal of government became not to deliver social justice or full employment, but to enable citizens to become consumers who can fend for themselves."

These economic and political developments filtered into the criminal justice system. A growing economic recession and rising crime rates during the 1990s produced a crime-control strategy that replaced the rehabilitation and welfare of offenders as the goals of the criminal justice system with "risk management": the policing and minimization of risk that offenders pose to the wider community. Under this neo-liberal "responsibilization" model of crime control (O'Malley 1992), criminals are to be made responsible for the choices they make; "rather than clients in need of support, they are seen as risks that must be managed" (Garland 2001: 175). In the correctional system, the focus has been on the development of risk-assessment instruments; the RNR (Risk, Need, Responsivity) model holds the status as "perhaps the most influential model for the assessment and treatment of offenders" (Bonta and Andrews 2007: 1).

Risk, need, and responsivity comprise a triad of key principles of correctional classification and are considered central to the delivery of correctional treatment programs (Andrews, Bonta, and Hoge 1990: 19). The risk principle refers to matching the level of service to the offender's risk to reoffend. The higher the risk assessment, the more security and treatment required. The need principle involves assessing an offender's criminogenic needs — "dynamic risk factors that are directly linked to criminal behaviour" (Bonta and Andrews 2007: 5) such as employment, marital/family, associates, substance abuse, and community functioning (Motiuk 1997) — and targeting them in treatment. The responsivity principle has two parts: general responsivity "calls for the use of cognitive social learning methods to influence behaviour," while specific responsivity "takes into account strengths, learning style, personality, motivation, and bio-social (e.g., gender, race) characteristics of the offender" (Bonta and Andrews 2007: 1). Reduction in recidivism constitutes the key empirical measure of effectiveness in the model.

Risk management is premised on the use of checklists of risk factors and actuarial tools such as the RNR model to fashion a scientific, "evidence-based" approach to crime control. Critics, however, have pointed to several issues plaguing this approach. One criticism relates to the diverse cultural meanings attached to the notion of "risk." As Pat O'Malley (2010: 15–16) explains:

> Risk emerges not just as a particular configuration of techniques,

nor as the effect of a grand unfolding of modern contradictions between science and survival, but as a matter of lived experiences, emotionally laden evaluations, expressions of inchoate feelings and so on. Such cultural considerations inform not only what are to be considered "acceptable" levels of risk, or what risks are worth taking, or even what risks are worth minimizing, but also whether something should be allowed to be dealt with as a "risk" at all.

The conception of risk that predominates in the criminal justice system, however, runs counter to other standpoints. As Haudenosaunee scholar Patricia Monture (1999) noted, when the "criminogenic needs" categories in the RNR model are applied to Indigenous people, they guarantee a poor score. In terms of community functioning, for instance, "Aboriginal people do not belong to communities that are functional and healthy (and colonialism is significantly responsible for this fact)." As such, "rather than measuring risk this dimension merely reaffirms that Aboriginal persons have been negatively impacted by colonialism" (p. 27). The same holds true for other categories such as substance abuse, marital/family, and associates. "Scoring higher on these categories is predetermined for Aboriginal prisoners because of the very structure of the instruments. What is being measured is not 'risk' but one's experiences as part of an oppressed group" (p. 27). In these terms, neo-liberal risk tools are not only individualized but racialized constructions.

Feminist criminologists have pointed to how both "risk" and the actuarial tools used to assess "riskiness" are also gendered (Hannah-Moffat and Shaw 2001; Hannah-Moffat 1999, 2009; Chan and Rigakos 2002; Pollack 2010). In feminist terms, criminalized women are more likely to be "at risk" than to pose a risk to community safety, especially given the inordinately high percentage of women in prison who have histories of abuse and victimization. As well, risk-assessment instruments were initially designed based on male prisoner populations and tend to overstate the risk to the public posed by women prisoners. Moreover, while gender is acknowledged as a "responsivity" factor in the assessment of risk, it is treated as a binary, "bio-social" variable (male/female) as opposed to a fundamental component in shaping individuals' identities, opportunities, and experiences. Further, feminists took pains to underscore the importance of assessing criminalized women's needs and experiences in a holistic manner so that resources could be provided to address those needs in a meaningful way. But under the logic of the RNR model, needs become linked to the risk to reoffend — and to the point where a history of abuse stands as a marker for a woman's increased likelihood of violent recidivism.

Moreover, while recidivism or reoffending is the empirical measure of effectiveness in risk models, "There is no generally accepted or standardized way to calculate recidivism rates" (Office of the Auditor General–Manitoba 2014: 278). Rates of recidivism for women, for instance, vary widely — from 4 percent to 47 percent — in part because studies have used different methods and measurement approaches (Gobeil and Barrett 2007). Renée Gobeil and Meredith Barrett found that federally sentenced women had a 38 percent recidivism rate when the figure included a revocation of their conditional release; the rate was reduced to 30 percent when only new convictions were counted, and 5 percent when only new convictions for a violent offence were counted.

In Ontario, recidivism is defined as a return to provincial correctional supervision on a new conviction within two years of completing a jail sentence of six months or more. In 2013/14, the recidivism rate for Ontario adults was 37.4 percent (Ontario Ministry of Community Safety and Correctional Services 2017). Prior to 2012, recidivism rates in Manitoba were tracked in terms of whether a person received new criminal charges in the two years following release from custody. Using that method produced a whopping 72 percent recidivism rate. After 2012, however, recidivism was tracked in terms of whether a person was convicted of a new offence and returned to custody within two years of release from jail. As of March 2013, 31 percent of those released from jail later faced a new conviction, a figure that had increased from 22 percent in March 2007 using this method of measurement (Office of the Auditor General–Manitoba 2014: 279 and 289). Either way, these data suggest that incarceration does not reduce the risk of an individual encountering further charges and more time in custody down the road.

Under the policies and practices of neo-liberalism, the precariousness of middle-income families provoked a social anxiety that easily translated into fear of crime, especially of those groups and individuals left less fortunate by virtue of the economic transformations. A neo-conservative rationality, premised on a concern for tradition, order, hierarchy, and authority, fostered crime-control policies aimed at "getting tough" on crime. Calls for more law and order became louder.

This "get tough" strategy was a key platform of the Conservative government under Stephen Harper during its time in power from 2006 to 2015. The changes implemented included: reducing the credit for time served in pre-trial (remand) custody that a judge could administer on sentencing; abolishing accelerated parole review, which entitled non-violent, first-time offenders a chance to seek parole after serving one-sixth of their sentences; imposing mandatory minimum sentences for drug-related and sex offences; and increasing restrictions on applying for pardons (Mallea 2012; CCPA–MB and John Howard Society of Manitoba, Inc. 2012; Comack, Fabre, and Burgher 2015). Significantly, in company with this "tough on crime" strategy, in 2012 the Harper government also implemented neo-liberal-inspired fiscal restraint measures through its Deficit Reduction Action Plan (DRAP). Aiming to cut federal government expenditures by at least $4 billion over three years, DRAP was expected to result in at least $295 million in "cost-saving" measures to Correctional Service Canada operations (CSC n.d.). To realize these reductions, access to programming, schooling, and work opportunities in federal prisons was restricted, prisoner pay was reduced, and other costs to prisoners (use of telephones, room and board) were increased. Meanwhile, to accommodate the increasing number of federal prisoners, the government commissioned 2,700 new or refurbished cells (OCI 2013: 38). The shift from rehabilitating to warehousing prisoners was put into motion.

The "get tough" strategy emerged when crime rates were already on the decline. According to Statistics Canada, the Crime Severity Index, which measures the volume and severity of police-reported crime, had been going down each year between 2002 and 2014. In 2014 the police-reported crime rate, which measures the volume of crime reported to police, was at the lowest rate recorded since 1969 (Boyce 2015). Yet despite declining crime rates, incarceration rates were on the increase. According to Public Safety Canada (2015: 36), 33,188 people were incarcerated in federal and provincial/territorial facilities in 2004/05. That number rose each year to 2011/12, when 39,958 people were incarcerated — a 20 percent increase over the eight-year period.

At the federal level, the incarcerated population increased by 14 percent (from 12,623 to 14,335) between 2005 and 2015. Increases were especially evident for women and Indigenous and Black people. The number of women prisoners increased by 77 percent (from 368 to 653), while for men the increase was 12 percent. The number of Indigenous prisoners went up by 52 percent (from 2,296 to 3,500), while the number of non-Indigenous prisoners increased by 5 percent (from 10,327 to 10,835). The number of Black prisoners increased by 78 percent (from 792 to 1,406), while white prisoners actually decreased by 6 percent (from 8,815 to 8,281) (OCI 2015: 2).

In recent years Manitoba had the highest incarceration rate among the provinces. In 2013/14, 242 adults on average were incarcerated in Manitoba's correctional centres for every 100,000 adults (Correctional Services Program 2015). The vast majority (90 percent) of adults held in custody in the province were men, but the number of women had increased rapidly, growing from 78 in 2003 to 260 in 2012 (a 233 percent increase). While Indigenous people make up 15 percent of Manitoba's population, they accounted for 70 percent of the province's incarcerated adults in 2011 (Office of the Auditor General Manitoba 2014: 242). These increases led to serious overcrowding in Manitoba's jails and remand centres. According to Manitoba's Auditor General (2014: 245–47), the occupancy rate in the province's correctional centres on May 15, 2013, was 126 percent, and ranged from 110 percent to 145 percent in the different centres. This was despite an increase in capacity of 52 percent since 2008, with 651 beds added at a cost of $182 million, including the construction of the wcc, which was at 126 percent capacity on May 15, 2013.

Assessing how things have changed since *Women in Trouble*, therefore, involves attending to the impacts of capitalist globalization, economic restructuring, and a shifting socio-political terrain on the social conditions that bring women into conflict with the law and their experience of imprisonment.

WOMEN'S PATHWAYS TO CRIME

Over the past two decades feminist criminology has developed a substantial body of research and theorizing about the lives of criminalized women. In particular, what came to be known as the pathways approach to understanding women's law violations — of which *Women in Trouble* was a part — became more predominant as a way of making sense of women's involvement in criminal activities, to the point where Joanne Belknap (2010: 1080) deemed this approach to be "perhaps the single most important contribution of feminist criminology."

The pathways approach aimed to better understand the lives of women and girls and the particular features that led to their criminal activity. Using qualitative methodologies, pathways researchers placed the standpoints of the women — their voices — at the centre of inquiry. Principal in much of this research were links made between women's victimization and their criminal involvement (see, for example, Chesney-Lind and Rodriguez 1983; Miller 1986; Daly 1998; Arnold 1995; Heimer 1995; and Chesney-Lind and Shelden 1998).

Mary Gilfus (1992), for instance, conducted life history interviews with twenty incarcerated women about their entry into street crime. Most of these women had grown up with violence; thirteen of them reported childhood sexual abuse, and fifteen had experienced "severe childhood abuse" (p. 70). Among them were eight African-Americans. While there were no race-based differences in reported abuse, the African-American women were more likely than their white counterparts to have grown up in poor families. Violence and neglect were prevalent themes in the women's narratives about their childhoods. Violence was also a common feature of their relationships with men: sixteen of the twenty women had lived with violent men. Repeated victimization experiences, drug addiction, involvement in the sex trade, relationships with men involved in street crime, and the demands of mothering: these themes marked the women's transitions from childhood to adulthood.

In a similar fashion, Beth Richie (1996) focused on African-American battered women in prison, developing a theory of "gender entrapment" to explain the "contradictions and complications of the lives of the African-American battered women who commit crimes" (p. 4). According to Richie, gender entrapment involves understanding the connections between violence against women in their intimate relationships, culturally constructed gender-identity development, and women's participation in illegal activities. In these terms, battered Black women were "trapped" in criminal activity in the same way that they were trapped in abusive relationships.

Other feminist researchers extended the pathways approach to women's involvement in the illegal drug trade. Lisa Maher, Eloise Dunlap, and Bruce Johnson (2006), for instance, drew on in-depth life history interviews with eighty-seven Black women living in New York City to explore how the emerging street-level trade in crack cocaine in the 1990s opened up economic opportunities for these marginalized women. Having grown up in impoverished inner-city communities, the women came to see the informal economy of the drug trade as an alternative to their social and economic exclusion from the mainstream society. An immersion in street life from an early age meant that the women "were brought into situations wherein they acquired the various skills and networks of associates that enabled them, not only to generate income, but also to survive in hostile and often dangerous environments" (p. 26). For Maher and her colleagues, understanding the experiences of the women involved attending to "macro-level structural forces which constrain participation in legal labor markets and the role of the institutionalized informal economic activities at the neighborhood level" (p. 27). As well, they cautioned that a single gendered lens needed to be avoided since "sex/gender clearly does not operate in a vacuum isolated from race and social class and their effects on women's lives" (p. 27).

As the pathways approach gained prominence, it became one of the planks on which "gender-responsive" programming in women's prisons and jails developed. Gender-responsive programming emerged from the recognition that correctional policies and practices were male-centred — that they were devised for men yet adopted for women prisoners. Feminist researchers had demonstrated significant gendered differences between men and women in their social locations, their pathways to crime, and their experiences of imprisonment; correctional policies and practices needed to be reconfigured to reflect those gendered differences.

In 2003 the U.S. National Institute of Corrections published "Gender Responsive Strategies: Research, Practice and Guiding Principles for Women Offenders," a report by Barbara Bloom, Barbara Owen, and Stephanie Covington. The report maintains that "understanding the contexts of women's lives, both in the general population and in the criminal justice system, is an important first step in developing gender-responsive policy and practice" (p. vii). In promoting a new "vision" for the criminal justice system, Bloom and her colleagues (2003: ch. 4; Covington and Bloom 2006) mapped out six principles as "building blocks" for improving the management, supervision, and treatment of women:

(1) Acknowledge gender differences in the life experiences of male and female offenders;
(2) Create an environment of safety, respect, and dignity;
(3) Centre policies, programs, and practices on women's relational needs, including the importance of children in the women's lives and the impact of interpersonal violence;
(4) Address substance abuse, trauma, and mental health issues as interconnected;
(5) Address the social and material realities in the lives of women offenders;
(6) Address the challenges women encounter on re-entry into the community in a holistic way.

In addition to pathways theory and its attention to the gender-specific adversities in producing and sustaining women's involvement in crime, the gender-responsive approach was predicated on relational theory and trauma and addiction theories. Following on the work of psychologist Carol

Gilligan (1982), relational theory posits that women's and men's psychological development differs; relationships are more central to women's sense of identity and self-worth. As such, "The primary motivation for women throughout their life is the establishment of a strong sense of connection with others" (Covington and Bloom 2006: 16). Trauma and addiction theories underscore the interrelations between these two issues in the lives of criminalized women and the importance of ensuring that criminal justice and other service providers are "trauma-informed," especially since "the standard operating practices (searches, seclusion, and restraint) may traumatize/retraumatize women" (Covington and Bloom 2006: 17).

Bloom and her colleagues (2003) also advocated for a two-tiered gender-responsive approach to treatment programs and services composed of: (1) structure (recognizing women's strengths and competencies, using women-only groups, and employing gender-responsive treatment tools); and (2) content and context/environment (including practical needs such as housing, employment, transportation, and childcare) of treatment. The gender-responsive strategy being advocated for the treatment of criminalized women "would involve comprehensive services that take into account the content and context of women's lives. Programs need to take into consideration the larger social issues of poverty, abuse, and race and gender inequalities, as well as individual factors that impact women in the criminal justice system" (Covington and Bloom 2006: 30).

In learning more about the lives of women and the "miles of problems" (Comack 1996: 134) that bring them into conflict with the law — histories of violence and abuse, lack of formal education and job skills, struggles to provide and care for their children, and problems with drugs and alcohol use — initial pathways researchers took pains to distance their work from formulations that located the source of women's problems in individual pathologies or personality disturbances. Instead, the intersecting structural inequalities in society — of gender, race, and class — that contour and constrain the lives of women provided the backdrop for understanding women's involvement in crime. Nevertheless, the pathways approach has developed into quantitative, "evidence-based" analyses of large data sets that seek to draw out empirical correlations between a host of variables — including abuse histories — and women's offending behaviours (Resig, Holtfreter, and Morash 2006; Salisbury and Van Voorhis 2009; Brennan et al. 2012). In the process, the focus shifted away from interrogating the structural barriers and systemic processes that come to bear on women's lives. Instead, the focus now appears to be more keenly fixed on the individual pathologies and personality disturbances that the initial pathways researchers sought to avoid in their formulations (see, for example: DeHart et al. 2013; Lynch, Fritch, and Heath 2012; Schnittiker, Massoglia, and Uggen 2012; Trestman et al. 2007). Much of this quantitative research draws its energy from the burgeoning neo-liberal risk-management industry and the effort to fashion actuarial risk tools to identify the risk of reoffending and corresponding treatment needs.

In response to criticisms that risk models were based on research involving only male populations, researchers and correctional officials turned to the pathways approach in order to devise a "gender-responsive risk/needs assessment instrument" (Salisbury and Van Voorhis 2009: 547). While onlookers deemed the qualitative research on women's pathways to crime to have "enriched" understandings of women's involvement in crime, others saw the pathways approach as being in "its relatively early stage of research development" because it had not yet been determined "whether such gendered pathways withstand statistical testing" (Salisbury and Van Voorhis 2009: 542).

As such, in what is described as "one of the first quantitative attempts to explicitly examine women's gendered pathways" (p. 561), Emily Salisbury and Patricia Van Voorhis (2009) undertook a statistical analysis of "gender-responsive pathways" to women's offending behaviours. Drawing on a sample of 313 women probationers in Missouri derived from the Women's Needs and Risk Assessment Project, they utilized a number of scales and devised a number of path models for testing the factors that lead to women's recidivism (the empirical measure of effectiveness in risk models). While the authors pointed to a variety of different factors identified in the literature, findings from their quantitative analysis showed support for three pathways to crime: a pathway from childhood victimization to mental illness and substance abuse; a relational pathway in which women's "dysfunctional intimate relationships" facilitated their victimization, reductions in self-efficacy, and mental illness and substance abuse; and a social and human capital pathway in which challenges in education, family support, and self-efficacy as well as "relationship dysfunction" contributed to their imprisonment. In their subsequent work, Salisbury and Van Voorhis further entrenched gender responsivity into an individualized risk logic. Working with three other colleagues, they developed a "person-centred paradigm" in which the individual is the unit of an analysis geared towards identifying the proper treatment modalities to be adopted "to treat risk factor patterns of separate pathways" (Brennan et al. 2012:1502).

Gender responsivity has also been put to work in Canada in conducting risk assessments of women prisoners. In 2004 Correctional Service Canada implemented an updated Program Strategy for Federally Sentenced Women Offenders. The strategy essentially folded a gender-responsive approach into the RNR model. Kelly Hannah-Moffat (2008: 204), however, maintains that the 2004 Program Strategy failed "to capture the complex and intersectional character of women's problems" that had been revealed in feminist research and had led to the gender responsivity approach. According to Hannah-Moffat (2008), the gender-responsive approach and the RNR model are fundamentally incompatible. While gender is "a central organizing principle for correctional reform" in the gender-responsive strategy, the RNR model relegates gender to a "responsivity" factor; gender is not central to a needs assessment. "Gendered concerns are compartmentalised, de-legitimated and only superficially addressed" in the RNR model (p. 205). Then too, while the gender-responsive strategy is premised on a theoretical foundation that "allows for consideration of the complexity and multiplicity of diverse women's experiences" (p. 200), the RNR model is concerned with "effectiveness" in terms of targeting and reducing recidivism.

Moreover, the RNR model discusses abuse and trauma within the context of women prisoners' mental health needs — and their corresponding need for cognitive behavioural therapy. Cognitive behavioural therapy is premised on the notion that "criminal offending is a result of the offender's inability to think logically, reason appropriately and to make rational decisions" (Pollack 2004: 694). Structural inequalities — poverty, racism, or gendered experiences (such as sexual violence) — are deemed to be irrelevant. Centred squarely on self-regulation, cognitive behavioural therapy is "consistent with neo-liberal strategies of individualizing social problems" (Kendall 2002: 183). As Hannah-Moffat (2008: 212) emphasizes, "The discussions of [gender] responsivity that filter into penal policy discussions focus on *individual* factors not structure."

In keeping with the shifting socio-political terrain, then, pathways research has expanded to include quantitative analyses that produce a variable number of routes leading women into the criminal justice system, and feminist pathways theorizing and research have been absorbed into neo-liberal risk-management regimes, with the focus squarely fixed on addressing the individualized mental health needs of criminalized women. In the process, the initial efforts of feminist criminologists to draw attention to the structural processes and systemic factors that come to bear on women's lives got lost from view.

Perhaps part of the difficulty has been the language of "pathways" to make sense of women's law violations. The metaphor slips too easily into individualization, as a woman is seen as "choosing" to take a particular path and not another. As well, the metaphor easily loses sight of the terrain on which a pathway is located; in particular, the ways in which the landscape of race, class, and gender inequalities conditions and contours the very choices that are made available. Adding to the difficulties, there is a tendency in much of the quantitative research on pathways to take crime categories as a given, to incorporate them unproblematically into the research. In the Salisbury and Van Voorhis (2009: 553) study, for instance, the measure of recidivism used was "incarcerations for any reason." Only 17 percent of the sample (52 women) were deemed to have recidivated; the majority of those women (73 percent) were readmitted to prison for violations of their release conditions rather than for new convictions — and some of those women had managed to abide by those conditions for up to two years before they were reincarcerated.

The women I met with at the WCC had been accused (for those on remand) or convicted of a wide range of criminal offences — from man-slaughter, aggravated assault, robbery, and drug offences to violations of their probation and bail conditions. These crime categories constitute the "official version" of criminalized women's actions or behaviours. One telling example of the problems encountered in relying on an official version of events comes from Sarah's story. One of the charges for which Sarah had been convicted in her encounter with the woman who came to her house for a visit was forcible confinement. When I asked her, "What's the forcible confinement about?" Sarah explained:

> Well, they charged me with forcible confinement because she had said that I forced her to stay there. There was a key to my door that came out. The key was knocked off. We couldn't find the damn key. So that's the forcible confinement. You know those doors that lock from the inside? The key's always there. But they were fighting right by my door, all of them, when I came out of the bathroom.
>
> [Yeah. And then it got lost?]
>
> Yeah. And we couldn't find it. So everybody was locked in my house until we found it.

In combination with the charges of aggravated assault and uttering threats, a forcible confinement charge gives the impression of serious wrongdoing — even though in this case it was simply the result of a lost key.

Moreover, many of the women I interviewed at the WCC indicated that they were charged with offences they did not commit. Some of the women, for example, said they were charged after being found in dwellings where drugs or guns happened to be present; others "took the rap" for friends and family members. As well, more and more people across the country are being taken into custody on remand — to the point where the majority of those held in provincial lock-ups have not been convicted of a criminal offence (Correctional Services Program 2017; Deshman and Meyers 2014). This situation is especially pressing in Manitoba, which has one of the highest percentages of adults held in remand custody among the provinces. "Un-sentenced" prisoners, those being held on remand awaiting their trials, accounted for 64 percent of the province's total adult custody population in 2010/11 — a figure on the increase since 1993, when only 26 percent of the custody population was being held on remand status (Office of the Auditor General Manitoba 2014: 251). Many of the women I interviewed at the WCC were being held in remand custody, and in some cases they had been held for more than a year. The women being held in these cases are motivated to plead guilty to an offence "just to get it over with" and return to their community.

It would be a mistake, therefore, to simply take as a given the "official version" of criminal offences. To do so misses the social contexts in which women's law violations occur and the often complicated situations that produce their criminal charges or convictions. It also misses the role of the criminal justice system not only in constructing crime but also in its handling of those individuals who get caught in the criminal justice net. In short, we need to focus on the structural barriers and systemic processes, especially as they relate to the experiences of Indigenous women in Canada.

INDIGENOUS WOMEN

The past few decades have witnessed the increasing overrepresentation of Indigenous women in Canadian prisons and jails — a condition even more acute than that of Indigenous men. While Indigenous men represented 24.1 percent of the 14,189 men held in federal custody in 2014/15, Indigenous women represented 35.5 percent of the 676 women held in federal custody in that same period (Public Safety Canada 2016: 53, 54). In 2015 Indigenous women represented less than 5 percent of the total female population in Canada (Statistics Canada 2017).

Although small in comparison to men, the number of women held in federal prisons has been increasing in recent years. According to the Office of the Correctional Investigator (2013: 37, 38), the federal female inmate population increased by 61 percent (from 359 to 579 inmates) between March 2003 and March 2013. One in three federally sentenced women is Indigenous; since 2003 their number has increased by 84 percent (from 104 to 191). At the provincial/territorial level, Indigenous women represented 13 percent of female adults admitted to provincial and territorial sentenced custody in 1998/99. By 2007/08 that figure had risen to 24 percent (Perrault 2009: 20) and by 2014/15 to 38 percent (Statistics Canada 2017). The proportions are highest in the Prairie provinces. In 2008/09 Indigenous women comprised more than 85 percent of women's admissions to adult provincial sentenced custody in Manitoba and Saskatchewan and just over half in Alberta. Yet in 2006 Indigenous adults represented only 11 percent, 12 percent, and 5 percent of these provincial populations respectively (Mahony 2011: 36). This overrepresentation is clearly evident at the Women's Correctional Centre: 90 percent of the forty-two women I interviewed — including Sarah — identified as First Nations or Métis; only four of the women identified as non-Indigenous (a mix of German, Scottish, Ukrainian, Romanian, and Irish heritages) (see also MacDonald 2016).

To understand this overrepresentation requires attending to the role of colonialism and its continuing impact on the lives of Indigenous women, their families, and their communities. One way of accomplishing that understanding is through the lens of trauma.

SITUATING THE WOMEN'S NARRATIVES

One of the insights gained from my meetings with the women at the WCC was that experiences of abuse were not the only feature to stand out in their narratives. Many of the women had also experienced incredible losses — of parents and caregivers, of sisters and brothers, of partners and children. Many of those losses were the result of a premature death due to suicide or violence encountered at the hands of an assailant. Several of the women had lost sisters or friends who are counted among the many missing and murdered Indigenous women and girls in Canada. These events have generated a profound sense of grief for the women. To understand the women's lives and their troubles with the law, therefore, requires a framework that attends not only to their experiences of abuse, but also to how experiences of loss figure into their lives.

Women in Trouble offered a particular understanding of women's law violations. But it is not the only way. Here, in *Coming Back to Jail,* I situate the lives of the WCC women within a broader trauma framework, one that locates the women's abuse experiences and their loss and grief in the structural barriers and systemic processes that impinge upon their lives, including their involvement with the criminal justice system.

Recent years have seen a growing interest in the subject of trauma, especially in relation to Post-Traumatic Stress Disorder (PTSD), including the impacts of PTSD on the lives of criminalized women (Bloom and Covington 2008; Derkzen et al. 2012). A trauma lens has also been used to explore the impact of colonialism on Indigenous peoples, especially historical or intergenerational trauma (Duran and Duran 1990, 1995; Duran, Duran, and Yellow Horse Brave Heart 1999; Wesley-Esquimaux and Smolewski 2004; Haskell and Randall 2009). Nevertheless, the overriding tendency has been to reduce the systemic impacts of colonialism on Indigenous peoples to the psychological level, as manifested in PTSD, the implication being that this colonial trauma can be remedied through appropriate counselling and therapy.

A trauma lens can assist in understanding the lives of the WCC women. My framing of trauma, however, is decidedly sociological, intended to make sense of the women's stories by keeping the focus squarely on the structural barriers and systemic factors — of race/class/gender — that have contoured and conditioned their lives. In this framing, trauma is understood not as a psychological disorder or disease but as the lived experience of residing in a settler colonial, capitalist, patriarchal society. One advantage of adopting this sociological framing is that it avoids the tendency to construct the women as "psychologically damaged" or as "embodying victimization." Despite the life-altering experiences of trauma they have endured, there is much more going on in a woman's life than can be captured in the label of "victim." To cast the women as "survivors" only captures part of their stories. It fails to adequately encompass their incredible resilience in being able to contend with the ongoing, socially created sources of trauma in their lives.

Bringing those socially created sources of trauma to the foreground means mapping out the structural processes and systemic factors that have come to bear on the women's lives — and in particular the ways in which settler colonialism has generated trauma for Indigenous families and communities. The processes and practices of colonialism (and their intimate connections to capitalist development) appear not only in the legacy of the residential school system but also in the social and economic conditions confronting many First Nations communities in Canada. Lake St. Martin First Nation, home to several of the women at the WCC, is one of those communities. The situation for people living in inner-city communities is often no better, as capitalist globalization and neo-liberal economic restructuring have created a complex, racialized poverty and incubated the conditions for the emergence of street gangs and a thriving trade in sex and drugs. Drugging and drinking become ready coping strategies for alleviating the pain generated by this lived experience of trauma.

The women's narratives that form the foundation of this book detail how the social conditions that produce trauma have worked their way into their lives. For most of the women, the trauma trails laid down in previous generations — including the "ripple effect" of the residential school system — continued to move forward into their experiences as children, teenagers, and adults. In their early years the women had common experiences: unsettled home lives, being taken into care, troubles at school, pregnancy at an early age, and initiation into the world of street gangs and the drug and sex trades — to the point at which exposure to sexual exploitation, violence, and drugging and drinking became part of their "normal." They followed those trauma trails into their adult years as they encountered abuse in their intimate relationships. The trauma of loss and its impacts as they grieved the loss of family members and friends added yet another pitfall to this journey.

This lived experience of trauma provides the necessary context for an appreciation of the messy and complicated social situations that draw the women into the criminal justice net. The women's accounts of the conflicts, problems, and dilemmas that bring them to the attention of the criminal justice system expose the often blurred boundaries between "offender" and "victim" and the limits of law's official version of events. Also exposed are the challenges — and further trauma — encountered once the women are caught in the criminal justice net. In particular, the imposition of restrictive bail conditions essentially requires them to refrain from living the life that they know, their "normal." Such restrictions have the effect of setting the women up to fail, thereby dragging them further into the net as they collect more criminal charges and are taken into remand custody to await their trial.

The prisoning of women, especially in these neo-liberal times, is another source of trauma. The provision of gender-responsive programming and other resources in prison is essentially designed to empower the women to become responsible, self-reliant, and conforming neo-liberal citizens.

Nevertheless, prison is a contradictory site: at once a treatment centre and a form of punishment. The women relay their experiences of imprisonment in this contradictory space, including the challenge of doing time in overcrowded cells or in segregation. They talk about their efforts to negotiate relationships with each other and with correctional officers and their attempts to maintain relationships on the outside, especially with their children. The women speak to the project of engaging in their own self-improvement and of trying to heal from their lived experience of trauma while incarcerated — made all the more difficult given the limited choices and the onerous conditions under which they are to undertake that project. Some of the women have managed to engage in a healing process while incarcerated. Even so, the sources of their trauma are not strictly individual or psychological but *social*. Awaiting these women upon their release are the very same systemic processes and social and economic conditions that created their lived experience of trauma and led them into prison.

After hearing from the women, we still face the difficult task of finding a way forward. To begin making change, we need first of all to adopt strategies of decolonization to address the damage that colonialism has caused in Indigenous communities. We need to resist the neo-liberal ideals of how citizens should live their lives, and continue the feminist efforts to break the silence and address the gendered violence that women and girls so regularly encounter in our patriarchal society. Making change also means questioning why we are sending women to prison, and in increasing numbers. Primarily, it means changing women's circumstances on the outside — so that they no longer keep coming back to jail.

CHAPTER TWO

UNDERSTANDING TRAUMA

Criminalized women are more likely to be diagnosed with mental health disorders than are women in the general population. One U.S. study found that 73 percent of females in state prisons, 61 percent in federal prisons, and 75 percent in local jails display symptoms of a mental disorder compared to 12 percent of females in the general population. Women prisoners are also more likely than male prisoners to be diagnosed with mental health disorders; 23 percent of females in U.S. state prisons and local jails said they had been diagnosed with mental disorders in the past year, compared to just 8 percent of male prisoners (James and Glaze 2006: 4).

In Canada, 94 percent of federally sentenced women have experienced symptoms consistent with a diagnosis of a psychiatric disorder; 52 percent displayed diagnostic symptoms of Post-Traumatic Stress Disorder (PTSD), 69 percent of Major Depressive Episode, and 83 percent of Antisocial Personality Disorder (Derksen et al. 2012). While comparable data for provincially sentenced women are not available, several of those I spoke to at the Women's Correctional Centre said they had been diagnosed with a variety of mental health disorders. One of them, Lynne, said she had just recently been diagnosed with schizophrenia. Heather had been diagnosed with "bad anxiety" and Obsessive Compulsive Disorder (OCD), Melody with depression and anxiety, Jackie with PTSD, Lori with bipolar disorder and PTSD, Avery with ADHD and depression, Jennifer and Harmony with anxiety, and Alyson with bipolar disorder. When asked about her health Christine commented:

> They told me I have Attention Disorder due to all the trauma and, like deaths and trauma, family trauma, that's happened in my life in the last five years. So it's like my brain's not functioning the way it should be. It's all over the place. I try to take on everything all

at once or I want all my problems to be solved by the end of the day, which would never, like, that won't happen. That's what the psychologist said, anyways.

Framing the trauma that criminalized women encounter in their lives as a mental health issue flows easily from a more general societal trend towards understanding personal challenges in psychological or psychiatric terms. As Rebecca Dobash and Russell Dobash (1992: 213) note, the overarching tendency in North America has been to consider most social problems "in terms of faulty individual traits and personalities requiring therapy." They describe the United States as a "therapeutic society" in which "almost all social, economic and even political problems are seen as 'personal troubles' requiring therapy" (p. 216; see also Wright 2011). Dobash and Dobash attribute the prominence of this therapeutic ethos to the "extreme individualism" and "perpetual concern about one's status and position" that pervades the United States (p. 216). In recent times that ethos has been strengthened with the advent of neo-liberalism and its individualistic focus. Nowhere is that trend more evident than in regard to the understanding of trauma.

The word "trauma" has become a regular part of everyday conversations. An Internet search easily produces 118 million hits for the word, with a number of common definitions: "A deeply distressing or disturbing experience: *a personal trauma like the death of a child*" (Oxford Dictionary); "An event or situation that causes great disruption or suffering" (The Free Dictionary); "An emotional response to a terrible event like an accident, rape or natural disaster" (American Psychological Association).

In variously referring to an "experience," an "event or situation," and a "response," these definitions of "trauma" reflect the term's contested meanings. Increasingly, however, trauma has become understood as a dominant feature of Post-Traumatic Stress Disorder or PTSD, one of the disorders featured in the *Diagnostic and Statistical Manual of Mental Disorders* (DSM), the bible of the psychiatric profession.

While PTSD might be a popular way of framing our understanding of trauma and its effects, it is nonetheless limited by its focus on the micro or individual level of analysis. In essence, PTSD places the emphasis on trauma as a psychological "response." As such, employing PTSD to understand trauma means individualizing and pathologizing the issue: trauma becomes located within the individual and is constituted as a mental disease or psychological disorder. In the process, the systemic processes that generate it and its social contexts get lost from view. This is especially the case for understanding trauma in the lives of Indigenous women. While a growing literature explores the impact of colonialism on Indigenous peoples through the lens of trauma, the overriding tendency has been to reduce the systemic impacts of colonialism on Indigenous peoples down to the psychological level, as manifested in PTSD.

To counter this tendency, we need to understand trauma not as a "response" but as "lived experience." We need to see it as being located within the particular historical and social conditions in which individuals live their lives. In doing so, we can come to appreciate that trauma is not strictly a psychological phenomenon; it has distinctly social determinants. Achieving this fuller understanding of trauma requires connecting "private troubles" and "public issues." In other words, it requires adopting what C. Wright Mills (1959) called the "sociological imagination" — the quality of mind that enables us to grasp the relation between biography and history. Following Mills, to fully grasp an issue as significant as trauma we must situate personal experiences within the context of a wider society. Fully comprehending the role and impact of trauma in the lives of the women who are at the heart of this work entails an explanation, then, of not just the micro (individual) but also the meso (institutional) and macro (structural) levels. In the process, the social basis of their trauma comes into fuller relief — and so too does the acknowledgement that trauma leaves its mark not only on the women but also on their families and their communities.

This exploration starts with an examination of how trauma is most commonly understood — as PTSD — and the shortcomings involved in adopting that understanding.

POST-TRAUMATIC STRESS DISORDER

The American Psychiatric Association (APA) first officially recognized PTSD in 1980, when the third edition of the *Diagnostic and Statistical Manual of Mental Disorders* (DSM-III) entered the condition under the category of "Anxiety Disorders." The DSM, first published in 1952, has since undergone a series of revisions, the most recent being the DSM-5, published in 2013. The Association intends each of these revised versions of the DSM to reflect the developments in clinical knowledge and scientific research about mental disorders. As the APA's website explains, working groups deliberate on advancements pertaining to specific disorders, field-test studies are conducted, and panels made up of psychiatric experts then determine the revisions or alterations to be made to the DSM.

Political considerations also influence the revisions to the psychiatric understanding of mental health issues. The inclusion of PTSD in the DSM-III, for instance, was prompted by the experience of U.S. soldiers exposed to a variety of battle-related traumas during the Vietnam War. Veterans and their organizations lobbied the APA to construct a diagnosis that would enable them to gain access to medical insurance and treatment (Guina et al. 2016). In a similar fashion, feminist therapists and clinicians lobbied on behalf of their clients to have child abuse and violence against women more adequately recognized in the DSM (Herman 1992a, 1992b, 2012).

The political considerations come into play in other ways, too. For instance, of the 170 panel members responsible for revisions to the DSM-IV and the DSM-IV-TR, 56 percent (95) had one or more financial associations with companies in the pharmaceutical industry. Indeed, a full 100 percent of the panel members considering "Mood Disorders" and "Schizophrenia and Other Psychotic Disorders" had financial ties to drug companies—diagnostic areas in which pharmacological interventions are standard treatment. The psychotropic drug market is extremely profitable: "Antidepressants and antipsychotics were the fourth and fifth leading therapy classes of drugs in 2004, with annual global sales totaling USD 20.3 and USD 14.1 billion in sales in 2004" (Cosgrove et al. 2006: 159). These close associations lead to care "that unduly emphasizes drug treatments," downplaying the harmful effects of drugs (Bloom and Covington 2008: 25).

The initial formulation of PTSD conceptualized trauma as an event that would evoke stress in almost anyone (Burstow 2005: 430). The DSM-III-TR revised the criterion to stipulate that "the person has experienced an event that is outside the range of usual human experience and would be markedly distressing to almost anyone" (APA 1987: 250). As Matthew Friedman (2016) explains, "The framers of the original PTSD diagnosis had in mind events such as war, torture, rape, the Nazi Holocaust, the atomic bombings of Hiroshima and Nagasaki, natural disasters (such as earthquakes, hurricanes, and volcano eruptions), and human-made disasters (such as factory explosions, airplane crashes, and automobile accidents)." In these terms, trauma events were considered to be fundamentally different from the normal stresses of everyday life, such as "divorce, failure, rejection, serious illness, financial reverses, and the like." The revised criterion drew strong criticism for its ambiguity and bias. Commentators raised questions about the meaning of "usual human experience" and the standpoint to be taken in judging it. In response, the DSM-IV, published in 1995, omitted the criterion, and PTSD was subsequently broadened to include not only survivors of war, rape, and disaster but also child abuse and domestic violence (Luxenberg, Sinazzola, and van der Kolk 2001: 374).

PTSD is unique in comparison to other psychiatric diagnoses because of the importance placed on the causal agent: exposure to a traumatic event. The trauma need not be directly experienced. According to the DSM-IV-TR, the person can have "experienced, witnessed, or was confronted with an event or events that involved actual or threatened death or serious injury, or a threat to the physical integrity of the self or others." Another defining criterion spelled out in the DSM-IV-TR was that the person's response needed to involve "intense fear, helplessness, or horror" (APA 2000).

The DSM-IV-TR also mapped out three diagnostic clusters of symptoms resulting from exposure to a traumatic event: (1) intrusive recollections (such as dreams and flashbacks); (2) avoidant or numbing symptoms (such as feelings of detachment or lack of recall); and (3) increased arousal symptoms (such as hypervigilance, insomnia, or outbursts of anger). The manual also specified the number of symptoms in each cluster that had to be present for a diagnosis of PTSD. A fifth criteria cited the duration of symptoms, and a sixth stipulated that PTSD symptoms must cause "significant distress or impairment in social, occupational, or other important areas of functioning" (APA 2000).

In 2013 the DSM-5 moved PTSD from the category of "Anxiety Disorders" to "Trauma- and Stress-or-Related Disorders." The defining feature of PTSD became the "exposure to actual or threatened death, serious injury, or sexual violence." Emotional reactions to the event — "intense fear, or helplessness, or horror" — were no longer part of the defining criteria. The exposure must result from: directly experiencing the traumatic event; witnessing the traumatic event in person; learning that the traumatic event occurred to a close family member or close friend; or experiencing first-hand (not including through media or pictures unless work-related) repeated or extreme exposure to "aversive details" of the traumatic event. This new version specifically includes sexual assault as a source of trauma, as well as recurring exposure to trauma of the type that police officers and first responders might encounter (APA 2013).

The DSM-5 expanded the criteria for diagnosis of PTSD from three to four diagnostic clusters: (1) intrusion (distressing memories and dreams, flashbacks, psychological distress or physiological reactions); (2) avoidance (of distressing memories, thoughts, feelings or external reminders of the event); (3) negative cognitions and mood (inability to remember aspects of the event, persistent and negative beliefs of self, others or the world, estrangement from others, markedly diminished interest in activities); and (4) arousal (aggressive, reckless or self-destructive behaviour, sleep disturbances, hypervigilance, or related problems). Again, the manual specified for each cluster the number of symptoms required for a diagnosis of PTSD. It also eliminated a distinction made in the DSM-IV-TR between acute and chronic phases of PTSD, which pertained to the duration of symptoms. Now a disturbance associated with PTSD must continue for more than one month (APA 2013).

In its form as of 2017, therefore, PTSD is considered to be a response to a trauma event that is evidenced by the characteristic psychological symptoms that an individual manifests.

THE PREVALENCE OF PTSD

Studies estimate that anywhere from 6 to 30 percent of people who experience trauma develop PTSD (*New York Times* Health Guide 2016). While estimates of its prevalence in the population vary, PTSD is thought to be relatively common.

According to the APA (2013: 276), the projected lifetime risk for PTSD in the United States is 8.7 percent of the population. In a country of almost 324 million people, that translates into over 28 million people. The disorder is also gendered. According to the APA (2013: 278):

> PTSD is more prevalent among females than among males across the lifespan. Females in the general population experience PTSD for a longer duration than do males. At least some of the increased risk for PTSD in females appears to be attributable to a greater likelihood of exposure to traumatic events, such as rape, and other forms of interpersonal violence.

Another source estimates the lifetime prevalence of PTSD in the adult population of the United States at 6.8 percent; women (at 9.7 percent) are more likely to be diagnosed with PTSD than are men (at 3.6 percent). In 2016 the previous year's prevalence of PTSD was estimated at 3.5 percent; 5.2 percent among women and 1.8 percent among men (Gradus 2016).

A Canadian study by Michael Van Ameringen and his colleagues (2008) estimated the prevalence rate of lifetime PTSD for adults to be 9.2 percent, or some 3 million Canadians. Similar to U.S. findings, significantly more Canadian women (12.8 percent) than men (5.3 percent) met the criteria for being diagnosed with PTSD. Based on the responses, the researchers estimated that at any given time 2.4 percent of the Canadian adult population is experiencing the disorder; again, more women (3.3 percent) than men (1.3 percent). The study also found that 76.1 percent of the respondents reported exposure to at least one trauma event sufficient to cause PTSD (such as the unexpected death of a loved one, sexual assault, or seeing someone badly injured or killed), leading the researchers to conclude, "A large portion of the Canadian population has been exposed to trauma in their lifetime, making it a relatively common occurrence" (p. 179). While in most cases individuals are able to overcome their trauma experience, "There is a subgroup of Canadian individuals (approximately 10%) who appear to be particularly vulnerable and develop full-syndromal PTSD" (p. 179).

In addition to gender (being female), several "risk factors" are thought to be associated with vulnerability to developing PTSD: a pre-existing mental disorder (especially depression); drug or alcohol abuse; a family history of anxiety; a history of physical or sexual abuse; neglect or early separation from parents; lack of social support; and poverty (*New York Times* Health Guide 2016).

THE LIMITATIONS OF PTSD

The widespread public acceptance of PTSD as a way of framing trauma is understandable. In addition to offering a ready-made construct for making sense of people's experiences, it locates the source of the trauma not in personal flaws or individual shortcomings but in external causes (Waldram 2004). As such, people diagnosed with PTSD tend not to experience as powerful a stigma as that often attached to people encountering mental health issues.

Despite its popularity, however, utilizing PTSD as a way to frame our understanding of trauma has its shortcomings. As the Canadian study revealed, most people experience a trauma event at one time or another in their lives. In that sense, trauma is a *normal* feature of social life; it is an inherently *social* phenomenon. Moreover, PTSD is not only deemed to be a gendered phenomenon (females are more likely to be diagnosed with the disorder); but also, among the "pretraumatic factors" it spells out, the DSM-5 lists "lower socioeconomic status" and "minority racial/ethnic status" (APA 2013: 277), suggesting that PTSD has distinct social determinants rooted in gender, class, and race inequalities. Trauma clearly occurs in a broader social context.

Yet, when framed in terms of PTSD the focus is decidedly an individualized one. As Bonnie Burstow notes, "PTSD is a grab bag of contextless symptoms, divorced from the complexities of people's lives and the social structures that give rise to them. As such, the diagnosis individualizes social problems and pathologizes traumatized people" (2003: 1296). James Waldram (2004: 214) makes a similar point: "DSM focuses in one way or another on *individual* experience, with the individual body as the locus of distress; the 'social body' and the 'body politic' play no meaningful role within the psychiatric conceptualization of the disorder."

In the same way that trauma is a relatively normal feature of social life, some of the coping strategies that individuals adopt — such as avoiding activities, places, or people associated with the trauma event — are normal adaptations in response to a trauma experience. A woman who has been sexually assaulted, for instance, might well be inclined to avoid certain activities (solitary walks), places (bars and nightclubs), or people (men) because of that trauma experience. Nonetheless, such responses are translated in the DSM into symptoms or manifestations of PTSD. As Burstow (2005: 433) notes, "By negating the person as an integral whole, that is, by isolating the behavior into discreet units covered in separate criteria, the diagnosis turns these useful and often vital ways of coping into symptoms of a disease."

Similarly, despite the finding that a large majority of the population is likely to encounter a trauma event, "the underlying assumption embedded in a PTSD diagnosis, and, indeed, in many other diagnoses, is that the world is essentially a safe and benign place. In this view, there is something wrong with people who see or respond to the world as if it were otherwise" (Burstow 2005: 434). Burstow goes on to explain:

> People who are not traumatized maintain the illusion of safety moment by moment by editing out such facets as the pervasiveness of war, the subjugation of women and children, everyday racist violence, religious intolerance, the frequency and unpredictability of natural disasters, the ever-present threat of sickness and death, and so on. People who have been badly traumatized are less likely to edit out these very real dimensions of reality. Once traumatized, they are no longer shielded from reality by a cloak of invulnerability. They now know that the world can get at them. What essentially the diagnostic label [of PTSD] does is define the cloak of invulnerability as normative and define the knowledge and knowledge-based responses of the survivor as symptoms. (Burstow 2005: 435)

For example, women who have been sexually assaulted may well develop a heightened sensitivity to their sexual safety and act accordingly (see Stanko 1990). But within the framework of PTSD, it is their heightened sense of vulnerability and danger that becomes the problem (and requires clinical intervention), and not the social relations between men and women that set the stage for sexual assaults to occur.

COMPLEX PTSD

In its initial formulation, PTSD focused on exposure to circumscribed trauma events, such as combat, disaster, and rape. Critics soon pointed out that this formulation failed to appreciate situations in which the trauma is prolonged and repeated, such as the trauma that Holocaust survivors endured in concentration camps during World War II. Feminist therapists were also dealing with caseloads of women and children who had been exposed to prolonged and repeated violence in their homes, most often at the hands of the men in their lives. In her 1992 book *Trauma and Recovery*, Judith Herman called attention to another war: "There is a war between the sexes. Rape victims, battered women, and sexually abused children are its casualties" (1992a: 32).

Herman pointed out that in cases involving long-lasting, recurring trauma — especially when the perpetrator was known to the victim and in a relationship of trust — the symptom picture is often far more complex: "Survivors of prolonged abuse develop characteristic personality changes, including deformations of relatedness and identity. Survivors of abuse in childhood develop similar problems with relationships and identity; in addition they are particularly vulnerable to repeated harm, both self-inflicted and at the hands of others" (1992a: 119). Nevertheless, Herman argued, "the diagnostic concepts of the existing psychiatric canon, including simple PTSD, are not designed for survivors of prolonged, repeated trauma, and do not fit them well" (1992b: 388). As a means of capturing the sustained effects of this kind of trauma, Herman therefore proposed a new diagnostic category called "complex post-traumatic stress disorder." She defined this new category as:

> A history of subjection to totalitarian control over a prolonged period (months to years). Examples include hostages, prisoners of war, concentration-camp survivors, and survivors of some religious cults. Examples also include those subjected to totalitarian systems

in sexual and domestic life, including survivors of domestic bat-
tering, childhood physical or sexual abuse, and organized sexual
exploitation. (1992a: 121)

A diagnosis of Complex PTSD comprised six symptom clusters reflecting
alterations in emotional regulation, consciousness, self-perception, per-
ception of the perpetrator, relations with others, and systems of meaning
(Herman 1992a: 121; Resick et al. 2012: 241). Yet despite considerable
lobbying efforts on the part of its advocates, both the DSM-IV and DSM-5 did
not include an entry for Complex PTSD, although they did offer a constellation of symptoms spelled out under the heading "Disorders of Extreme
Stress Not Otherwise Specified (DESNOS)," which approximates Complex
PTSD (APA 2013; van der Kolk et al. 2005).

Nevertheless, Herman's work was instrumental in the development of
feminist therapies employed in addressing the trauma of male violence in
women's lives. As Burstow (2003: 1293) notes, Complex PTSD was positioned as a kind of "counterdialogue" to the more male-centred formulation
of simple PTSD, albeit while still accepting its psychiatric underpinnings.
Nevertheless, as she says, even though "the popularization of PTSD has
resulted in greater awareness of the long-term harm of violence against
women and children, the diagnosis itself turns the aftermath of the violence
into a disorder and turns the violence itself into nothing but a preceding
event" (Burstow 2005: 443).

As such, notwithstanding Complex PTSD's greater attention to the gendered nature of trauma and its effects when sustained and repeated over
time, the psychiatric framing of trauma predominates. For writers such as
Burstow (2003), this framing is problematic, and for a number of reasons.
For one, using psychiatric diagnoses such as PTSD means accepting the
power of the psychiatric profession to name people's experiences (thereby
denying people the power to do their own naming). For another, imposing
the psychiatric label opens the way for more substantial psychiatric interference, "for diagnoses are an entry point to more intrusive measures" (p.
1300) such as drugging, electroshock, and restraints. For Burstow, therefore,
"Psychiatry alienates people from their capacity to name, invalidates people's
conceptualizations, imposes a stigmatized identity on them, places them
on paths not of their own choosing, deprives them of liberty, and imposes
harmful treatments on them" (p. 1307).

Burstow also notes that the psychiatric model understands trauma in
binary terms; that is, as a yes or no to a diagnosis of PTSD. In her view, it

makes more sense to conceptualize trauma "as a complex continuum in which we are all located" (pp. 1302–3). To broaden the understanding of trauma, she draws on the work of sociologist Kai Erikson (1995), who rests his analysis of trauma on the Greek origins of the word, meaning "wound." As Burstow notes, "Trauma is not a disorder but a reaction to a kind of wound. It is a reaction to profoundly injurious events and situations in the real world and, indeed, to a world in which people are routinely wounded" (p. 1302). A wound connotes violence. Violence can occur at the interpersonal level, between individuals — but it can also take a structural or systemic form, that is, when "the violence is built into the structure [of society] and shows up as unequal power and consequently as unequal life chances" (Galtung 1969: 171). Moreover, the routine nature of trauma suggests that the resulting injury can have a broad social impact.

Indeed, in his earlier work Erikson (1976) used the notion of "collective trauma" to understand the aftermath of a flash flood that wiped out an entire valley in West Virginia that was the home of a number of small, close-knit Appalachian communities. Erikson noted that on the eve of the disaster, "Buffalo Creek was home for a close nucleus of people, held together by a common occupation, a common sense of the past, a common community, and a common feeling of belonging to, being part of, a defined place" (p. 131). While the loss of homes and family members was devastating for the survivors of the flood, the loss of "communality" — their network of relationships and shared state of mind — was, Erikson argues, every bit as devastating. As Waldram (1997: 44) explains, "In effect, the flood washed away the culture of the valley. With it went the ability of the people to deal with the disaster as a collective and, therefore, their ability to cope with the trauma as individuals."

Erikson's formulation of "collective trauma" has the advantage of extending our understanding: not just individuals but entire communities can be exposed to trauma. This formulation has a special relevance for understanding trauma in Indigenous communities.

TRAUMA AND INDIGENOUS PEOPLES

In his book *Revenge of the Windigo*, Waldram (2004) notes that despite all the evidence of Indigenous peoples being exposed to considerable trauma in their lives, the research on the prevalence of PTSD among Indigenous populations has not produced consistent findings: "While some have discovered relatively high rates of PTSD, many others have been troubled by apparently low rates" (p. 216). Studies on the prevalence of PTSD, as well as diagnoses arrived at by clinicians (see, for example, the PTSD Checklist 1994), are based upon individuals' self-reports of their trauma experiences and responses to those experiences. Most of the studies surveyed by Waldram (pp. 216–18) involving Indigenous populations found that the majority of respondents reported having experienced or witnessed a traumatic event (including experiencing intimate violence or witnessing someone's injury or death), yet only a small proportion met the criteria for a PTSD diagnosis.

Some researchers attribute this disparity to the possibility that the degree of trauma in Indigenous communities is so much higher than in non-Indigenous communities that trauma has become normalized, thereby resetting the individual threshold for a clinical diagnosis of PTSD. For Waldram, the problem with this idea of an elevated threshold for developing PTSD is that it "clearly suggests the existence of a comparative standard of normative experience against which the Aboriginal population is being measured." Such an approach, he says, "fails to comprehend the inherently cultural nature of life experiences such as personal misfortune and disaster" (p. 220).

To address the role of culture — and of history, especially in relation to colonialism — in understanding trauma in the lives of Indigenous peoples, several scholars have embraced the notion of historical or intergenerational trauma. Bonnie Duran, Eduardo Duran, and Maria Yellow Horse Brave Heart (1999; see also Duran and Duran 1990, 1995), for instance, locate trauma in the context of the effects of colonialism on Native Americans. They argue that "intergenerational trauma exists and that its effects manifest themselves through present-day symptomatology," including "alcoholism, poverty, learned helplessness and dependence, violence, and the breakdown of values that correlate with healthy living" (p. 61). Duran and her co-writers situate their analysis in the context of the "trauma of colonialism," which involved the loss of territory and means of livelihood, the loss of loved ones through the introduction of diseases and warfare, the "colonization of the lifeworld" through the dominance of European rationality, and the loss of identity and family stability through the forced removal of children and other assimilationist colonial projects (pp. 62–63). What transpired, according to Duran, Duran, and Yellow Horse Brave Heart, was a "cultural genocide" that threatened the integrity and viability of Native Americans as a social group (p. 63).

These colonial practices created a historical trauma or "soul wound." As the authors explain, colonialism produced a "multigenerational, collective, historical, and cumulative psychic wounding over time" (p. 64). Indigenous peoples pre-contact had "systems in place to deal with and resolve problems in a way that ensured the healthy functioning of the family and culture" (p. 67). Colonialism disrupted those systems, leading to an unresolved trauma that is "intergenerationally cumulative, thus compounding the mental health problems of succeeding generations" (p. 64). Like the children of Holocaust survivors, Native Americans have encountered "depression, suicidal ideation and behavior, guilt and concern about betraying the ancestors by being excluded from their suffering, as well as internalized obligation to share in the ancestral pain" (p. 65).

Given that "researchers and practitioners using western methodologies fail to realize how incompletely their methods capture the truth of Native American tribal lives and pathology" (p. 69), Duran and her colleagues advocate for a postcolonial practice that "integrates indigenous knowledge and therapies with Euro-American models of therapy" (p. 70). This "hybrid therapy," while adding "the strengths of Native American family structures" into the mix, is nonetheless situated within a psychiatric framing of trauma as pathological. In particular, the model uses the notion of the "soul wound" to capture the historical and collective trauma embedded in colonialism; more specifically, in referencing cultural bereavement, the grief over the loss of the culture of one's people, it locates trauma as a wounding of the Indigenous psyche resulting from historical injustices perpetrated by the colonizers. For these writers, historical trauma "encompasses the aftereffects of racism, oppression, and genocide" (p. 65). It produces a repressed anger that manifests in "anesthetic self-intervention behaviors such as alcohol abuse, drug abuse, domestic violence, or suicide" (p. 67).

While their work has the benefit of drawing attention to historical colonial practices and the devastating effects on Indigenous communities and individuals, Duran, Duran, and Yellow Horse Brave Heart focus their understanding of trauma on its psychic manifestations; they position substance abuse, violence, and even poverty as part of the "symptomatology" of this trauma. Similarly, they situate colonialism as a historical artefact that has produced "aftereffects" in the form of a soul wound, which belies its effects as an ongoing, contemporary process. In that regard, while the Holocaust has emerged as a "paradigm for trauma" and the narratives of Holocaust survivors have provided a benchmark for understanding the impact of trauma experiences (Maxwell 2014: 412), Waldram (2004: 223) cautions against setting up the Jewish experience as "a set standard against which all other collective trauma should be measured." Indeed, as Laurence Kirmayer, Joseph Gone, and Joshua Moses (2014: 301) note, the Holocaust and contemporary Indigenous communities display striking differences. For one thing, "The persistent suffering of Native peoples in North America reflects not so much past trauma as ongoing structural violence."

Canadian writers have also adopted the notion of historical or intergenerational trauma to understand the experiences of Indigenous peoples. In a report written for the Aboriginal Healing Foundation, Cynthia Wesley-Esquimaux and Magdalena Smolewski (2004) develop a model for understanding the intergenerational transmission of historic trauma. Similar to the notion of "soul wound," these authors conceptualize trauma in psychiatric terms. Drawing on the work of Herman (1992a), they propose the notion of "complex or endemic post-traumatic stress disorder," which is posited as a "direct result of historic trauma transmission" (p. iii). They define historic trauma transmission as "a cluster of traumatic events and as *a disease itself*. Hidden collective memories of this trauma, or a collective non-remembering, is passed from generation to generation, as are the maladaptive social and behavioural patterns that are symptoms of many social disorders caused by historic trauma" (p. iv; emphasis added).

Wesley-Esquimaux and Smolewski (2004) purposely universalize the historic experience of Indigenous peoples "as a means to explain the basis for the creation of a nucleus of unresolved grief that has continued to affect successive generations of Indigenous people" (p. iii). This experience is also globalized — it includes Indigenous nations of North, South, and Central America. For these authors, "This global context of trauma and suffering produces similar psychological and social reactions in trauma victims, regardless of their cultural background or direct experience with the original source of the trauma" (p. 5). "Cumulative waves of trauma" have been created as colonization passed through its various periods: an early period of cultural transition, a middle period of cultural dispossession, and a late period of cultural oppression. It is in the late period that the psychological effects have been most heavily experienced as the transmission of historic trauma was passed down through the generations by means of different channels: biological (hereditary predispositions to PTSD); cultural (storytelling); social (inadequate parenting, lateral violence, acting out of abuse), and psychological (memory processes). This historic trauma transmission has resulted in an unresolved grief in the "collective psyche" of Indigenous peoples (p. 76).

Despite its attention to the impacts of colonialism on Indigenous peoples, the model of historic trauma transmission put forward by Wesley-Esquimaux and Smolewski has a number of troublesome features. For one, as in the work of Duran, Duran, and Yellow Horse Brave Heart, it conceives of colonization as a historical process "in the past" that has created unresolved trauma for Indigenous peoples "in the present" — as opposed to being an *ongoing* process that continues to generate trauma for Indigenous individuals, their families, and their communities. For another, it again individualizes and pathologizes trauma. For Wesley-Esquimaux and Smolewski (2004: 1), trauma is psychogenic (of mental origin); it manifests in the Aboriginal psyche (collective memory) and in psychiatric disorders, including not only PTSD but also alcoholism, learned helplessness, and Battered Woman Syndrome (BWS).

Among these disorders, "learned helplessness" is a psychological construct that derives from the laboratory research of psychologist Martin Seligman (see Seligman and Maier 1967). In conducting his research, Seligman placed dogs in cages and administered electric shocks to them at random and variable times. Over time, the dogs ceased all voluntary escape activity and instead developed coping skills to minimize the pain (such as lying in their feces). This learned helplessness response was said to consist of trading the unpredictability of escape for the more predictable coping strategies. Learned helplessness became a key component of the Battered Woman Syndrome, as advanced by clinical psychologist Lenore Walker, who used the construct to address the question of why women do not simply leave an abusive relationship. According to Walker (1977–78: 525), learned helplessness provides "a psychological rationale for why the battered woman becomes a victim, and how the process of victimization further entraps her, resulting in psychological paralysis to leave the relationship." Like Seligman's laboratory animals, therefore, abused women are thought to develop coping strategies rather than escape responses to the violence they encounter (Walker 1989: 50–51). Similar to other psychiatric constructs (such as PTSD), then, learned helplessness and the BWS translate a broader social issue — male violence against women — into a pathology applied to the *victims* of the violence and not the perpetrators.

Wesley-Esquimaux and Smolewski (2004) adopt the construct of learned helplessness to explain how trauma enters into the psychological makeup of Indigenous people:

> [Learned helplessness] occurs when an individual (or a group) perceives that his or her behaviour cannot control events and that no action on his or her part will control outcomes in the future.... In consequence, even if a person finds herself or himself in a situation

where she or he could act and react to outside pressures, she or he fails to make any attempt to do so. A person or a group becomes passive, inactive and hostile, ascribing social failures to personal, internal causes and blaming themselves for their helplessness (internal attribution). It is this internal attribution of failure that results in decreased self and social esteem. (Wesley-Esquimaux and Smolewski 2004: 66)

Moreover, much as in the work of Duran, Duran, and Yellow Horse Brave Heart, this model, given its focus on the impact of historical trauma on cultural identity formation for Indigenous people, translates the social into the cultural — a focus that also contains a distinct problem: it obscures "the ongoing forms of material dispossession and political domination" and thereby deflects attention away "from the fundamental causes of distress." It frames healing "in terms of therapy for psychic wounds ... rather than in terms of how people might find meaningful livelihoods within increasingly difficult constraints and imagine a viable future rooted in the material realities necessary for reproducing thriving communities at the local level" (Kirmayer, Gone, and Moses 2014: 311).

As well, the authors deliberately essentialize indigeneity by positing historic trauma transmission as a global phenomenon encountered by Indigenous peoples, "regardless of their cultural background or direct experience with the original source of the trauma" (Wesley-Esquimaux and Smolewski 2004: 5). Also troublesome, the picture that too easily emerges from this account is one of "damaged minds and crippled souls" (Wesley-Esquimaux and Smolewski 2004: 1), which elides the incredible resiliency of so many Indigenous individuals, families, and communities. As Renee Linklater (2014: 25) notes, "The mere fact that Indigenous people exist today and many are experiencing vibrant and healthy culturally connected lives is clear evidence that Indigenous people are extremely resilient."

Other writers have been more attuned to the limitations of the psychiatric model of trauma for understanding the lives of Indigenous peoples. Lori Haskell and Melanie Randall (2009), for instance, acknowledge that trauma has typically been framed as an individualized issue, which "disengages from a broader awareness of the ways in which people's individual experiences are inextricably connected to their broader social contexts" (p. 50). In particular, they note that "an exclusively individualized approach fails to account for the ways in which social injustice, discrimination and colonialism have systematic and far-reaching effects on entire communities" (p. 50). Haskell and Randall are also attuned to some of the difficulties with the notion of "historical trauma":

> This concept of "historical trauma" in relation to Aboriginal peoples makes the trauma in the lives of the peoples of Canada's First Nations appear to be only "historical," when in reality the trauma in their lives remains contemporary and current. In fact, many Aboriginal communities are in contemporary crisis, and are currently traumatized as a result of their current, and not only historical, social conditions. (Haskell and Randall 2009: 73)

These authors therefore propose a "social context complex traumatic stress framework" — a "socio-psychological framework" that draws on constructs from trauma theory, attachment theory, and the literature on historical trauma to provide a "multi-levelled way of understanding collective trauma in communities" (p. 49). Similar to Burstow (2003, 2005) and Waldram (2004), Haskell and Randall point to the limitations of the disease model of trauma: "The language of traditional psychological, psychiatric and medical accounts of trauma and victimization is replete with pathologizing and stigmatizing terms. These include the idea that traumatic responses are best characterized as 'disorders,' and use of descriptors like dysfunction, maladaptive and pathological" (p. 52). Their remedy, therefore, is to opt for the terms "adaptations," "effects," and/or "responses" to refer to the ways in which people cope with abuse and other traumatic events in their lives.

Haskell and Randall come closer to a more sociological understanding of trauma in their effort to bring the social contexts of colonialism and social inequalities into the mix. Nevertheless, their model is still caught within a psychiatric framing. For instance, they retain the notion of "complex post-traumatic stress" — but refer to it as a "response" rather than a "disorder." That semantic switch may not be quite enough to distance their work from the psychiatric model of trauma.

Haskell and Randall, define trauma as "the range of possible, typical and normal responses people have to an extreme and overwhelming event, or series of events" (p. 49). As in the psychiatric framing, then, trauma is a "response," leading to an individualized focus on how individuals respond and what manifestations the response takes within the individual. Indeed, the "social context complex traumatic stress framework" they map out consists of six "diagnostic criteria" that mirror the criteria spelled out for Complex PTSD: (1) affect dysregulation (difficulties regulating emotional states); (2) dissociation (an inability to integrate information and experiences); (3) disruptions in relationships with self and others (including overwhelming feelings of guilt, shame, and inadequacy); (4) disrupted attachment to others (including individuals, community, and a sense of cultural identity); (5) somatization (the physical ailments associated with trauma); and (6) loss of meaning (feelings of hopelessness and despair) (pp. 78–85). While they do pay some attention to the social contexts in which these trauma responses occur, the focus is squarely on individual adaptations to exposure to trauma events.

The question remains, then, as to whether it is possible to understand trauma and the devastating effects it can have on people's lives without recourse to psychiatry; that is, without framing or conceptualizing trauma in terms of a medical disease or psychological disorder. A sociological framing of trauma offers that understanding.

TRAUMA AS SOCIOLOGICAL

Framing trauma in sociological terms involves understanding how the broader social contexts of people's lives play a role in generating the conditions for trauma, as well as delimiting the strategies available to individuals for coping with its effects. As the research on PTSD shows, trauma is a social phenomenon; it is a normal feature of social life encountered by large numbers of people. In a similar fashion, suffering is a normal reaction to trauma. Nevertheless, people's exposure to trauma — and their abilities to manage the suffering it produces — will be very much governed by their social position; that is, their race, class, and gender.

Race, class, and gender inequalities abound in our society: white people accrue privilege on the basis of their race, while Indigenous peoples and other racialized groups experience dispossession and marginalization; wealth is concentrated in the hands of a relative few while poverty restricts the life chances of millions; and men occupy the vast majority of seats in the corporate boardrooms and political offices while too many single-parent mothers struggle to feed their children. As Roxanna Ng (1989: 10) noted, however, "There is a tendency to treat gender, race and class as different analytic categories designating different domains of social life." Yet that separation does not reflect people's actual experiences. Patricia Monture-Angus (1995: 177–78) pointed out:

It is very difficult for me to separate what happens to me because of my gender and what happens to me because of my race and culture. My world is not experienced in a linear and compartmentalized way. I experience the world simultaneously as Mohawk and as woman.... To artificially separate my gender from my race and culture forces me to deny the way I experience the world.

Feminist and critical race theorists have used the term "intersectionality" to capture the multiple and complex nature of these social relations. People's social positioning is not singular or fixed but derives from the relationship between interlocking systems of power (Crenshaw 1989). Accordingly, "forms of subordination such as classism, racism, and patriarchy are enacted in repetitive ways that leave tracks through which the 'traffic' of power and decision-making travel, creating patterns and conditions where these dynamics are replicated and become systemic" (Kaiser-Derrick 2012: 85). Adopting the notion of intersectionality, therefore, means that rather than treating race, class, and gender as additives (race + class + gender), we need to think about these concepts and the relationships they represent as simultaneous forces (race X class X gender) (Brewer 1997).

An individual's positioning within the axis of race/class/gender will very much contour and condition their life experiences, including their ability to exercise autonomy, power, and control in their lives. As Michel Foucault (1978) reminded us, "Power is everywhere." Rather than simply being an instrument or tool that some individuals or groups use to alter the action of others, power is dispersed throughout society. Clarissa Hayward (2000) suggests that we understand power as boundaries that enable and constrain possibilities for social action. "Power's mechanisms include laws, norms, standards, and personal and social group identities. They demarcate fields of action. They render possible and impossible, probable and improbable, particular forms of conduct, speech, belief, reason, and desire" (p. 8). In these terms, "the social capacity to help shape the terms of one's life with others" (p. 10) will be enabled or constrained according to an individual's social positioning within society and the prevailing power mechanisms.

An individual's social positioning will also put them in jeopardy of encountering trauma. In this sense, while trauma may be a normal feature of social life, some individuals and groups will be more exposed to the social conditions that generate trauma than are others. In a society rife with gender inequalities, women and girls will be disadvantaged. Research has shown, for instance, that females are much more likely than males to encounter sexual violence in their lives. Official crime statistics confirm that females are overwhelmingly the most common victims of sexual assault and other sexual violations (such as sexual interference, sexual exploitation, and incest), representing 87 percent and 80 percent, respectively, of those incidents reported to police (Mahony 2011: 7). Girls are more at risk of encountering sexual violence in their homes than boys are. Police-reported data on family violence against children and youth show that girls and boys have similar rates of physical assault perpetrated by a family member, yet the rates of sexual assault against female children and youth are four times higher than they are for males (Juristat 2016: 25).

Research on domestic violence also shows that while men and women are equally likely to report some form of physical or sexual violence by a current or former intimate partner, the scope and severity of the violence they experience differ. Women are more likely than men to report a physical injury (42 percent versus 18 percent) or fear for their lives as a result of the violence (33 percent versus 5 percent). Women are also more likely to report experiencing chronic violence, that is, eleven or more incidents of violence, than are men (20 percent versus 7 percent) (Mahony 2011: 9, 10). Domestic violence is not only gendered, but also racialized. Indigenous women are more likely to report experiencing intimate partner violence than are non-Indigenous women (15 percent versus 6 percent) (Mahony 2011: 12). Data from the 2009 General Social Survey also indicate that Indigenous women experience more serious forms of intimate partner violence than do their non-Indigenous counterparts.

> In 2009, 58% of Aboriginal women who experienced spousal violence reported that they had sustained an injury compared to 41% of non-Aboriginal women. Almost half (48%) of Aboriginal women who had experienced spousal violence reported that they had been sexually assaulted, beaten, choked, or threatened with a gun or knife. A similar proportion (52%) of Aboriginal women who had been victims of spousal violence reported that there were times when they feared for their life. (O'Donnell and Wallace 2011: 41)

Feminists argue that such gender-based violence is neither random nor circumstantial. Rather, they locate the sources of this violence in systemic or structural terms; more specifically, in the patriarchal nature of society. Patriarchy is a system of male domination, the historical structuring of society by men and for men (see, for example, Brownmiller 1975; MacKinnon 1983; Walby 1989; and Price 2005). Violence against women, therefore, both reflects and reinforces women's inequality in society in relation to men. As *The War Against Women* (1991: 9), a report of the Canadian House of Commons Standing Committee on Health and Welfare, Social Affairs, Seniors, and the Status of Women, noted, "The vulnerability of women to violence is integrally linked to the social, economic and political inequalities women experience as part of their daily lives."

Gendered-racialized violence is a significant source of trauma in women's lives. Accordingly, a woman's ability to manage that trauma will be variable, according to the social capital — the resources embedded in the social structure — that she has at her disposal. In order to capture this social nature of trauma, therefore, we need to locate trauma within the historical and cultural context in which individuals live their lives. In other words, we need to reconceptualize trauma as "lived experience." Rather than simply an event or a response, prolonged and repeated exposure to trauma shapes the "personalities, values, attitudes and behaviours" of individuals (Waldram 1997: 46). It also gravely influences the lived experience of the families and communities of which they are a part. In this sense, conceptualizing trauma as "lived experience" draws our attention to collective trauma, "a blow to the basic tissues of social life that damages the bonds attaching people together" (Erikson 1976: 154). In other words, collective trauma impairs what Erikson calls the "communality" of a group: their social networks and shared sense of community.

Framing trauma as "lived experience" also has implications for understanding the notion of "historical trauma." As Aaron Denham notes, "Too often, historical trauma is regarded as both the history or experience of trauma and the resultant impact or constellation of behaviors." A more useful (and accurate) conceptualization of historical trauma "would refer only to the conditions, experiences and events that have the potential to contribute to or trigger a response, rather than referring to both the events and the response." This conceptualization of historical trauma opens the way to acknowledging not only various "expressions of suffering" but also "expressions of resilience and resistance" in response to trauma exposure (Denham 2008: 410–11).

In that regard, the psychological symptoms often associated with reactions to trauma (dissociation, numbing) can actually constitute constructive ways of getting by — and with a proven track record. Burstow (2003) offers the example of survivors of child abuse who use cutting as a way to distract themselves, to calm down, and to remind themselves they are human — and "it works for them" (p. 1305). The same could be said of individuals who turn to drugging and drinking to cope with the trauma in their lives as a way of numbing its effects in order to get by. As the billions of dollars spent each year on prescription medications and alcohol attest, drugging and drinking are socially sanctioned resources in our society. While turning to drugs or alcohol may well generate further troubles, they do have the benefit of ena-bling individuals to manage their pain, at least in the short term. Traumatized people are therefore "actively coping. As such, the so-called symptoms are best theorized as survival skills." They represent their ability "to navigate a world in which terrible things really do happen" (Burstow 2003: 1311)

Framing trauma as "lived experience," therefore, avoids constructing individuals who encounter trauma as possessed of "damaged minds and crippled souls" (Wesley-Esquimaux and Smolewski 2004: 1). Rather, trauma can be said to bring out both problems — and strengths, includ-ing "the development of profound survival skills, an enhanced ability to understand other traumatized and oppressed individuals and groups, a passion for justice, a desire for a different kind of society, a certain critical realism, and what is particularly significant, a less distorted view of the world" (Burstow 2003: 1310).

Moreover, rather than a dualism (yes or no to a psychiatric diagnosis), a sociological understanding of trauma incorporates the notion that trauma exists on a complex continuum. In that regard, "people or communities may be more traumatized in some respects and less in others" (Burstow 2003: 1303). In a sociological framing of trauma, this distinction is very much governed by the social conditions in which those individuals and communities exist and the social capital at their disposal. This is especially the case when the source of the trauma is systemic, as is the case for many (although not all) Indigenous people in Canada. As Linklater (2014: 22) notes, "Colonization has caused multiple injuries to Indigenous people, and therefore many Indigenous people experience trauma in a multi-traumatic context; thus living in and with trauma is a common experience." As well, trauma can be cumulative, both in an individual's lived experience and in the community of which they are a member. In that regard, Burstow speaks to the layering effect of trauma:

> Trauma occurs in layers, with each layer affecting every other layer. Current trauma is one layer. Former traumas in one's life are more fundamental layers. Underlying one's own individual trauma history is one's group identity or identities and the historical trauma with which they are associated. Underpinning this are the structural oppressions

and the institutions through which they operate. (Burstow 2003: 1309)

Finally, this sociological framing has implications for how we respond to trauma. The psychiatric framing of trauma as PTSD puts the emphasis on the individual as the locus for change (through therapeutic interventions by mental health professionals). Clearly, individuals do require supports and assistance in order to heal from their lived experience of trauma and to move their lives forward in a positive and healthy way. The sociological framing of trauma, however, is more expansive. In company with individual healing, it calls for the healing of families and entire communities. Moreover, in drawing attention to the broader social conditions that produce trauma, the sociological framing implicates the "tracks through which the 'traffic' of power and decision-making travel" (Kaiser-Derrick 2012: 85). Ultimately, therefore, alleviating trauma (and preventing its generation in the first place) requires challenging the forms of oppression — of racism, classism, and patriarchy — that are at the root of this lived experience.

STRUCTURAL BARRIERS AND SYSTEMIC PROCESSES

Psychiatric labels such as PTSD have become the dominant frame for understanding trauma and its effects on people's lives, especially on the lives of criminalized women. Indeed, many of the women at the WCC have been diagnosed with PTSD along with other psychiatric disorders. In adopting this individualized framing, however, the social conditions that produce trauma and contour and condition the women's abilities to manage its impact become lost from view. In contrast, a sociological framing of trauma directs our attention to the structural barriers and systemic processes that impinge upon the women's lives, including their involvement with the criminal justice system.

All of the women I met with at the Women's Correctional Centre — albeit to varying degrees and extents — had encountered trauma in their lives. For many of the women, trauma was a defining feature of their lived experience. The women's social positioning — their race, class, and gender — exposed them to social conditions that produce trauma. Most of the women identified as Indigenous. Many had struggled with the constraints of living in poverty. And the majority had encountered gendered violence (in the form of sexual assaults and intimate partner violence). To put this sociological framing to work, we need to explore the social conditions that played a role in generating trauma in the women's lives, especially in relation to the processes and practices of colonialism.

CHAPTER THREE

COLONIALISM, CAPITALISM, PATRIARCHY, AND TRAUMA

Initial pathways researchers were intent on showcasing the voices of criminalized women and locating the women's lives within the nexus of race/class/gender relations. More recent pathways researchers have embraced a risk discourse that seeks to draw the connections between the women's "risk factors" and their propensity for criminal involvement. This more recent work sees the gendered pathways that lead to women's law violations — including childhood victimization and so-called "dysfunctional" intimate relationships — as prompting women's substance abuse and mental health issues, which in turn set the stage for law violations and contact with the criminal justice system. The focus accordingly rests on the need to manage criminalized women's risk to reoffend with appropriate counselling and therapy (Salisbury and Van Voorhis 2009; Brennan et al. 2012), encouraging them to become self-reliant and law-abiding citizens.

Rather than reducing our understanding of women's law violations to their individualized risk factors, however, we need to reinvigorate the sensibilities of the initial pathways researchers and map out the terrain on which these gendered pathways are located. This work involves attending to how the landscape of race/class/gender inequalities — especially in these neo-liberal times — conditions and contours the women's lives.

The social characteristics of the women I talked to at the Women's Correctional Centre reflect those basic inequalities. The vast majority (38, or 90 percent) of the women identified as Indigenous; 30 (71 percent) identified as First Nation; and 8 (19 percent) as Métis, and their education and work histories reveal their class position. Only five of the women (12 percent) had completed high school; 19 (45 percent) had less than a Grade 10 education. Thirteen of the women (31 percent) had never worked for wages in the formal economy. The women who had been employed had worked in low-waged jobs — as factory workers, fast-food servers, home-care attendants, and telemarketers — and usually for only short periods of time. The majority (33, or 79 percent) were mothers, and one-third (11) of those women had five or more children; concerns for their children's welfare figured prominently in their lives.

These numbers — which begin to paint a picture of the women's race, class, and gender locations — are integral to the structural processes and systemic factors that bear on their lives — and that have brought them into conflict with the law. In particular, the women's race/class/gender positioning generates the conditions for trauma. Mapping out these broader trauma-producing social conditions bridges the gap between "private troubles" and "public issues," between individual biography and social history. While trauma is a normal feature of social life, exposure to trauma and the ability to manage its effects are governed by their lived experience in a settler colonial, capitalist, patriarchal society.

COLONIALISM'S TRAUMA TRAILS

Colonialism is, at its core, an economic phenomenon historically tied to capitalist development. In the words of John McLeod (2000: 7), colonialism represents "a lucrative commercial operation, bringing wealth and riches to Western nations through the economic exploitation of others." McLeod notes that seizing "foreign" lands for settlement — a process that began in the late seventeenth and early eighteenth centuries — was in part motivated by the desire to create and control markets abroad for European goods, as well as to secure the natural resources and labour power of different lands and people at the lowest possible costs. As he (2000: 7) emphasizes, colonialism and the erection of a new settler colonial society were "pursued for economic profit, reward and riches. Hence colonialism and capitalism share a mutually supportive relationship with each other." A key characteristic of colonialism is the effort to govern the Indigenous inhabitants of the occupied lands. At its heart, therefore, is the construction of unequal relations of power between the colonizers and the colonized.

In Canada, with the seizure of the territories of the Indigenous population, settler colonization became "a structure rather than an event," and settler colonialism remains in place as "a specific social formation" (Wolfe 2006: 390, 401). Indeed, the racialization of Indigenous people — "the process through which groups come to be designated as different and on that basis subjected to differential and unequal treatment" (Block and Galabuzi

2011: 19) — has continued into the twenty-first century. As Sherene Razack (2007: 74) notes: "As it evolves, a white settler society continues to be structured by a racial hierarchy."

Canadians are often averse to acknowledging our country as a settler colonial society. Indeed, even former Prime Minister Stephen Harper, in responding to a news correspondent during a press conference at the G20 Pittsburgh Summit in September 2009, remarked: "We also have no history of colonialism" (O'Keefe 2009). When public discourse does acknowledge colonialism, it is often as a historical artefact with no bearing on contemporary events. On the contrary, in the words of Patricia Monture (2007: 207), colonialism is "a living phenomenon…. The past impacts on the present, and today's place of Aboriginal peoples in Canadian society cannot be understood without a well-developed historical understanding of colonialism and the present-day trajectories of these old relationships."

The continuing impact of colonialism led to what Judy Atkinson (2002) calls "trauma trails." Examining the case of the Indigenous population of Australia (and with direct relevance to the Canadian experience), Atkinson (2002: 50) notes:

> Large-scale epidemics, massacres, removals of whole populations to detainment camps called reserves, removals of children, splitting apart of family groups, physical and cultural genocide — these formed layers of traumatic impacts down the generations. The cultural and spiritual ceremonial practices of repairing and healing human distress were in many cases outlawed and destroyed under the conditions and enforcements of colonization.

The trauma trails laid down by colonialism have disrupted and restructured relationships between Indigenous men and women, and between parents and children, with an intergenerational impact. "When physical, structural or psychological violence is used to achieve the objective of domination," Atkinson (2002: 92) writes, "the outcomes may not only produce acute trauma, but may set in place chronic conditions of ongoing victimization and traumatisation at different levels, compounding the traumatisation across generations." Colonialism's trauma and the trails laid down in the process alter the lives and conditions not just of individuals — but of families and entire communities.

In addressing the issue of trauma in Indigenous communities as settler colonialism took root and grew, Atkinson and other scholars have referred to what transpired as a "cultural genocide." That sort of naming has itself been the subject of considerable discussion. Genocide scholars have debated the appropriate definitions that apply to a determination of whether or not the treatment of particular groups can be described as "genocide." Andrew Woolford (2015), in a study of the residential school system, offers his own take on this issue. Drawing on the initial formulation of Raphael Lemkin, Woolford uses the term "genocide" to refer to "acts committed with the *intent* to *destroy* a *group*" (p. 31). One of the most important features of genocide, he says, is the "need to be sensitive to the relations and processes that sustain the group and make it a valued source of identity and meaning for individual members" (p. 34). A recognition of this feature draws us away from essentialized notions of group identity and treats the nature of the group and its potential for destruction as empirical questions. Woolford also broadens the notion of "intention" as a way "to better capture the complexity of social action, so that perpetrator actions and intentions can be considered diverse, albeit under a forceful and dominant collective action frame that pushes toward the destruction of a targeted group or set of groups" (p. 45). For Woolford, residential schools represented "an attempt at the genocidal destruction of Indigenous peoples" (p. 263). The concepts of "assimilation" and "civilization" provided the collective action frames around which different governmental and religious actors cohered to bring about that destruction.

Woolford also speaks to the wider colonial context that surrounded the residential school system. In keeping with the characterization of settler colonialism as a structure as opposed to an event, the primary factor animating this colonial structure is "the settler desire for Indigenous lands, not for Indigenous labor, which thus marks Indigenous peoples as dispensable and replaceable" (Woolford 2015: 43). As such, with settler colonial genocide, "the colonizer establishes a dominant settler population in the colonized territory and that population rules that territory from within while seeking the removal or disposal of the 'native'" (p. 42). Settler colonial genocide is therefore a process rather than an outcome. Similarly, "Like capitalism, colonialism is totalizing rather than a totality. It is always expansive and therefore always incomplete in its aspirations. It is a process. It spreads across regions and times in an often uneven and variegated manner, adapting to the local networks that give shape to colonialism on the ground" (Woolford 2015: 42).

THE TRAUMA TRAIL OF THE RESIDENTIAL SCHOOLS

One of the main planks of settler colonialism as it unfolded in Canada was the residential school system, which was initiated in the 1880s with the specific objective of undermining the cultures, languages, spiritual practices, and identities of Indigenous peoples. Duncan Campbell Scott, the Deputy Minister in charge of the Indian Affairs Branch from 1913 to 1923, put it starkly when he described the residential school project as an attempt "to kill the Indian in the child" (Paul 2006). Aboriginal children were forcibly removed from their homes and transported, often some distance away, to attend large, racially segregated industrial schools. Attendance was compulsory. Indian agents were empowered to commit children under sixteen to the schools and to keep them there until they were eighteen. Federal legislation passed in 1894 allowed for the arrest and conveyance to school of truant Aboriginal children, and for fines or jail terms for parents who resisted (Hamilton and Sinclair 1991).

The government delegated this civilizing project of the residential school system to religious organizations and churches, which were given the task of transforming the children from "savages" to "citizens" by inculcating the values of Christianity and industry so that the youngsters could take up positions as "functioning" members of the emerging capitalist society. As the 1889 Annual Report of the Department of Indian Affairs explained:

> The boarding school dissociates the Indian child from the deleterious home influences to which he would otherwise be subjected. It reclaims him from the uncivilized state in which he has been brought up. It brings him into contact day to day with all that tends to effect a change in his views and habits of life. By precept and example he is taught to endeavour to excel in what will be more useful to him. (Cited in Hamilton and Sinclair 1991: 68)

By the 1930s eighty residential schools were spread across the country, with children registered from every Indigenous culture (RCAP 1996: vol. 1 ch. 2). Eventually Canada had a total of 139 residential schools, with the last one closing in 1997. Some 150,000 First Nation, Inuit, and Métis children were forced to attend the schools (TRC 2015).

Several important expositions have been produced about the residential school system in Canada (Assembly of First Nations 1994; Miller 1996; RCAP 1996: vol. 1 ch. 2; Milloy 1999; Knockwood 2015; TRC 2015; Woolford 2015). The conditions at the schools were abysmal; they were built with the cheapest materials, employed untrained staff, and were overcrowded due to the government's financial inducements to increase enrolments (Blackstone and Trocmé 2004). The expressed goal was to produce educated graduates, but few of the children were enrolled beyond Grade 8 in any of the schools (TRC 2015). Children were poorly fed and clothed; so many of them died from preventable diseases (such as malnutrition, smallpox, and tuberculosis) that several of the schools even had their own graveyards. Physical punishment was the norm. Children were beaten for speaking their Indigenous languages; those who tried to run away were shackled to their beds. Suicide attempts were common. Not only were physical abuse and neglect rampant, but so too was sexual abuse — something that was never cited in all of the major reports on the residential school system and only became public knowledge once survivors began to break the silence and tell their stories (see, for example, Assembly of First Nations 1994).

Settler colonial programs of assimilation such as those embodied in the residential school system "can be seen as forms of prolonged terror perpetrated on Aboriginal peoples for generations" (Waldram 1997: 46). Through the residential school project, the Canadian government deliberately set out to destroy Indigenous families and cultures. The generations raised in the schools were not only traumatized by experiences of sexual and physical violence, but also denied their Indigenous identity and access to their language and cultural and spiritual teachings. Indigenous children were told repeatedly that they, their families, and their communities were inferior. Survivors were confronted with the difficult challenge of healing from years of abuse and neglect. Being deprived of healthy parenting role models also left them with diminished capacities as adults to raise and care for their own children, setting up the conditions for the trauma to be reproduced in subsequent generations.

In recent decades, largely in response to the activism of survivor groups and their allies, the Canadian state has taken steps to make reparations for the harms incurred by residential school survivors and their families. In 1998 the federal government designated $350 million for establishing community-based healing initiatives to address the legacy of physical and sexual abuse suffered in the schools, including its intergenerational impact. The Aboriginal Healing Foundation (AHF) was given an eleven-year mandate to administer the funds for conducting research and providing programming for healing initiatives in Indigenous communities. That term was extended in 2007 for another seven years, with $125 million in funds from the Indian

Residential School Settlement Agreement (IRSSA). The largest settlement in Canadian history, the IRSSA was the result of a class-action lawsuit under-taken by survivors against the government and the churches who ran the schools. In addition to providing some $1.9 billion in compensation to residential school survivors and funding to support their healing, the IRSSA initiated the Truth and Reconciliation Commission (TRC). Established in 2008 and issuing its final reports in 2015, the TRC's main purpose was to document the harmful experiences of the survivors in order to make those experiences known to the Canadian public (TRC 2015). Also in 2008 Prime Minister Harper issued a formal apology (albeit without ever mentioning the word "colonialism") for Canada's role in the Indian Residential Schools system (Harper 2008).

The residential school experience has become the singular focus of Canadian discussions of Indigenous trauma, with healing programs "tightly organized around alcohol, drug, and sexual abuse, and incest survival" offered as the appropriate response (Million 2013: 19). Healing, in this context, is positioned as "the afterward, as the culmination or satisfactory resolution of illness or, for the Indigenous, a promised safety and revitali-zation from prior colonial violence" (p. 8). In these terms, there is a ready fit between the need to heal from the historical injustices represented by the residential schools and an individualized understanding of trauma. As such, this therapeutic ethos "has often lent itself to a reconciliation that does not change the colonial structures but adapts the colonized to the colonial systems as they change" (p. 178). In the prevailing neo-liberal climate, "adaptation" came to mean becoming responsible, self-managing individuals who can contribute to the capitalist market.

Mental health and social welfare professionals have also taken up this indi-vidualized understanding of the trauma of the residential school experience. While earlier research and reports on the residential schools emphasized a diverse range of experiences, including "the myriad ways in which students and their families had challenged, subverted, and generally resisted the attempts by the schools to eradicate their language, world view, and familial relations," the adoption of a trauma discourse places the focus "more nar-rowly on experiences of physical and sexual abuse" (Maxwell 2014: 417). It essentially operates to "blame indigenous parents' dysfunction for their children's social suffering and failure to assimilate" (p. 420). Viewing the residential school experience through a psychologized trauma lens has led to "a decontextualized understanding of colonization in which indigenous people are always and only victims" and "disregard[s] how the continuation of colonial institutions, discourses, and practices disrupt indigenous family life in the present" (pp. 421–22).

Indeed, it would be a mistake to rest an understanding of Indigenous trauma solely on the harmful legacy of the residential school experience. To do so would tell only part of the settler colonial story.

THE "MYRIAD DIMENSIONS OF COLONIZATION"

Without a doubt, the residential school experience represents a significant source of trauma, of "prolonged terror," inflicted on Indigenous peoples. But it is not the only source of historical colonial trauma. There are "myriad dimensions of colonization which have had profoundly disruptive effects on social and intergenerational relations" (Maxwell 2014: 426).

One of these dimensions was the appropriation of Indigenous land through the treaty process, whereby the well-being of Indigenous peoples was promised in return for access to the land and other resources (Hart 2002: 25). As the Royal Commission on Aboriginal Peoples (1996: vol. 1 ch. 8) noted, "Treaties and other agreements were, by and large, not covenants of trust and obligation but devices of statecraft, less expensive and more acceptable than armed conflict." The interest of the colonial government in obtaining access to land was so that it could be populated by incoming settlers and utilized for capitalist development (including the building of a transcontinental railway). For many First Nations communities, therefore, the treaties facilitated their dispossession and displacement from traditional hunting, trapping, and fishing grounds, thereby disrupting their economic systems and means of livelihood.

A primary means by which colonization was embedded on Canadian soil, however, was the Indian Act. Enacted in 1876, the Indian Act represents the Canadian state's principal legal instrument of control over Indigenous peoples. The act was "based unashamedly on the notion that Indian cultures and societies were clearly inferior to settler society" (RCAP 1996: vol. 1 ch. 8). The 1876 annual report of the Department of the Interior expressed the assimilationist and paternalistic philosophy that prevailed at the time. Indians were to be treated as "children of the state":

> Our Indian legislation generally rests on the principle, that the aborigines are to be kept in a condition of tutelage and treated as wards or children of the State.... The true interests of the aborigines and of the State alike require that every effort should be made to

aid the Red man in lifting himself out of his condition of tutelage and dependence, and that is clearly our wisdom and our duty, through education and every other means, to prepare him for a higher civilization by encouraging him to assume the privileges and responsibilities of full citizenship. (Cited in RCAP 1996: vol. 1 ch. 8)

The Indian Act sought to "replace the traditional Indian political system by arbitrarily defining a process for the selection of chiefs and councils." It also "imposed upon Indian nations an artificial grouping called the 'band,' and sought to define who was legally entitled to be called an 'Indian' in Canada" (Hamilton and Sinclair 1991: 148). An Indian was legally defined as "any male person of Indian blood reputed to belong to a particular band, and any child of such person and any woman who is lawfully married to such a person" (Gibbins and Ponting 1986: 21). Under this definition, an Indigenous woman who married a non-Indigenous man ceased to be an "Indian" in legal terms, and both she and her children lost all claims associated with that status (for example, treaty rights, residence on a reserve, and participation in cultural and community activities). In contrast, an Indigenous man who married a non-Indigenous woman not only retained his legal status as an "Indian," but also conferred it on his wife and their children. This overt sex discrimination in Canadian law had significant ramifications for generations of Indigenous women and their children. As Gwen Brodsky (2014: 100) notes, "A foundational aspect of an individual's right to enjoy his or her culture is the formation of a sense of identity and belonging to a group, and recognition of that identity and belonging by others in the group. The capacity to transmit one's cultural identity to one's descendants is also a key component of cultural identity." While section 12 1 (b) of the Indian Act was amended in 1985 and 2010 to permit the reinstatement of membership status to Indigenous women, the women who were reinstated could only pass a limited form of status onto their children, which meant that sex discrimination remained in the law (Brodsky 2014; Monture 2014).

The Indian Act was also the mechanism by which Indigenous spiritual and cultural practices were outlawed. An amendment passed in 1884 prohibited the Potlatch (ceremonial gift-giving) and *Tamanawas* (medicine or healing ceremony) and imposed sanctions of two to six months' imprisonment for those found in violation. An amendment in 1885 banned Sun Dances, providing for imprisonment of two to six months for violators. Another amendment in 1914 "outlawed the wearing of any Aboriginal 'costume' and further restricted dances and gatherings" (Flynn 2011: 229). Missionaries — tasked with the "civilizing mission" of the colonial state — saw the persistence of these cultural practices as "devil worship." The hours taken to prepare for the ceremonies were considered to be time that could be better spent engaging in more "legitimate" economic pursuits. Moreover, the giveaways associated with them were inimical to the capitalist ethic — respect for private property and pursuit of individual accumulation — that the colonial government was endeavouring to instil in Indigenous people (McCalla and Satzewich 2002). While Indigenous people found ways of resisting these intrusions on their lives, such as holding ceremonies in secret and altering the practices to make them more "acceptable" to European eyes, the Indian Act continued long into the twenty-first century to hold sway over the lives of Indigenous peoples.

The phasing out of the residential schools began in the late 1940s, and the migration of Indigenous people to urban centres, increased access to isolated Northern communities, and the development of the social work profession brought greater attention to the issue of child welfare for Indigenous children. Because child welfare is primarily a provincial/territorial responsibility, these governments were reluctant to extend their growing social services to Indigenous people without federal funding. A 1951 amendment to the Indian Act provided that laws in force in any province would apply to Indigenous people both on and off reserve, including child welfare laws, although no monies were designated to support this change. In 1966 the Hawthorne Report, a federal government survey of Indigenous people living in reserve communities, documented the poor state of child welfare services on reserves. In the same year, with the passage of the Canada Assistance Plan, the federal government entered into a cost-sharing agreement with the provinces to extend child welfare services into Indigenous communities.

With this expansion of child welfare services into Indigenous communities, more and more Indigenous children were placed in care. As the Canadian Council on Social Development documented:

> In 1955, there were 3,433 children in the care of B.C.'s child welfare branch. Of that number it was estimated that 29 children, or less than 1 percent of the total, were of Indian ancestry. By 1964, however, 1,446 children in care in B.C. were of Indian extraction. That number represented 34.2 percent of all children in care. Within ten years, in other words, the representation of Native children in B.C.'s child welfare system had jumped from almost nil to a third. It was

a pattern being repeated in other parts of Canada as well. (Cited in RCAP 1996: vol. 3 ch. 2)

By 1977 almost 20 percent (15,500) of the total number of children in care across the country were Indigenous. The proportion was greatest in the Western provinces, where Indigenous populations are concentrated: 39 percent of the children in care in British Columbia were Indigenous; 40 percent in Alberta; 50 percent in Saskatchewan; and 60 percent in Manitoba (Hepworth cited in Kline 1994: 387). According to a 1983 study, First Nations children were being placed into care at a rate of almost *five times* that of other Canadian children. Once admitted into care (most often in urban, white homes), these children were much less likely than other Canadian children to be returned to their parents (Johnson 1983; see also York 1990: ch. 8).

The child welfare system essentially amounted to the same thing as the residential school system: a method of colonization, albeit in a different guise. Indigenous children were removed from their homes and communities and placed in non-Indigenous homes on the grounds that Indigenous parents were deemed to be "unfit" — and their children were seen to be in need of "values and lifestyles with which the child welfare workers themselves were familiar: white, middle-class homes in white, middle-class neighbourhoods" (Hamilton and Sinclair 1991: 520). As in child custody cases generally, this action was taken under the rubric of the "best interests of the child doctrine." As Marlee Kline (1994; see also Monture-Angus 1995) noted, this doctrine carried distinct racist tendencies. It relied upon a construction of the child's "best interests" as separate from, and abstracted out of, his or her familial and cultural context; it therefore minimized and even negated the importance of maintaining a child's Indigenous identity and culture. In this way, the "best interests of the child" doctrine offered "an interpretive framework in which the removal and placement of First Nations children away from their families and communities appear natural, necessary and legitimate" — rather than coercive and destructive (Kline 1994: 393–94).

One insidious practice came to be known as the "Sixties Scoop" (because it began in earnest in the 1960s). It involved the apprehension of Indigenous children from their home communities — often without the consent of their families and bands — and their subsequent adoption by non-Indigenous families, many of whom lived outside of Canada. The strongest demand for children came from the United States, where private agencies were making profits by finding children for middle-class white couples. From the early 1970s until 1982, more than one thousand Indigenous children from Manitoba were "scooped" from their families and sent to the United States for adoption (York 1990: 206; see also Hamilton and Sinclair 1991: 523).

As the colonial state's practice of "scooping" Indigenous children came more and more into the public light, Indigenous communities and their leaders reacted with anger and outrage, accusing the government of engaging in the practices of "selling babies" and "cultural genocide" (Hamilton and Sinclair 1991: 523). The Manitoba government responded in 1982 by ordering a halt to all out-of-province Indigenous adoptions. That same year, Associate Chief Judge Edwin C. Kimelman of the Provincial Court, Family Division, was appointed to head an inquiry into the province's child welfare system and its impact on Indigenous people.

In his report, *No Quiet Place*, Kimelman (1985) was sensitive to the class-related factors that led to Indigenous children's overrepresentation in the child welfare system: "There is a direct relationship between poverty and the stress caused by poverty, and the child welfare system" (p. 262). But a key theme in his report was the racism that permeated the system: "Cultural bias is practiced at every level from the social worker who works directly with the family, through the lawyers who represent the various parties in a custody case, to the judges who make the final disposition in the case" (p. 185). Kimelman noted, for example, that an Indigenous mother might leave an infant child with a member of her extended family for a period of time. But "a worker who did not understand the Indian concept of the child as a member of the total community, rather than as the exclusive property of a single set of parents, might perceive that child to be abandoned when it is, in fact, residing within its own 'family'" (pp. 161–62). Similarly, Indigenous parents tend to give their children a great deal of independence and freedom, and children are viewed as equal members of the community. Yet "a Native mother who does not provide constant eyes-on supervision of a child might be viewed by a social worker as negligent" (p. 162).

Kimelman's investigation revealed "an abysmal lack of sensitivity to children and families." Indigenous families approached agencies for help only to find that "what was described as being in the child's 'best interest' resulted in their families being torn asunder and siblings separated" (p. 274). He therefore deemed the problems encountered with the child welfare system as being systemic:

> It would be reassuring if blame could be laid to any single part of the system. The appalling reality is that everyone involved believed they

were doing their best and stood firm in their belief that the system was working well. Some administrators took the ostrich approach to child welfare problems — they just did not exist. The miracle is that there were not more children lost in this system run by so many well-intentioned people. The road to hell is paved with good intentions, and the child welfare system was the paving contractor. (Kimelman 1985: 275–76)

Kimleman recommended drastic changes to the province's child welfare system, including a legislative redefinition of the "best interests of the child" to include recognition of a child's cultural and linguistic heritage, the repatriation of "exported" Indigenous people to their home communities, and greater efforts to strengthen Indigenous families and to keep Indigenous children in their home communities. *No Quiet Place* was also influential in strengthening the move — begun in 1981 in Manitoba — to transfer responsibility for the welfare of Indigenous children to Indigenous agencies (Hudson and McKenzie 2003).

Cree scholar Michael Hart (2002) notes that the lives of Indigenous families have been dramatically altered by these myriad dimensions of colonization. "At one point Aboriginal families were well defined by extended family relationships which crossed generations and bloodlines. These relationships established intricate balances between the genders, generations and assigned responsibilities, and were the weave of Aboriginal communities." These relationships were "torn apart" as a result of the displacement and increasing impoverishment that accompanied colonization (p. 26).

Métis scholar Emma LaRocque (2002: 148) maintains that while colonization has taken its toll on all Indigenous people, "it has taken perhaps its greatest toll on women." She explains:

> Prior to colonization, Aboriginal women enjoyed comparative honour, equality, and given political power in a way European women did not at the same time of history. We can trace the diminishing status of Aboriginal women with the progression of colonialism. Many, if not the majority, of Aboriginal cultures were originally matriarchal or semi-matriarchal. European patriarchy was initially imposed upon Aboriginal societies in Canada through the fur trade, missionary Christianity and government policies. Because of white intrusion, the matriarchal character of Aboriginal spiritual, economic, kinship, and political institutions was drastically altered.

At bottom, the dimensions of colonization amount to the perpetuation of racism towards Indigenous people. Robert Miles (1989) defines "racism" as "ideas that delineate group boundaries by reference to race or to real or alleged biological characteristics, and which attribute groups so racialized with other negatively evaluated characteristics." But racism involves more than just holding particular negative beliefs or attitudes about certain groups of people. Racism is a social practice connected to power; it organizes, preserves, and perpetuates the power structures of society (Henry et al. 2009); it rationalizes, legitimates, and sustains patterns of inequality (Barrett 1987: 7). Speaking of racist ideas, Stuart Hall (1997: 35) explains they are "not a set of false pleas which swim around in the head."

> They're not a set of mistaken perceptions. They have their basis in real material conditions of existence. They arise because of concrete problems of different classes and groups in society. Racism represents the attempt ideologically to construct those conditions, contradictions, and problems in such a way that they can be dealt with and deflected at the same moment.

LaRocque (2002: 149) states: "One of the many consequences of racism is that, over time, racial stereotypes and societal rejection may be internalized by the colonized group. The internalization process is one of the most problematic legacies of long-term colonization." LaRocque draws on the work of Howard Adams (1975), who in *Prison of Grass* refers to the problem of "internalization." According to LaRocque, "By this [Adams] meant that as a result of disintegrative processes inherent in colonization, Aboriginal peoples have subconsciously judged themselves against the standards of white society, often adopting what he called the White Idea. Part of this process entails internalizing or believing — swallowing the standards, judgements, expectations, and portrayals of the dominant white world" (p. 149).

As LaRocque notes: "A lot has changed in Aboriginal communities since Adams wrote *Prison of Grass*. A lot more Aboriginal people are aware of the whys and wherefores of their position in Canadian society. As more Aboriginal people grow in political awareness, they are less prone to judge themselves or act by outside standards. However, the damage has been extensive" (p. 149).

While the original trauma trails of colonialism were laid down decades ago, settler colonialism as a process and a social formation persists into the present day.

CONDITIONS ON FIRST NATIONS RESERVES

Contemporary manifestations of settler colonial dominance and the inequities it produces are many, especially for those who reside on First Nation reserves. One manifestation is the disparities in educational achievement.

The completion of high school is beyond the reach of many First Nations youth living on reserves (Drummond and Rosenbluth 2013). "Among young adults aged 20–24, nine of 10 non-Aboriginals have at least high school, as do eight of 10 Métis and seven of 10 First Nation living off-reserve. In stark contrast, only four in 10 First Nation young adults living on-reserve graduated from high school" (Anderson and Richards 2016: 4). A large part of the reason for these educational disparities is the chronic underfunding of education on First Nations reserves. Funding for reserve schools is a federal matter, while the provinces are responsible for funding the education of other Canadian children. For their primary school education, Indigenous students on reserves receive about a quarter less funding for their primary school education than do other Canadian children; in Saskatchewan the funding gap is estimated to be as high as 40 percent per student. Member of Parliament Charlie Angus has described this practice as a form of "educational apartheid" (Sniderman 2012).

Another manifestation is Indigenous child poverty. Using data from the 2011 National Household Survey and the 2006 Census, researchers David MacDonald and Daniel Wilson (2016) applied the After Tax Low Income Measure to discover an overall child poverty rate of 18 percent, putting Canada in twenty-seventh place out of thirty-four Organization for Economic Co-operation and Development (OECD) countries (p. 6). Indigenous children fared the worst: 60 percent of status First Nations children were experiencing poverty (p. 19), with the highest figures for status First Nations children in the Prairie provinces; 76 percent in Manitoba and 69 percent in Saskatchewan were living in poverty (p. 6).

In company with the alarming rates of Indigenous child poverty, living conditions on many First Nations reserves have long been defined as a matter of crisis proportions. Substandard and overcrowded housing is one pressing issue. In 2006, 28 percent of First Nations people were living in a home in need of major repairs, compared with just 7 percent of the non-Indigenous population; First Nations people were five times more likely than non-Indigenous people to live in crowded homes (Statistics Canada 2008). Access to potable water, adequate sanitation, and waste disposal services are resources that many Canadians take for granted, yet in the fall of 2015,

120 First Nations communities were under drinking-water advisories; some of those advisories have been in place for nearly twenty years (MacDonald and Wilson 2016: 21; Perry 2016). Many reserve communities still do not have running water or sewer lines.

Impoverished living conditions undermine the health of a community. Indigenous people have shorter life expectancies and a higher risk of suffering from infectious diseases such as tuberculosis and chronic illnesses such as diabetes. The Royal Commission on Aboriginal Peoples (RCAP: 1996 vol. 3 ch. 3) found that rates of tuberculosis infection were forty-three times higher among status First Nations people than among non-Indigenous Canadians born in this country; the incidence rate for diabetes was at least two to three times higher among Indigenous than among non-Indigenous people.

These impoverished social conditions generate trauma. One indicator is the suicide rate. While varying widely, the youth suicide rate in First Nations communities is still between three and seven times greater than in Canada overall (Campaign 2000 2010). In March 2016, for instance, Pimicikamak Cree Nation in Northern Manitoba declared a state of emergency after six members of the community — many of them youth — committed suicide and another 170 students at the local high school were placed on a suicide watch list (CBC News 2016a). Sheila North Wilson, Grand Chief of Manitoba Keewatinowi Okimakanak, attributed the crisis to "despair and poverty in our communities. The opportunities and resources that are afforded to the rest of Canadians are not being afforded to our people" (CBC News 2016b).

As the prevalence of suicide attests, individual trauma is evident in First Nations communities. But trauma also prevails at a collective level. Kai Erikson's account of the collective trauma experienced by members of an Appalachian community bears a close resemblance to that experienced in several First Nations communities in Canada.

COLLECTIVE TRAUMA

In his study of the "collective trauma" that resulted from a massive flash flood in a West Virginian valley in 1972, Erikson (1976) provides a historical account that looks at how capitalist economic development altered life in the region as lumber and coal companies moved in to extract the natural resources. As he summarizes: "The people of Appalachia have been the victims of one long, sustained disaster brought about by the pillaging of the timber reserves, the opening of the coal fields, the emergence of the Depression, and the introduction of welfare as a way of life" (p. 250).

In the early 1970s the community was relatively stable. Most of the men were employed and earning good wages in the coal mines and people owned their own homes, which they had bought from the coal company and renovated to accommodate their growing families. All of that came to an abrupt end on February 26, 1972 when after a heavy rain the dam holding back water and silt from the mining operation breached, sending 132 million gallons of black water into the valley and washing away almost everything and everyone in its path. The flood killed 125 people and left another 4,000 Buffalo Creek residents homeless.

In the aftermath of the flood, the National Guard was called in and the Nixon administration authorized $20 million for emergency relief (p. 43). The U.S. Army Corps of Engineers came in to dismantle the houses that could not be repaired; other houses had to be cleared of mud and debris. The residents left homeless were moved to mobile homes. The U.S. Department of Housing and Urban Development (HUD) set up thirteen trailer camps that sheltered some 2,500 people, a decision that further disrupted the social networks in the community.

> HUD assigned applicants to vacant spaces on a first-come, first-served basis, the theory being that people should be moved under a secure roof as soon as possible. The net result of this procedure, however, was to take a community of people who were already scattered all over the hollow, already torn out of familiar neighbor-hoods, and make that condition virtually permanent. (Erikson 1976: 47)

Even though the flood was a natural disaster brought on by rain, it had human causes. A lawsuit was filed against the coal company on behalf of some 650 survivors on the grounds that the company was negligent in its handling of the water and waste produced from the mining operation. Some two years after the disaster, in 1974, the plaintiffs won their court case and were awarded $13.5 million in damages against the coal company (p. 248). But as Erikson notes, the task of restoration for the residents of Buffalo Creek was still very much ahead of them.

In detailing the various trauma symptoms experienced by the Buffalo Creek survivors — including fear, apathy, and demoralization — Erikson makes the case that these symptoms were not simply a reaction to the disaster itself, but a result of being ripped out of a meaningful community (p. 194). Moreover, this breakdown of "communality" — the network of social relationships or shared state of mind — was in evidence several years after the disaster. The use of alcohol increased among the residents, and drugs found their way into the community. The theft rate was rising, and teenagers finding themselves with little to do were engaging in delinquent acts (p. 205).

Like the people of Appalachia, First Nations communities in Canada have also been devastated by flooding and experienced collective trauma as a result. Also like the experience of the people of Appalachia, the cause of the flooding was not simply a matter of nature; it had distinctly human-made determinants rooted in capitalism and its unrelenting drive to increase profitability through the exploitation of land and labour. Hydroelectric developments carried out in the name of "economic progress" have led to the disintegration not only of livelihoods and social cohesion but also of the self-worth of Indigenous individuals and communities. But unlike the Appalachian flood, First Nations communities have been subjected to the incursions of both capitalism but colonialism (see, for example, Waldram 1988; Kulchyski 2007). One of those communities is the Lake St. Martin First Nation, home to several of the women I met with at the Women's Correctional Centre.

LAKE ST. MARTIN FIRST NATION

In 2011 Manitoba experienced what was deemed to be "the largest spring runoff in the province's history" (Galloway 2012). Concerns over high water levels led the provincial government to divert water into Lake St. Martin in Manitoba's Interlake region. The decision saved summer vacation cottages and agricultural areas near Lake Manitoba and the Assiniboine River, but flooded three First Nations communities. Lake St. Martin First Nation was hardest hit by the flooding, and the entire community had to undergo an emergency evacuation on May 8, 2011.

Lake St. Martin First Nation is a community of some 2,400 people located on the northeast shore of the lake, 225 kilometres northwest of Winnipeg. Indigenous people have resided on those shores for generations. Their traditional land, home to abundant fish and wildlife, also had fertile soil for agriculture. After the treaty process reduced the community's once vast territory to about 24 square kilometres, the community found it more challenging to maintain its traditional means of livelihood (Thompson,

Ballard, and Martin 2014), yet managed to hold its own. At the beginning of the 1960s, as Grand Chief Derek Nepinak (2012) of the Assembly of Manitoba Chiefs later wrote, "The lands around the Lake St. Martin First Nation supported a strong agricultural economy bolstered by a strong fishery. One could observe that the community was a prime example of being ideally situated for long-term stability with a diversified economy. Flooding was not a concern for the Lake St. Martin community members."

In 1961 the province changed all that by constructing the Fairford water-control structure upstream at the Fairford River, which receives its water from Lake Manitoba. The resulting elevated water levels on Lake St. Martin threatened agricultural lands and fishing livelihoods. Annual spring flooding also damaged the local housing stock, with mould becoming a perennial problem. Further exacerbating the situation, in 1970, to keep the city of Winnipeg safe and dry the province created the Portage Diversion, which elevated water levels in Lake St. Martin even more (Ballard and Thompson 2013: 48). The reoccurring flooding had severe consequences for the members of the First Nation community.

As the water levels increased, so too did poverty in the community. As Shirley Thompson, Myrle Ballard, and Donna Martin (2014: 80) note, Lake St. Martin First Nation community members had a median annual income of only $1,636 in 2006, a figure that was drastically below that of Manitobans in general ($24,194), First Nations people living off-reserve ($22,500), and First Nations people across Canada living on-reserve ($14,000). The low figure so surprised these authors that they were prompted to contact Statistics Canada to confirm its accuracy.

In Lake St. Martin, as in other First Nation communities, educational attainment is low. Only about 11 percent of Lake St. Martin youth had graduated from high school in 2006 (Thompson, Ballard, and Martin 2014: 80). Part of the reason for this low educational attainment is that schooling in the community was available only to Grade 9. For another thing, Thompson and her colleagues note, the federal government had determined the school's location against the advice of the community. Soon after it was opened, the school was closed by public health officials because of health hazards. The children were then housed in portables that were prone to dampness and mould, making conditions for learning even more challenging.

In response to the "superflood" of 2011, the Fairford control structure was opened to its maximum to divert water from the Assiniboine River towards Lake St. Martin. The rising water levels prompted an emergency evacuation of the Lake St. Martin First Nation community. The evacuation required the residents to leave most of their possessions behind. They were relocated to hotels in Winnipeg and to temporary housing in the Interlake region and other locations. For those living in hotels, the lack of access to a kitchen meant relying on restaurant food. With limited funds, that proved problematic.

> The daily evacuee allowance of twenty-four dollars per adult per diem did not cover the costs of having to eat in restaurants. Families had to make tough choices, deciding each day who would eat and who would not, as the money would not cover three meals a day for all family members. This initial stipend was drastically reduced to four dollars per adult per day, and many people spiralled into debt, taking loans from friends and family. Families were forced to access food banks to supplement their basic needs and often went hungry. (Thompson, Ballard, and Martin 2013: 82)

Access to education was also an issue. The majority of the children were evacuated to Winnipeg in May 2011, but a school building was not made available for them until October "despite many closed schools identified by band staff as possibilities" (p. 80). The children were moved to a different school in September 2012, although the city closed it down for several weeks because the landlord had violated a number of city bylaws regarding fire hazards and asbestos exposure (CBC News 2012). Moreover, since pets were not allowed in hotels and other temporary housing, family pets often had to be taken to the Humane Society for adoption, creating further distress for the children.

While the province established a $200-million relief plan for farmers and cottagers who had suffered losses as a result of the government's decision to cut a hole in a dike during the flood (Paperny 2011), the Lake St. Martin families did not have access to similar compensation. Given the communal land and home-ownership model on reserve lands, band members do not own their homes. As a result they could receive no compensation for the loss of their houses, even if they had made significant upgrades and investments in the property.

The individual trauma created by the evacuation was considerable. Being relocated far from home and disconnected from their social networks left people emotionally unhinged. As one woman described it, "I get very lonely. I want to cry all the time" (Ballard 2012). Relationships came under stress. One man said that he and his wife now "argue more than we ever did" (Ballard 2012). Community members reported various health issues, including "premature deaths, increased rates of suicides, miscarriages, mental health issues, and worsening of chronic disease" (Thompson, Ballard, and Martin 2014: 84).

The collective trauma was also evident in experiences after being relocated to Winnipeg. As one of the Elders reported, "We're not used to living in the city" (Ballard 2012). Compounding the matter, several community members reported being subject to overt racism on a daily basis (Thompson, Ballard, and Martin 2013). Parents became concerned for their children's welfare as youth accustomed to rural life were exposed to drugs and alcohol and lured into the street gangs that operate in the city (Paul 2013; CTV News 2015).

The loss of a deep sense of communality was yet another concern. As one of the Elders remarked, "We've lost our traditional way of life. We've also lost our culture" (Ballard 2012). With the community dispersed and separated from their traditional land, spiritual activities and cultural practices (such as Sun Dances) were curtailed. "Visiting each other is an important part of native culture, but now people are so dispersed that they have lost track of each other. This dispersal has also meant that people are not able to visit and communicate in their *Anishinaabe* language" (Ballard and Thompson 2013: 60).

Some five years later, the members of Lake St. Martin First Nation were still without a permanent home. By May 2016 the costs to temporarily house the evacuees had ballooned to $136 million (Rabson 2016). While the federal and provincial governments and First Nations finally reached an agreement on a new site for resettlement of the community, plans for the construction of new homes and services were still not finalized. The community remained displaced and reeling from the collective trauma resulting from the human-made flood.

As the experience of the residents of Lake St. Martin First Nation documents, deteriorating living conditions in many First Nations communities have prompted increased migration between First Nations communities and urban centres. Indigenous people began to move from rural and reserve communities to urban centres in the 1960s; the numbers of those migrants increased significantly in the 1970s and 1980s (Loxley 2010). As of 2006, over half (54 percent) of the Indigenous population of Canada now live in urban centres (Statistics Canada 2008). While many of the women at the WCC spent their childhoods residing in their First Nation community, just as many grew up in Winnipeg's inner city, and most of the women ended up living there as adults.

LIVING IN THE INNER CITY

Much like other Prairie cities in Canada, Winnipeg is home to a large number of Indigenous people. In 2011 about one-third of all Indigenous persons in Manitoba lived in Winnipeg. Of major cities in Canada that year, Winnipeg had the highest number of Indigenous people (72,335), representing 11 percent of the total Winnipeg Census Metropolitan Area population (Statistics Canada 2011). Many Indigenous people have taken up residence in Winnipeg's inner-city communities, making up some 21 percent of the population there (MacKinnon 2009: 32); in some inner-city neighbourhoods Indigenous people make up 50 percent or more of the total population (Silver 2015: 228). Jim Silver (2006: 17) observes, "The spatial distribution of Aboriginal people in cities … parallels their spatial distribution outside urban centres." That is, just as they have historically been confined to rural reserves, now in cities they are being set apart from mainstream Canadian life. Their "move to the city is too often a move from one marginalized community to another."

Like other inner-city communities in North America, Winnipeg's inner city has undergone drastic changes with the advent of capitalist globalization — the integration of national economies into a global network — and the accompanying shift from industrial to "non-standard" and service-sector jobs (Broad 2000; Broad, Cruikshank, and Mulvale 2006). Large firms have relocated many industrial jobs that were unionized, paid a living wage, and offered reasonable benefits — jobs that could support a family — to other, lower-wage jurisdictions. The jobs have been replaced by "precarious" employment that is non-union, low-wage, and part-time, and carries with it neither benefits nor security — positions that cannot support a family (Silver 2016: 14). At the same time, the process of suburbanization that began in the post–World War II era has seen large numbers of people who can afford to do so moving away from inner-city locations to the suburbs. Many businesses followed suit. Those left behind in inner-city communities have been, for the most part, those least financially able to move.

The abandonment of Winnipeg's inner city by the more financially well-off placed downward pressure on housing prices in an area in which housing was already the oldest and in need of repair (Deane 2006). Cheaper housing attracted people with the lowest incomes, not surprisingly, thus concentrating poverty in large numbers in the inner-city neighbourhoods. Some ten percent of Winnipeg dwellings are in need of major repair, which significantly exceeds the national average of 7 percent and is the highest percentage among Canada's twenty-five metropolitan areas (Skelton, Selig, and Deane 2007: 55). In many cases cheap inner-city housing was acquired by absentee landlords who used it as a "cash cow" while allowing it to deteriorate. Close to two-thirds of Winnipeg's inner-city residents rent their living accommodation, and are therefore reliant on landlords to ensure that buildings are properly maintained (Cooper 2011: 22).

In more recent years, growing numbers of immigrants and refugees from war-torn countries arrived in Winnipeg. Many of them had low levels of formal education as a result of poverty and war, and most of them located in the inner city — for the same reason that low-income people had, for decades, located there. Refugees tend to look for central locations, access to services, and a proximity to others from their homelands. "But many refugees stay in the inner city simply because that is where housing is affordable and available, although not always adequate in size or condition" (MacKinnon, Salah, and Stephens 2006: 5; see also Silver 2010; Kazemipur and Halli 2000).

When Indigenous people began arriving in Winnipeg in the 1960s, many of them came unprepared for urban industrial life, in large part because the reserve and residential school systems had left them without adequate formal educational qualifications (Knockwood 2015; Milloy 1999). After the initial arrivals became concentrated in Winnipeg's inner city — because of its inexpensive housing — those who came in subsequent decades went to the same areas because that was where other Indigenous people already lived. But they were moving to neighbourhoods in which jobs — and particularly the kinds of industrial jobs that had historically been available to those with limited formal educational qualifications — had disappeared. With few well-paid jobs available, and facing a wall of systemic racism and discrimination, many Indigenous people became effectively locked out of the formal labour market (Silver 2016; Cheung 2005).

The result of these various processes — globalization, deindustrialization, suburbanization, immigration, and migration — has been the concentration of complex, racialized poverty in Winnipeg's inner city (Silver 2016, 2017). Meaningful well-paid jobs are scarce, housing is frequently inadequate, and opportunities (recreational and otherwise) are limited. As a result, very large numbers of inner-city people have been "raised poor." They have never known anything but poverty and joblessness.

Statistics offer a picture of life in Winnipeg's inner-city communities. The rate of poverty in the inner city is almost twice as high (39.6 percent) as in the rest of Winnipeg (20 percent) (MacKinnon 2009: 30). As Silver (2015: 228) notes, "The median household income in the inner city is just under two-thirds — about 64 percent — that of Winnipeg as a whole." Almost half (49 percent) of the large numbers of Indigenous people living in Winnipeg's inner-city communities were living in poverty in 2011 (Lezubski and Silver 2015: 33). Unemployment explains some of this disparity. Unemployment rates for Indigenous people in Winnipeg are double those of the non-Indigenous population, and the labour-force participation rate for Indigenous people aged fifteen to twenty-four is just over 50 percent. Almost half (49 percent) of Indigenous children under the age of six in Winnipeg are living in families with incomes below the poverty line (Lezubski 2014: 77, 82, 120, cited in Silver 2015: 228–29).

Educational attainment is also lower in the inner city. A study produced by the Manitoba Centre for Health Policy (Brownell et al. 2012: 207) found that while 99 percent of urban students in the highest income quintile graduated from high school on time, only 55 percent of those in the lowest income quintile did. In some inner-city neighbourhoods in Winnipeg, the proportion of young people graduating from high school on time is only around 25 percent (Silver 2015: 234).

Health outcomes are much worse in Winnipeg's inner city. As another Centre for Health Policy investigation (Brownell et al. 2003: 7, 44) found, "The least healthy populations tended to be closest to the city centre and the most healthy populations generally toward the south and outskirts of the city." The same tendency occurred in incidences of deaths from cancer, heart disease, and respiratory illness. Between 2001 and 2005 infant mortality rates were almost three times higher in the lowest-income areas of Winnipeg (Brownell et al. 2008: 87–88). These health outcomes are worse for Indigenous than for non-Indigenous people (Hart 2010; Brownell, Fransoo, and Martens 2015).

This complex poverty and the hardships it produces constitute a major source of disruption for families. Silver (2015: 228) notes that the proportion of lone-parent families, most of which are headed by women, is "two-thirds again as high in the inner city as in Winnipeg as a whole." The struggles of these families to make ends meet can lead to involvement in the child welfare system, especially for Indigenous families.

First Nations and Métis children continue to be overrepresented in child welfare caseloads. Over a decade ago Cindy Blackstock (2003) estimated that as many as *three times* more Indigenous children were in the care of child welfare authorities as compared to children placed in residential schools at the height of those operations in the 1940s. Both the number of children in care and the proportion of Indigenous children in care have been growing steadily; Manitoba has the highest rate of children in care among the provinces (McKenzie and Shangreaux 2015: 162). While Indigenous children make up some 26 percent of the child population of Manitoba, in 2015 they made up 87 percent of the children living under the care of the child welfare system (Manitoba Family Services 2015: 94).

This overrepresentation of Indigenous children in the child welfare system is especially evident in Winnipeg's inner-city communities. A 2008 Manitoba Centre for Health Policy study found: "The proportion of children receiving services from Child and Family Services was eight times as high, and the proportion of children in care was almost thirty-four times as high in Winnipeg's lowest income quintile neighbourhoods — neighbourhoods roughly equivalent to the inner city — when compared with the highest income quintile neighbourhoods" (Silver 2015: 228). For Pete Hudson and Brad McKenzie (2003: 50), such figures are not surprising, "in that the effects of colonization, including underlying socio-economic issues as well as family breakdown and parenting problems, are not erased simply by the creation of community-based child and family services agencies." As the RCAP (1996: vol. 3 ch. 2) noted, most of the parents who have lost their children to the child welfare system were themselves clients of that system — which suggests a historical process that is difficult to disrupt.

EVERYDAY RACISM AND RACIALIZED SPACES

Impoverished social conditions and children being taken into care are significant components in the generation of trauma; racism is another key component. As the Amnesty International *Stolen Sisters* report notes, "The difficult struggle to get by is compounded by many Indigenous peoples' experience of racism, both subtle and overt, within the dominant society" (Amnesty International 2004: 19).

While racism takes a systemic form — as evidenced by the history of settler colonial laws and practices — it also manifests at the level of everyday experience. "Everyday racism" is a complex of practices (both cognitive and behavioural) that integrate racism (and its underlying power relations) on a daily basis (Essed 2002: 188). These daily situations become part of the expected, of the unquestionable. They are what the dominant group in society sees "as normal." To this extent, everyday racism becomes part of our common sense. Racist comments or interactions may involve "a few words exchanged, words not exchanged, gestures, glances, tone of voice, rumours, coincidences, inclusions and exclusions" (Das Guptas 2009: 19). On their own, these comments or interactions may not seem overly problematic. Considered collectively, they can reveal a pattern of marginalization and exclusion.

Statistics Canada's 2009 General Social Survey found that a large percentage of Indigenous people reported having faced some type of discrimination in the previous five years, and in a number of everyday situations, including in stores, banks, restaurants or schools, at work or when applying for a job, and on the street (McCaskill 2012: 17–18). Josh Brandon and Evelyn Peters (2014: 24–25) document experiences of everyday racism that Indigenous people in Winnipeg encounter in their efforts to secure housing: "A commonly reported experience was that individuals would go to view an apartment, and once the landlord realized they were Aboriginal, they were told it had already been rented."

These experiences of everyday racism are bolstered and sustained by racist discourses. While past racist discourse cast Indigenous people as "savage," "inferior," and "child-like" (and therefore in need of a civilizing influence and the benevolent paternalism of the colonial state), more contemporary discourses include the notions of the "welfare recipient" and the "criminal Other" (and therefore in need of heightened surveillance and control). The most invidious of these racist stereotypes are the "squaw" and the "drunken Indian."

As Emma LaRocque put it so powerfully to the Royal Commission, "The portrayal of the squaw is one of the most degrading, most despised and most dehumanizing anywhere in the world. The squaw is the female counterpart of the Indian male savage and, as such, she has no human face. She is lustful, immoral, unfeeling and dirty." LaRocque draws a direct connection between "this grotesque dehumanization" and "these horrible racist, sexist stereotypes and violence against Native women and girls" (cited in RCAP 1996 vol. 3 ch. 2).

The racist stereotype of the "drunken Indian" works in a similar fashion. Bolstered by a dominant, regularly reinforced discourse that is content to explain private troubles as being rooted in individual circumstances (as opposed to systemic processes), the common view is to see Indigenous people as being intoxicated and "out of control." Such representations merely function to objectify and devalue Indigenous people. Ignored are the historical processes by which alcohol was introduced into Indigenous life and the social conditions that have fostered its continued use. In the view of the Royal Commission (RCAP 1996), alcohol abuse and the violence that often accompanies it are parallel means of dealing with deep distress. In a similar fashion, Aboriginal Justice Inquiry commissioners Alvin Hamilton and Murray Sinclair (1991: 498) state: "Ultimately, it must be recognized that the presence and influence of alcohol and substance abuse in Aboriginal communities and among Aboriginal people are a direct reflection of the nature and level of despair which permeates that population."

Moreover, physical spaces are also subject to racialization. Sherene Razack (2002) and her colleagues have explored how "place becomes race," that is, how the constitution of spaces reproduces racial hierarchies" (Razack 2007: 74). Contrary to familiar, everyday notions, spaces do not simply "evolve, are filled up with things, and exist either prior to or separate from the subjects who imagine and use them" (p. 76). Rather, spaces are abidingly social. They have not only a materiality in that they connect to social relations that produce and use them but also a symbolic meaning attached to them. Spaces can variously come to represent places of home, work, or leisure, sites of comfort and the familiar, or places of danger and disorder. Together, the material and the symbolic "work through each other to constitute a space" (p. 77). From this standpoint, racialization can be directly experienced as a spatial process:

> When police drop Aboriginal people outside the city limits leaving them to freeze to death, or stop young Black men on the streets on in malls, when the eyes of shop clerks follow bodies of colour, presuming them to be illicit, when workplaces remain relentlessly white in the better paid jobs and fully "coloured" at the lower levels, when affluent areas of the city are all white and poorer areas are mostly of colour, we experience the spatiality of the racial order in which we live. (Razack 2007: 75–76)

As such, it is through everyday routines and experiences that space "comes to perform something in the social order, permitting certain actions and prohibiting others. Spatial practices organize social life in specific ways" (p. 77).

Over time, certain spaces become identified as places in which crime and violence are most likely to occur. Inner-city communities populated by impoverished Indigenous people and new immigrants are more likely to be seen as "disordered" and "dangerous" places, whereas suburban white middle-class neighbourhoods — with their tree-lined streets, manicured lawns, and spacious homes — become spaces of "civility" and "respectability." Such is the case with Winnipeg.

VIOLENCE AND THE SEX AND DRUG TRADES

Given the trauma-producing conditions of inner-city communities, violence, not surprisingly, "is a day-to-day reality in many impoverished and racialized spaces" (Comack et al. 2013: 26) — creating a vicious circle that produces ever more trauma. In Winnipeg's inner-city communities, violence is intimately connected to the sex and drug trades, and the advent of street gangs.

For many impoverished — and disproportionately Indigenous — women, working in the street sex trade is often their only recourse for getting by. Jason Brown and his colleagues (2006) conducted focus groups with women who were actively and formerly involved in the street sex trade in Winnipeg's inner city. They learned that the women turned to the sex trade "out of economic necessity" and because of the "multiple barriers to employment" they experienced (p. 43). "The women wanted to find employment so that they would not have to rely on welfare benefits. But, discrimination [and] lack of education and job experience were common experiences and barriers to finding employment" (p. 44). The women who had recently left the sex trade continued to experience low-income and poor jobs due to their lack of work experience and formal education. "They had families and noted that the kinds of jobs they needed had to fit with being a single mother and supply enough money to adequately care for their children and, in some cases, other family members" (p. 50).

Similarly, Maya Seshia's (2005) Winnipeg research on street sexual exploitation — or coercion into the sex trade — revealed that poverty and homelessness, colonialism and the legacy of the residential schools, childhood victimization, gender discrimination, and generational sexual exploitation (having a family member who has been sexually exploited) all combined to lead women and girls to become involved in the sex trade. Other Winnipeg research showed that "63 percent of sexually exploited youth have had experiences with the child welfare system and 77.8 percent had been in agency care and lived in foster and group homes for years" (p. 17), suggesting a link between the trauma of family disruption and entry into the sex trade as a means of economic survival.

Violence is endemic in the street sex trade. When Maya Seshia and I did a study of an inner-city newsletter reporting on "bad dates" and "street hassles" encountered by Winnipeg sex trade workers, we found that the targets of the violence detailed in the reports were overwhelmingly female, while the perpetrators were predominantly male, and most often white. In many of the events, the violence occurred after the women were driven to isolated industrial areas of the city or outside of the city limits. We concluded:

> One of the risks encountered by those who work in the Winnipeg street sex trade is violence in its various forms. The social circumstances in which they carry out their work — standing on street corners, getting into cars with clients, and then being driven to isolated or secluded areas — make street sex trade workers especially vulnerable to violence. (Comack and Seshia 2010: 210)

Violence in the sex trade also persists in other Canadian cities. In a Vancouver study, Melissa Farley, Jacqueline Lynne, and Ann Cotton (2005) interviewed one hundred women involved in the street sex trade, finding: 90 percent of them had been physically assaulted while working the street; and 78 percent had been raped, with 67 percent having been raped more than five times. Some 75 percent of the women reported physical injuries from violence (stabbings and beatings) encountered in the sex trade, causing concussions, broken bones, cuts, and black eyes. As Farley, Lynne, and Cotton (2005: 254) noted, "Violence seemed to be in the very air they breathed." Violence had become so routine in the women's lives that they tended to minimize their experiences: "One woman told us that since she had no broken bones and had not been assaulted with a weapon, therefore her rape and strangulation by a john did not count as much" (p. 260). The women working in Vancouver's street sex trade were "in a state of almost constant revictimization" (p. 256) because the violence they encountered was part of a lifetime of victimization and abuse: 89 percent had been sexually assaulted as children, and 72 percent reported childhood physical assault (p. 252). The overwhelming majority (95 percent) of the women told the researchers that they wanted to escape prostitution, "while also telling us that they did not feel that they had other options for survival" (p. 261). Adding to their challenges, 86 percent of the women whom Farley and her colleagues interviewed were currently or previously homeless (p. 257).

Over half of the women (52 percent) interviewed were Indigenous, while only 7 percent of Vancouver's population is made up of Indigenous people. The researchers assert that "an analysis of the intersections of race, class and gender is crucial to an understanding of prostitution" and that given the overrepresentation of Indigenous women in the Vancouver street sex trade, "Prostitution is one specific legacy of colonization although it is infrequently analyzed as such" (pp. 246–47, 258). Nevertheless, a key focus of their analysis rests on the incidence of PTSD among the women they encountered. Respondents were asked to complete a PTSD checklist. Some 72 percent of them were deemed to have met the criteria for a PTSD diagnosis (p. 251), a rather unsurprising finding given the extensive victimization and trauma they had encountered in their lives.

Many of those working in the street sex trade, Winnipeg's included, turn to drugs and alcohol as coping mechanisms. As Seshia (2005: 21) notes, "Sexually exploited youth and adults use [drugs] in order to cope with the harsh realities in their lives. Degradation, humiliation, and violence are experienced on a daily basis and substance use can temporarily help numb the pain inside them and help them escape their reality." As in other inner-city spaces, the drug trade has become more and more insidious in Winnipeg's inner city. Supplied mainly by organized crime networks that bring the drugs into the city, the types of drugs being sold and the methods of sale have changed over time, largely due to the economics of supply and demand. While injecting Talwin and Ritalin (Ts and Rs) was prevalent in the 1980s, injecting cocaine grew in popularity in the 1990s. Crack cocaine came onto the drug scene in Winnipeg in the late 1990s, and then crystal methamphetamine appeared not long afterward. Financed largely by biker gangs, fortified drug dens and shooting galleries (where customers could buy flaps of cocaine to freebase) gave way to crack houses and crack lines or "dial a dealer" operations run by street-gang crews. Dealers would set up their operations in rental houses in the inner city or run their businesses over cellphones. As a number of us (Comack et al. 2013: 115) found in our research into Aboriginal street gangs, street sex workers are the "perfect customer" for these operations: "They just keep coming back for more. It's a symbiotic relationship: the street sex workers need the drugs to dull the pain, and then need to do more work to earn the money to buy the drugs that dull the pain."

The drug trade constitutes a major source of income and activity for street gangs. In the mid-1990s Winnipeg gained the reputation as the "gang capital of Canada," and the names of particular Indigenous street gangs became part of the public discourse. This emergence of Indigenous street gangs in Winnipeg is a logical outgrowth of the impoverished conditions, social exclusion, and experiences of racism encountered by inner-city youth. It is a form of resistance (albeit a negative one) to colonialism:

> Creating or joining street gangs offered young Aboriginal men a
> means of exerting power, of resisting their impoverishment....

> Moreover, given the colonized space that the North End [one of Winnipeg's inner-city communities] had become, it is no accident that Aboriginal street gangs in Winnipeg adopted names such as Indian Posse, Manitoba Warriors, and Native Syndicate; their self-identity as "gangsters" is a racialized feature stemming from a recognition (however underdeveloped) of their colonial condition and their resistance to that condition. (Comack et al. 2013: 62)

More globally, the proliferation of street gangs in racialized inner-city spaces became yet another facet of the sweeping changes wrought by global economic restructuring and the neo-liberal response of the state to the deepening inequality between rich and poor produced by these economic changes (Hagedorn 2008; Bourgois 2003; Rios 2011). Rather than being passive victims of social forces largely beyond their control, young Indigenous men have formed "resistance identities" that involve the performance of a "hypermasculinity" centred around "being hard" and "tough." Violence, including violence against women, is a key component of this performance (Comack et al. 2013: 82–88).

Sexual exploitation and violence against women are common aspects of street-gang life (see, for example, Bourgois 2003). In an important sense, girls involved with gangs strike a "patriarchal bargain" that allows them to reconcile the negative aspects of their gang affiliation with the perceived benefits. As Jody Miller (2001) pointed out, the lives of young girls growing up in inner-city neighbourhoods are complicated by contradictory messages: young women can gain status through their sexual appeal, yet be denigrated for their sexual activity. As well, the sexual victimization and exploitation of young women, both in their homes and on the streets, mean that "the world around gang girls is not a particularly safe place, physically or psychically" (p. 193). As such, the gender hierarchy and inequality that girls encounter in street gangs are not unlike what they experience more generally in the larger world around them. When young women in that social world are seen as such ready targets of violence and victimization, affiliation with a gang can offer at least a semblance of protection. Nevertheless, Miller found that "many young women's means of resisting gender oppression within gangs tended to be an individualized response based on constructing gendered gang identities as separate from and 'better than' those of the girls and women around them in their social environments. It meant internalizing and accepting masculine constructs of gang values" (p. 197).

In her research involving Indigenous girls in Winnipeg, Nahanni

Fontaine (2014) found that there were no female gang members or female gangs operating in the city. Rather, females were connected to street gangs by virtue of their relationships with male gang members as "old ladies," "bitches," and "hos." Old ladies are the "women or girls with whom male gang members have some semblance of a committed and loving relationship" (p. 121). As such, they are accorded a certain status and respect by the gang members. Bitches and hos were lower on the rung of the gender hierarchy. "These women and girls were not looked upon favourably and were always described in pejorative ways" (p. 124). Regardless of social status in relation to the gang, violence was a pervasive feature of that relationship.

The gendered and racialized nature of violence has become more of a public issue now that attention has begun to focus on the numbers of missing and murdered Indigenous women and girls in Canada. In 2004 in *Stolen Sisters*, Amnesty International called attention to the violence encountered by Indigenous women and pointed to the role of cultural and systemic discrimination in perpetuating this violence, thereby impeding their basic human right to be safe and free from violence. The report noted that Indigenous women were five times more likely to die as a result of violence (p. 23). It also documented many of the cases of missing and murdered women, including the disappearance of women from the streets of Vancouver's Downtown Eastside. In 2005 the Native Women's Association of Canada (NWAC) launched the *Sisters in Spirit* initiative, which was aimed at addressing the root causes, circumstances, and trends of missing and murdered Indigenous women and girls. By March 2010 NWAC had gathered information about the disappearance or death of more than 580 Indigenous women and girls across Canada (NWAC 2010b). Manitoba had the third-highest number of cases (79); 81 percent of those cases involved murder (NWAC 2010c). A more recent database compiled by the RCMP increased that figure to 1,181 missing or murdered Indigenous women and girls across the country (RCMP 2014; see also RCMP 2015).

WHY THE PAIN?

The broader trauma-producing social conditions attendant with colonialism, capitalism, and patriarchy form the necessary backdrop for an understanding of the lives of the WCC women. The "myriad dimensions" of settler colonialism — attempts at cultural genocide in the form of the residential school system, efforts to contain and control Indigenous people by means of the treaty process and the Indian Act, and the insidious practice of the

"Sixties Scoop" — set in process trauma trails that have continued into the present day.

The impoverished conditions on First Nations reserves provide evidence of these trauma trails. Those conditions have generated individual trauma, indicated by the high rates of suicide among Indigenous people, and especially youth. But settler colonialism — and its intimate connections to capitalism — has also provoked the conditions for collective trauma in Indigenous communities as residents contend with the impact of the breakdown of "communality" caused by their displacement due to hydroelectric developments and flooding. The experience of the members of Lake St. Martin First Nation provides a stark reminder that colonialism as a process continues even now.

For those who migrate to the city, life is often no better. Trauma-producing conditions also prevail for Indigenous people in urban centres like Winnipeg. The impact of capitalist globalization and neo-liberal economic restructuring has tended to be strongest in inner-city communities, including Winnipeg's. The widening gap between rich and poor has created a class of "urban outcasts" in cities throughout the West, leading to alienation and disaffection (Wacquant 2008). Complex poverty and the hardships that accompany it produce broken families as children are taken into care by the child welfare system, setting the stage for further trauma. Compounding the situation, "everyday racism" has become part of the "normal" for Indigenous people and newcomers living in the racialized space of the inner city.

The trade in sex and drugs and the presence of street-gang activity that prevail in Winnipeg's inner city, as in most Western cities, have become part of "normal" for the residents who live there. So too has the accompanying violence. Not surprisingly, drugging and drinking become one way of coping with the trauma. Gabor Maté (2008), a doctor whose work in Vancouver's Downtown Eastside placed him into "close encounters with addiction," notes: "All addictions always originate in pain, whether felt openly or hidden in the unconscious. They are emotional anaesthetics" (p. 34). Following Maté's lead, the question we need to ask about drugging and drinking is not "Why the addiction?" but "Why the pain?" The stories told by the women at the wcc reveal the lived experience of trauma — and the pain it generates.

CHAPTER FOUR

THE LIVED EXPERIENCE OF TRAUMA

Settler colonialism, capitalism, and patriarchy are interwoven in ways that produce "structural violence," the social injustices and systemic barriers that prevent individuals from realizing their full potential (Galtung 1969). These systemic processes also work to produce trauma, especially for those individuals whose race/class/gender position limits or denies them access to the social capital and resources that enable the realization of the good life — what the Cree refer to as *mino-pimatisiwin* (Hart 2002). Trauma can accumulate over a lifetime as an exposure to it becomes layered, with former traumas (especially if they are not reconciled) having a heavy impact on abilities to cope with current trauma. Experiences of sexual and physical violence in childhood, for example, can compound the impact of sexual and physical violence experienced in adulthood. The trauma encountered by families and communities can prompt and exacerbate individual experiences, especially when family and community members are themselves reeling from their own lived experiences of trauma.

This broader sociological understanding of trauma can help to reveal how the social conditions that produce the disturbance worked their way into the lived experiences of the women who ended up in custody at the Women's Correctional Centre. Most of those women encountered some form of trauma in early childhood; as they moved into their teenage years and later into adulthood, the experience became more layered. Based on their experiences, then, what forms did this trauma take? And how have these women managed to cope with, resist, and survive that trauma over the course of their lives?

TRAUMA IN CHILDHOOD

The women I met with at the Women's Correctional Centre came from diverse family backgrounds. While some had experienced the so-called "typical" nuclear family arrangement of mom, dad, and two or three kids, others came from families of ten or more children; in one case, a father had sired thirty-one kids with several women. Many of the women had grown up in single-parent homes. In several cases, fathers were absent because they were serving lengthy prison sentences. Some of the women had been raised by their grandparents or other relatives. Often, the women's sense of family extended to their many aunties, uncles, and cousins with whom they shared a close relationship. For many, childhood consisted of a number of different home situations. The Indigenous women in particular had often moved between the reserve and the city; many of them had been taken into care by Child and Family Services and placed in foster and group homes.

Certainly, not all of the childhood memories of the women were negative. They often talked warmly of their early relationships with caregivers. Cyndi spoke of her close ties to her mother: "To be honest I never grew up in an abusive home. My mom never drank. She worked her whole life, yeah. I probably only seen her drunk twice, yeah…. You know, we weren't rich or anything, but we had each other." Heather, who until the age of six was raised on the reserve by her grandmother, recalled: "I don't remember being spanked and getting in trouble…. It was very fairy tale for me." Melody wished that she could go back to her childhood, living with her grandparents, "'cause I felt more safe and more — human. I was never doing anything wrong when I was with them." Christine grew up in Winnipeg's North End. "I had a good childhood and I was spoiled. I didn't know I was on welfare or in the ghetto or anything, right. My mom made it seem all perfectly well."

Many of the women, however, were born into families in which parents and other caregivers were dealing with their own trauma, and those experiences spilled over into the youngsters' lives. Economic hardship, broken families, drugging and drinking, and violence more often than not coloured the women's early lives — to the point at which those conditions became part of their "normal." As Donna explained: "I saw a lot of stuff a kid shouldn't see. And when you're that age and you see it all the time, you think it's normal."

The experience of growing up in impoverished social conditions stood out for several of the women. Ashley remembered being "hungry all the time" as a kid. Mary recalled that when her parents split up when she was eleven, it was a turning point in her life: "We went from having everything I wanted as a child to having nothing and being on welfare." Dianne's parents separated when she was just two years old. The children remained with their mother, but were often left to fend for themselves: "I remember starving lots of times because she was out drinking and had taken the welfare cheque with her. One bag of groceries and it's like, 'Here you go,' and five of us were supposed to live on that for a week."

For many of the women, their parents' troubles meant having to assume responsibility for the care of their siblings. Doreen's story is one example.

Doreen's Story

Doreen, who grew up in a mining community, recalled not having "boundaries and rules and stuff. My mom was very heavy into alcohol and my dad wasn't home that often. He was always working, doing what he can to feed us."

Doreen took on responsibility for the care of her little sister at an early age. She was only six years old when her sister was born, and quickly learned how to prepare bottles of formula for the baby. "And once my mom knew I knew how to do that and I was doing stuff on my own she kind of got lazy and she started drinking again. And I remember taking my little sister upstairs a lot of the times and looking after her while my mom had parties. And my dad was at work, he worked the whole weekend sometimes." For Doreen, like Donna, it was all only a normal way of life: "I didn't understand at the time, you know, like alcoholism and partying and abuse and all that was bad. 'Cause it felt normal to me."

Doreen's home life began to unravel when she was just nine years old. The mine where her father worked closed down, leaving her parents struggling to make ends meet. "My family just fell apart from there," she said. Both parents became addicted to crack cocaine. The children were in and out of care. "I was in and out of CFS care but I knew what was going on. I knew where my home was and how to leave that home and then go back to find my parents. I was always so worried about how I was going to fix my parents' marriage and fix my family and how to get it back together. I never worried about myself."

Doreen wished that things could be like they were when she was born "'cause when I was born everything was together. Everything. We had a family. We had a house." When Doreen was four years old she burned down the family home. She had been playing with matches. "Even to this day I feel like it's my fault the way my family is 'cause I burnt down that house. And that's where our foundation was. That's where we lived." Her sense of responsibility took its toll at an early age. "I was so worried about what was happening with my family life. Even at a young age I had to worry about, you know, where's my little sister and if my parents were okay. I developed ulcers at age eleven from worrying too much."

Other women also felt the weight of responsibility at a young age. Many were left alone at home to care for their younger siblings. Molly told me:

> I couldn't have a normal childhood. I was always taking care of them [her sisters]. If there was no food sometimes I'd have to go steal food from Safeway to provide for them for a meal and Enfalac. 'Cause my sisters were still babies and I'm buying them Pampers. I was just always trying to cook for them and I didn't even know how to really cook. I was young still. Trying to clean. And I just felt like I lost out on my childhood.

Lynne's parents also often left her alone to look after her younger sister. "They would fill up the fridge with food and give me a hundred bucks and then leave me with the kid and they would just venture off.... Sometimes they'd be gone for three days, but the most they'd be gone was a week, a couple of weeks." As Lynne recalled: "I had food and money and stuff but I never really had a childhood, where I can have girls come over and have sleepovers and go do normal things. I was like a mom right away."

Child and Family Services (CFS) Involvement

Broken families and caregivers' troubles with drugs and alcohol meant that the women were often taken into care as children. Ellen spent many of her early years in foster homes. "I'd be back and forth in foster care and then I'd be back with my family and then I'd be back in foster care again." Ellen didn't know it at the time, but her mother was addicted to crack cocaine. In the times when she was at home, Ellen was the caregiver for her baby brother: "It's pretty sad 'cause I recall the times I'd go home and my little brother would be there alone and nobody was taking care of him. So I'd go home and have to feed him and bathe him and put him to bed, make sure everybody else is okay." At the age of thirteen Ellen ran away from home and ended up in Winnipeg. After that, she said, "I was bouncing back and forth from foster homes, group homes, shelters, and whatever."

Alicia was first apprehended by CFS when she was two years old. "My mom is the kind of woman that can't live without a man ... her boyfriend's a sex offender and CFS said that she can't have us girls if she's going to be with him. And she picked him over us." Alicia, who didn't see her mom from the ages of five to sixteen, ended up living in thirty-two different CFS foster homes, as well as in hotels: "CFS would put me in hotels because no one wanted to keep me 'cause I was bad and, yeah, no one wanted to keep me." Alicia said she "misbehaved" because she "wanted to be with my family." As she explained: "I was just mad at the world. I didn't understand why I was put with all these different people and I just didn't understand. I was young. I just wanted to be on my own. I didn't want people telling me what to do. You guys aren't my parents, why would I listen to you guys?"

Molly had a similar experience of being taken into care by CFS:

> It was confusing, it was scary. I felt alone and, I don't know, scared. I wanted to be with my family. I just felt like I was taken away and I didn't know why. I didn't understand why. And, I mean, my mom and dad were good parents. Well, I thought they were. Well, they were but they just had problems, yeah. But I just didn't understand at the time.

Molly ended up at a youth treatment centre when she was eleven. But she said she "was better off before I went there." As she put it, "It was supposed to help me but it just made things worse and I got connected with people that were more, worse than I was, yeah."

Schooling

Only five of the forty-two women I talked to had completed high school, and their unsettled home life as children helps to explain why. When asked about her schooling Doreen said she had only completed Grade 6 because she had not "really been given a solid foundation to stay in school." With her family on the move as her father looked for work, she was "pulled out of schools lots."

Helen had a similar experience. Her aunt and uncle, her caregivers, worked on farms. "I moved from farm to farm so I never got any education." Complicating Helen's schooling experience, she didn't speak English until she was eight years old — using her Indigenous language until then. Corrine only made it to Grade 8, and even then, she said, "I just felt like they were just passing me to the next grade just for nothing. I remember being in Grade 6 and my teacher told me, 'Oh, well, you're just going to the next grade 'cause you can do better than that.' And just really encouraged me and pushed me. So I went into Grade 7 and that was a big struggle for me."

Both of Tina's parents were alcoholics, and her mom "was very abusive." Tina and her sister, a year younger, were left alone to take care of the younger siblings when the parents "would leave us the whole weekend and go drinking." Both Tina and her sister "missed a lot of school because we had to stay home and watch the ones that weren't in school." Tina left school in Grade 9.

For Ashley, who managed to complete Grade 11, school became a means of escaping what was going on at home and a way of feeling good about herself:

> School was my only way to escape. It was my safe haven. 'Cause, you know, at home there was no food there or my mom would be drinking or there would be people I didn't even know who's in the house or, you know, even though I wasn't the best-dressed kid and I didn't have much stuff but, you know what, going to school was good for me 'cause it just got me away from home. So I was just really focused on my school and stuff like that and I knew that was kind of like my way out. So that's, yeah, I guess it did help me to cope? You know, knowing that — 'cause it did feed my self-esteem, too, because, you know, I'm getting good marks in school. So I was doing good, something good for myself.

The "Ripple Effect of Residential School"

The women's exposure and vulnerability to violence compounded their unsettled childhoods. In that regard, one theme evident in their narratives — absent in the original *Women in Trouble* study — was the intergenerational impact of the residential school system. Several of the women made a point of noting that their grandparents, parents, or siblings attended the schools.

Ashley's mother was emotionally and physically abusive towards her. Ashley believed that the abusive behaviour was what her mother had learned from her own mother, who was a residential school survivor:

> My grandmother went to residential school and she wasn't very healthy, mentally wise and emotionally. So I like to call it the "ripple effect of residential school." So, you know, my mom being hit by that ripple effect and she went through a lot of abuse in her life. My

mom has talked about insane things that happened to her when she was growing up. A lot of sexual abuse. And then her not knowing how to be a parent .... She wasn't a really good parent because she was giving them those same abusive, those abusive things to us.

Tannis lived on the reserve with her granny. Her mother had died of alcohol poisoning when Tannis was nine years old. Tannis remembers that her granny would get her boyfriend to go into the bush to find a willow stick to hit her with. "She was trying to discipline me, I guess. She'd hit me on the hand or something like that. Maybe 'cause she's been through it when she was younger. 'Cause she told me she was in residential schools, too." Dianne's father was also a residential school survivor. He would beat her up. "I was about eleven when he started first hitting me and the first time that he had done it he had knocked me out with his fist as I was waking up [from] sleeping."

Doris said she "grew up in violence and physical, sexual, emotional abuse." Her father was physically abusive towards her mother; he was also sexually abusive towards Doris when she was little. "When I was younger he used to make me dress up and do stuff with guys." He raped Doris when she was fourteen. Doris said she had forgiven her father because she understood that "he's been in residential school and he's been abused, raped, and all that."

Molly recalled that her dad "would always fight my mom and hit her and beat her up. He even put her through a glass window and stuff and he'd always hit her head on the corner of the table and stuff like that .... Yeah, even our Christmas, our turkey was on the heater and our Christmas tree was in the bathtub and our presents were gone. I remember a lot of crazy stuff, yeah." Molly's dad attended residential school "and he'd been through a lot of abuse. And he didn't know how to really love. He was closed off in a way."

Although she was the youngest of ten children, Helen, now in her early fifties, didn't even know she had siblings until they came out of the residential school when it was closed in the 1970s. "They were there when they were six years old. They walked out when it closed. So that's all they knew. They didn't know nothing else. They were being molested from the priest, you know." When she was seven years old, two of Helen's brothers raped her. But she did not place blame on her brothers:

That wasn't who they were. That's what they made them, you know. That's all they knew. And for me it was only, they only did it to me once. And then, but [for] them it was every night, you know. And

I don't think they meant to do it. Because they ended up committing suicide, my brothers, killing themselves.... I think they only did that when they were drunk and then when they were sober they regretted it. So they took their lives. I always wished that they would have got help.

Silencing and Social Censuring

One of the insights to emerge from the original *Women in Trouble* study was the silencing and social censuring that occurred around the women's abuse experiences. While silencing has been used to refer to the difficulty that women have in finding the language to speak about what happened to them, social censuring refers to the obstacles that exist around the very telling of stories of abuse — not only the feelings of guilt and shame that often accompany the experience but also the inability of others to hear the women's stories and take action to support them.

The silencing and social censuring that was in evidence when I interviewed the women at the Portage Correctional Institution over two decades ago continue to prevail. Corrine, now in her early twenties, shared an experience of being sexually molested in her bed when she was a child.

It feels like a dream but I don't know if it happened. But I remember being a little kid and someone, I can't even remember who it is, I just remember being in my room.... Someone came into my room and touched me where I wasn't supposed to be touched. And it was so dark in the room I didn't even know who it was. And I started crying, I just remember laying there and I started crying and that person just got up and ran out of the door. And I didn't even know who it was. But it was an older person and I didn't know who it was.

And so the next day I was just so quiet and my grandpa's wife kept asking me what was wrong and stuff. And I never told her 'cause they were very abusive to me and my brothers. So I never, I didn't really trust them as a kid. So I didn't really say anything. And so I kept that with me, probably 'til now. I never talked about it.

Wanda, also in her early twenties, was raped by her sister's boyfriend when she was twelve. When asked, "How did you deal with that?" she replied: "I don't know. I didn't deal with it. I just held it in."

In her early forties, Carol finally felt ready and able to tell her story. As she explained when we met:

> I have this friend inside the unit. She's the one who told me about you. She says that, "Well, I opened up to her." She said that I should tell my story. And for some reason I listened to her. I would just feel — it's funny but I knew I was going to tell someone and — but all these years I didn't know who. People asked me but I would be, like, "No," and then, I don't know.

Through her tears (and some laughter) Carol was finally able to talk about her life.

Carol's Story

Carol grew up in a small and isolated First Nations community in Northern Manitoba. Both of her parents were residential school survivors. "So they were really strict with me," Carol said. "I wasn't allowed to make a mistake."

The oldest of five children, Carol believed that her mother treated her differently than the other children when she was growing up. "Basically all my life I was just, I was abused. I had to clean up after everybody. I felt like a slave. My mom would literally splash a bucket of water — mop pail water, dirty water — on me if I was sleeping — 'Get up already' — to start cleaning and stuff like that. And then, so I just basically knew how to follow orders."

Carol spent most of her time in the family home. "If I did go out I'd always have to be with my mom." She had a kind of invisibility in her community. "A lot of people don't know me on the reserve. When they ask me who I am and I tell them who my parents are, and they're like, 'Really?' I say, 'Yeah.' They know about my brothers and sisters but not me."

Carol felt that her mom was "never a mother" to her. "I was just there [chuckles]. I don't know. I was her extra arm, I guess you'd say. And I would just do the work." Perhaps as a remnant of her residential school experience, Carol's mother was very religious. "Sometimes she'd read quotes from the Bible and she'd tell me that I'd have to be punished. I grew to hate — not to hate, I was afraid of this person called Jesus." Carol said that she would try her best to please her mother, "but nothing was ever good.... I felt she hated me. I felt like she hated me. She just hated me. And to this day." Carol's mom wasn't like that with the other siblings. But "she let them beat me up too, my brothers. One, he was cruel to me. I'd be sleeping. I'd try to get a little sleep here and there. He'd come up to me and just pour a bucket of water over me and I'd be gasping for air. Or he'd start hitting me with a mop or a broom. And there was nothing I could do." The only sibling Carol felt close to was her baby brother. She looked after him. "I think that was the only fun I ever had was just playing with him [chuckles]." Carol's relationship with her father was more positive: "My dad would try to do things with me, like take me fishing. He'd be the only one. He'd tell me he loved me. I don't know if he knew what was really going on 'cause he was always at work."

Violence was all around Carol as she was growing up on the reserve: "I saw lots of horrible stuff. Some people getting stabbed, assaulted with axes, rape. I saw lots of stuff." Violence was also directed at her. As a child, in addition to encountering physical and emotional abuse from her mother and siblings, Carol was raped by relatives. "I didn't know what was happening to me. It was twice, three times." Carol said she had "tried to tell people about things that happened but they just said it's something that I'm not supposed to talk about. Just to keep quiet and don't say anything." Asked how she coped with those traumatic experiences, Carol replied, "I guess I just grew numb because I was always beaten. I just took it."

Like Carol, other women shared experiences of social censuring when they tried to seek help after being victimized. Jackie, now in her early thirties, was sexually molested by her uncle when she was six. She said that she "tried to tell someone and then I got in trouble for telling." Maxine, in her early twenties, was sexually abused by her mom's boyfriends and some family members, including her auntie when she was twelve. She tried to tell after the first experience, but no one would listen. "So I just never said anything about the other ones. And I just thought no one would want to hear me. So I just never told anyone."

Tina and her sisters were sexually abused by their brothers.

> It started before I was a teenager and it went on for quite a few years. And we couldn't go to my mom and tell her stuff like that. And actually they were doing it to two of my other sisters. And finally my one sister did go to my mom and tell her what was happening. And she said, "Well, what are you doing in their bedroom?" 'Cause the girls all had one bedroom and the boys all had one bedroom. She said, "I'm not going in their bedroom. They're coming to our bedroom."

Her mother, Tina said, responded to all of this by saying, "Quit your fuckin' lying" and slapping her. "That's how she deals with things."

Coping, Resisting, and Surviving Strategies

When it comes to children, the resources available for dealing with trauma experiences are especially restricted. Their physical size, dependency on adults, and limited knowledge and awareness of what may be happening to them (as in the case of sexual assault) not only make children easy targets for abuse, but limit the range of options for dealing with it as well.

In some cases, the trauma was so acute that the women coped by simply trying to ignore the memories. When asked about her time growing up, Cheryl replied: "I don't remember my childhood. I blocked it out. All I remember is being hit all the time." When she was asked, Annette commented: "I don't really recall much memories from seven and under. It's all suppressed." Alyson remarked: "Something had to go on when I was younger 'cause I don't remember my childhood." Cyndi said: "To be honest, I don't really remember anything up until I was fourteen, 'til I had my oldest son. I just have little bits of memories. I think it's a memory block I have." Cyndi believed that her memory block was due to a "tragic experience" that happened to her when she was four years old. She was sexually molested by her grandfather. "I don't know if it happened more than once or what, but, yeah."

One coping strategy that occurs at the time of the abuse is to mentally remove yourself from the situation. That was Dianne's experience. She was raped at the age of six. Her mom and her auntie had met up with a "fish," which she explained was "some guy that they pick up at the bar who's willing to spend some money on them. So I guess a cheaper version of a trick or a john, right." The "fish" drove them around to different places, and when her mom and auntie went into a house party Dianne and some younger siblings were left in the van with him.

> And when they were inside [the house] he had said to me, "Will you fuck me if I give you a dollar?" And I said, "Well, what does fuck mean?" And then the next thought that I have is remembering the floor, you know, what the floor looked like and being very cold and, yeah, and then just kind of leaving my body and, you know — yeah.

When asked whether she was able to tell her mom or her auntie about what had happened to her, Dianne replied: "No, they were drunk. And it was really kind of like always, 'It's all about me' with my mom, you know. She as well came from not a very good background, you know, a lot of drinking."

In other cases, the women were able to break their silence and tell someone in authority. Natalie didn't meet her mother until she was seventeen years old. She and her two sisters grew up with her father. She described him as "a really angry individual and, yeah, we spent most of our childhood on eggshells, trying not to make him mad." Natalie said, "I probably got beaten on almost every day. My sisters had it worse, though. He molested two of them." When she was twelve, Natalie took the initiative and told her school principal, who contacted Child and Family Services:

> I had gotten my report card and I went home and my dad was screaming at me and throwing stuff at me. And I think I had gotten a B, which wasn't good enough. I had the best marks. Not 'cause I cared, because I was scared not to. And one of my older sisters had come through the door right behind me and she had a failing mark. And he turned his attention to her. And when he was giving her a lickin' I ran back to school — we lived across the street from the school — and I just told the principal what was going on. And they kept me there until someone from Child and Family came and got me. And I guess they picked up my other two sisters. And I didn't see my dad again until I was already an adult.

While Natalie managed to escape her situation at home, the abuse from her father drove a permanent wedge between the siblings:

> I have no relationship with any of my siblings because of our upbringing. We used to put the blame on each other, you know, in order to keep him from beating on one of, say, me. We would try to focus his attention on somebody else. So we all hate each other. None of us, we've tried occasionally through the years to talk but there's too much hurt there. And none of us care to put in the work to try to be a family.

Wanda grew up with her mom; she didn't meet her dad until she was sixteen years old. Wanda's mother was an alcoholic and abusive towards her. "My mom was always violent when she was drunk and I was scared of her. She was mean to me." Her mother made Wanda stay home from school to help out. "And I had to stop going to school at some point because she wanted me to stay home and clean the house, whatever, and just stay home with her." When the school phoned about her absence, Wanda was returned to school. "I phoned CFS from there. I didn't want to stay at home with my mom anymore. It was too hard 'cause I didn't like how she was treating me and stuff."

Heather's mother was a solvent abuser. Heather said that she used to call CFS on her mom, "hoping that if they took us away she'd realize that we were gone and she'd miss us and stop. But it never worked. [pause] And then we just stopped calling 'cause we would have rather been at home with her than in CFS."

In some cases, the effort to disclose the abuse to someone in authority was subverted. Added to her experience of being sexually molested as a young child, Corrine encountered sexual abuse from her mother's boyfriend, who came to live with them when they were in the city.

> I remember him living there with my mom and stuff. And so I was about, I think I was like twelve, thirteen years old, and I remember being a little kid. And I can't remember the first time but I just remember him touching me and stuff. And I was so scared. I was so scared 'cause it kind of just brang me back, that memory when I was a little kid.

> [In your room and not even being able to see who it was?]

> And being, yeah, and being frozen and I just wouldn't say anything. And I was like, "Okay, he'll go away." And it just kept happening after that. And I was so scared and I wanted to tell my mom but I was scared that she'd get mad at me or something. So it kept happening.

> And one day when I was going to [name of school] I told one of my friends what happened. And she was really close to me and she said, "You have to tell the teacher. If you don't tell the teacher I'm going to tell the teacher." I was like, "Okay, then you tell the teacher." And then she told the teacher and the teacher took me to the library and asked me if that was true and I said "Yeah."

> And then the cops came and took me to the CFS place on Portage [Avenue]. And so we're sitting there and then the ladies were talking to me and they were telling me where was he was touching me and stuff. And it was so weird because my mom came there and he came there. And it was so weird. I can remember as a kid, I was wondering, "Why are they here?" And my mom told me to tell them that I was lying and that — told me not to tell anybody and that everyone would hate me and stuff if I told. So it got me really scared and I told those people that I was lying and they said, "Are

you sure that you're lying?" And I said "Yeah, I was lying." And I remember that lady telling me, you know what, she told me "never to cry wolf." And I asked her what that meant. She said "If you tell us that someone's bothering you again we're not going to believe you." And I said "Okay."

And then so that was that. And after that it kept happening.

Without support within their home environments, the children did what they could to resist the abuse they encountered. Helen said that her aunt and uncle, her caregivers, would drink when they got their paycheques — and that's when the sexual molestation started. People they brought to the house "used to bother her." Helen found ways to resist the abuse:

> When I knew they were going to drink I would — we used to have this shack in the back of the house. And I used to fix that up and put locks in it. And that's where I used to go when they partied, so nobody could bother me, you know. Or I'd hide under the bed, you know what I mean. Sleep under the bed so they wouldn't know where I was. It's just something I started to pick up to protect myself.

Many of the women took one of the few options left to children for resisting the abuse: they ran away. Brenda said she ran away from her foster home "because my foster father used to sneak into my room at night." Lori left home at the age of thirteen because of the physical and sexual abuse from her stepdad. When she tried to tell her mom about the abuse, "She refused to admit that it was happening." Lori was able to call on her grandmother for support. "She tried to keep me away as much as possible. She would just keep me at her house." But when her grandmother died, Lori was left with few options. She "took off" and "hit the streets." "I just slept wherever I could, friends' houses, in parks, who the hell cared, anything was better than being at home at that point." She supported herself by panhandling and doing odd jobs.

In some cases, the children learned to deal with the abuse — and the anger it engendered — with aggression of their own, especially towards other children. Ashley said she was a "bully" in elementary school because "I was really angry." She was suspended from school twenty-six times because of her aggressive behaviour. Helen said, "I learned to protect myself in fighting. 'Cause I was always picked on and all that." But her aggression got Helen expelled from school on several occasions: "I must have been retaliating from the things that were happening to me. So that was the only way I knew how to protect myself. People wouldn't bother me if I fought them." Cyndi was bullied by the kids at school. "But one day I just had enough of it and I started fighting back. And they left me alone ever since."

Corrine also experienced a lot of bullying in grade school. She attributed the bullying to racism: "My whole life I would always wish that I was white for some reason as a kid. I used to wish I was white so I wouldn't be picked on. I'm like, 'Oh, maybe if I was white I wouldn't be picked on' or something. So it was really tough around those times." But Corrine soon learned to fight back against her bullies: "Every time someone would say something mean about me I would lash out or get violent. And it made me feel better but it made me kind of feel worse at the same time. It made me feel better because I felt like I was sticking up for myself, and they didn't bother me after I hurt them or something."

TRAUMA IN TEENAGEHOOD

Trauma followed the women into their teenage years. The women also carried with them their sense of what was "normal." Given their parents' troubles, drugging and drinking and violence were all too routine in their lives. Many of the women were growing up in the racialized space of Winnipeg's inner city, with its flourishing sex and drug trades and street gangs. Exposure to these social conditions — and to the violence that went along with it — was another part of their "normal."

While Heather described her early years growing up with her grand-parents as a "fairy-tale" existence, moving to the inner city to live with her mother meant exposure to "a completely different lifestyle" — one she described as "ghetto" and "survival of the fittest, you know, if you don't end up dead in the end, you're on top of things. You're doing a lot better than anybody else." One feature of that lifestyle was exposure to the drug trade:

> I grew up in the heart of going to shooting galleries. My aunties' houses were shooting galleries. I was nine years old watching some hooker get shot in the neck leaning over an ottoman. That was where I grew up. That was where I played with my toys and stuff like that.... It sounds kind of weird but what I grew up with I thought was just normal.

Heather started working in the sex trade when she was twelve years old.

When asked how she got involved, she replied:

> All my aunties are hookers. And my aunties have all been hookers for as long as I can remember. They're still hookers. So I grew up around it. I grew up seeing it. And, um, I started doing it 'cause I needed stuff. I needed clothes and I wanted to go places and do things with my friends and stuff. And their mothers all gave them money and stuff. My mom never gave me anything.

Heather said that she "picked it up very quickly. I'm a fast learner."

> At first I was just scared and I would cry and stuff and I was very uncomfortable. And then, I don't know, after — I remember this one time, the first time I got scared and cried, the man gave me the money and he says, "Don't worry." He's like, "I'm not going to make you do anything you don't want to do." And then he dropped me off. And in my eyes that was like the greatest thing to do but yet the worst because it taught me that if I cried I could get what I wanted without having to do much, which helped me later on in manipulating men. And then I would just, it turned into a hustle and survival mode.

Family members sometimes had a part in the women's entry into the sex trade at a young age. Alyson's mom put her on the street to work in the sex trade when she was sixteen. Like Heather, Alyson found it to be a scary experience: "The first time I didn't do it 'cause I was scared." Alicia's older sisters "were all into drugs and partying and stuff like that, and yeah, I got into that at a young age. And then I started working the streets." Alicia, who began working the streets at the age of thirteen, also said that working the streets was "scary." She was "surprised that I'm still alive."

Violence is endemic in the street sex trade. Alicia had experienced several violent encounters with johns:

> I took money upfront for this guy and he pulled a knife on me and he stabbed me in the face and I almost lost my eye. And I was in the hospital for three days. And then there was another incident just a couple of years ago.... I was with a john and then he didn't want to pay me my money and I was really determined to get my money. And I was so doped up it wasn't even funny. And he pulled me by my hair and he dragged me up an alley and I was wearing

short-short shorts and just a tank top and flip flops and he dragged me a whole block on a vehicle. I had road burn on the whole side of my body.

Annette's mother and sister were involved in the sex trade, so she "got hooked right away." But working the streets also put her at risk of ever-present "street hassles" and "bad dates" (Comack and Seshia 2010). As Annette told me:

This one time I was on Jarvis, I was sitting there waiting to be picked up and these kids walked by and then they walked by this way again and then they met up with another group of kids and this guy, he had a pole, and they came up to me and they're, you know, talking like, "Where's your money?" and shit. I was like, "Well obviously I ain't got no money. Look, I'm on the street, right." I was like, "What makes you think we make money and come back out here?" I was like, "We're out here 'cause we have no money." I was like, "But here"—I threw them my purse, right. I was like, "Take it." I was like, "If you guys want it, you guys obviously need it more than me, take it." And then they searched me, this girl searched my bra and everything, I had nothing. So, whatever, and they left.

And then another time too I was on Selkirk and Parr working and these two girls, I've never seen them, ever, 'cause when you work the streets you get familiar with the faces and whatever, right.... They were walking around and that's what, they were kind of young, and that's what the young girls do, they walk, they don't just stand. And so they were walking around and they come up to me with a hammer, like, "Give me your money." It's like, "I don't got no money." Like, "Well, we're watching you," and I was like, "Yeah," I was like, "If you guys are watching me you guys wouldn't be stupid and you would know where I'm going, you know, I'm not coming out here with my money." And like, "Well, we're watching you, just know, okay, just know we're watching you." And I was like, "Holy, okay." And then after that I never seen them again.

So that happened. And then one time with this guy that picked me up he took me by the Perimeter [Highway, on the outskirt of the city] and we were on the Perimeter and he offered me forty bucks for a blow job. So I was "Okay," right. And I don't like it when guys put their hands on my head when I'm doing that and he tended to do that a lot and I kept pushing his hand away. I was like, "Don't, don't," you know, and he kept doing it, and I ended up puking on him 'cause of my gag reflex, okay [chuckles]. And he got mad at me and he cleaned himself off and he's like, "Okay, here, finish," right. I was like, "No." I was like, "I'm done." I'm kind of crying now. I was like, "I'm done. I'm not doing this no more." And he's like, "Well," he's like, "you're either going to finish or you can get out." I was like, "No." I was like, "I'm not going to finish and you're going to drop me off." And he's like, "Get the fuck out," and he raised his hand to me, hey, so I got out. I was like, "Okay, whatever." I'm stuck on the Perimeter and I walked all the way back 'cause it was late and there was no buses.

For Heather, the violence of both the sex trade and the drug trade con-stituted an "occupational hazard, as horrible as it sounds."

I've had arguments with women about it. I've been in prostitution. I believe strongly that if a girl is going to perform a sexual act and the man doesn't pay her after that, that's occupational hazard. You should have gotten your money first, because anybody can do that to you, right. If a woman gets raped, I understand it's a very horrible thing and it shouldn't happen to anybody. But again, occupational hazard. You put yourself in that risk when you get into that car whether or not you feel that you need to be in that position, you know. Whether you're working for money or you're working for drugs or you're working to feed your kids or you're working to feed your brother or you're working to buy a new shirt or whatever the purpose is, right. It's an occupational hazard.

Drug dealers are the same thing. They don't know when they go to sell their drugs that they're not going to sell it to a cop and end up in jail for four years or sell to somebody who's feening [craving] that has no money that's going to kill them or stab them with a dirty needle or, you know … it's an occupational hazard.

I grew up like that. I was raised very 'hood style, ghetto. But I like to think that I was raised specifically for my surroundings.

Susan was also attentive to the violence surrounding the sex trade, especially since so many of the girls and women involved were also dealing with drug addictions:

> I know a lot of guys that are getting violent out there. That's why there's a lot of murders. And it's because a guy can sit in a car and hold a piece of fuckin' foil and say, "Hey, do you want to come for a ride? I've got rock for you." One of those girls will go follow that little piece. And, you know, she doesn't care. She's just looking for a piece, her next hit. A lot of girls don't think about that.

Street sex workers are the "perfect customer" in the drug trade business because they "need the drugs to dull the pain, and then need to do more work to earn the money to buy the drugs that dull the pain" (Comack et al. 2013: 115). Pamela Downe (2002: 55–56) frames this issue in a similar way: the use of drugs by young women in the sex trade both contributes to their vulnerability and provides a means of coping with that vulnerability.

Ashley's experience reflects this complicated relationship between doing drugs and working in the sex trade. She moved from her reserve community to Winnipeg to live with her dad when she was seventeen years old. That's when things "started going downhill." She started "hanging out with really bad people" because, she said, "I wanted to be accepted." Part of being accepted involved trying crack cocaine. "I gave it a try and I really liked it. And then I just kept on smoking and I just, 'I need more, I need more.' And I told myself I was never going to do that to myself. And it was kind of freaky 'cause all of a sudden it was just happening right before my eyes…. It was really scary how much of a control that drug could have on you." To pay for her drugs, Ashley began working in the street sex trade. She said that it wasn't difficult to get involved in the trade:

> It was something that was already there. You know, there's guys everywhere that are like that. You can just go to Sargent [Avenue], you could just go stand there for a while and someone would look out for you and you'll get picked up. And then once you get those people's numbers and then it just kind of goes from there. And you could have regulars. You could have people that you've met before. And you just keep doing what you're doing.

Molly's experience was somewhat different. She was exposed to the sex trade first and then became involved in using drugs. Molly lost her virginity to a john when she was eleven years old. "And that's when I first, the time

I did my first hoot of crack 'cause that guy gave us crack and money and stuff.... I got really bad into crack for a while there, for a couple of years. And then I just remember a lot of bad stuff happening. Yeah, it was a pretty rough life." One of the bad things that happened was Molly's best friend was murdered in 2009. "Somebody picked her up and I guess she jumped in the wrong car. I don't know how it happened. All I know is that she was found outside the city and she was raped and beaten." Bad things also happened to Molly.

> I got raped when I was at my friend's. They took me to some apartment and I got raped by some guys. I only drank one cup of vodka and well, half a cup, and I blacked out. And I was really spinning, my head was spinning. I started puking, I remember that, and blacked out. And then when I was sleeping, then I remember coming to and there was different guys on me and I couldn't do anything. And then I didn't know where my friends were, and they disappeared on me. I woke up and no one was there the next day. I can't even remember what happened.... And then when I was on the streets I got raped, too.

Losing her best friend and encountering sexual violence left Molly with severe anxiety and a concern for her safety. "I just couldn't trust anyone. I felt unsafe. Everyone was out to get me too."

Peer Groups and Street Gangs

As teenagers, the women knew the importance of being accepted by their peer group. Annette explained: "I'm thirteen, fourteen years old and my friends, the crowd I hung out with, they were like the 'cool kids' and I wanted to be part of the cool crowd, right. So I started doing stuff they were doing, which was smoking cigarettes, smoking weed, and drinking. So I started smoking weed and drinking and stuff just to fit in, right." For some of the women, fitting in with their peer group meant involvement in street gangs.

A popular explanation for why young people turn to gangs is that they provide a sense of family. For youngsters lacking both emotional and economic supports at home, the gang becomes the missing family. For Australian criminologist Rob White (2009: 47), the street gang's "family-like role" falls into place "particularly when it comes to material support, emotional refuge, psychological well-being, physical protection and social belonging" (see also Short and Hughes 2006; van Gemert, Peterson, and

Lien 2008). For many of the women I spoke to, the street gang was also quite literally their family because they had relatives deeply entrenched in the lifestyle. Molly's dad was a gang member. "He used to sell drugs and he lived a pretty rough life." Most of Brenda's family remained gang members, with many of them serving time in prison because of their involvement. Heather reported "lots of gang involvement" in her life. She explained:

> A lot of my aunties have kids with gang members, my sisters have kids with gang members. Um, my second daughter's dad's gang-affiliated. He's IP [Indian Posse]. My last baby daddy he was, the last gang he was in was Vendetta, but he used to be a Bloods before that. Yeah. I have a lot of family in Familia. My cousin's the captain of Ruthless Posse.

Christine likewise had "a lot of family that are gang members." She hung around with them and started selling weed for a street gang when she was eight years old. "It was an after [school] thing." She found it "cool" to be collecting "two dollar bills here and there all the time."

Street gangs, though, share an important similarity to the women's families: fraught with tensions and producing hardships, they too become another source of trauma. The women find themselves in a group centred squarely on the performance of a hypermasculinity that emphasizes dominance, toughness, physical strength, and compulsory heterosexuality (Comack et al. 2013: 21; also see Connell 1987, 1995, 2000; Messerschmidt 1993, 2004, 2005, 2013, 2015; Connell and Messerschmidt 2005). Complications arise because, as R.W. Connell and James Messerschmidt (2005) point out, different forms of masculinity are defined in relation not only to each other but also to femininities. Connell (1987: 188) refers to "emphasized femininity," which is organized as an adaptation to men's power and stresses compliance, nurturance, and empathy as womanly virtues. In the context of street gangs, Jana Grekul and Petrina LaRocque (2011: 152) note, "For many gang-involved girls, the hypermasculine environment means an emphasized femininity for themselves that leads to abuse, lack of power, and dependence on men." In other words, like the family, the street gang constitutes a source of violence and abuse for the women.

While street gangs engage in various types of criminal endeavours — assaults, break and enters, robberies — the main focus of their activities and the primary source of their incomes are sales of illegal drugs (Comack et al. 2013: 181). For several of the women, therefore, their involvement in street-gang activity in the form of drug sales led to their own use of drugs. Corrine, who started hanging out with gang members as a teenager, began selling drugs when she was fourteen years old. "And they made me feel like they were there for me and they kept telling me, 'Oh we're your family now' and all this stuff." Her association with the street gang put her on the path to an addiction with prescription drugs. "I started smoking weed and stuff, and it kind of escalated from there and I started drinking. And I didn't really like the drinking thing because it reminded me of my mom." Because of her mother's drinking, she said, she "wasn't really into drinking as a kid. And then I started getting into prescription pills. And that was probably the worst." Corrine was using Restoril, Valium, and Xanax. She said, "It made me feel better. It made me forget about my mom."

Molly sold crack for a street gang. Because she "had a good name with the gang," she said, "I could get anything I wanted. I had everything I needed and stuff, yeah. They would protect me. So I never felt unsafe." She was also using cocaine: "I felt like I needed drugs to feel happy." But Molly's involvement with the gang brought with it a lot of violence. "I started running around with guns and home-invading people. I was just doing a lot of crazy things and things I wouldn't do normally, punching out people and seeing them do, fuck, they were shooting at people. I was doing a lot of stuff I shouldn't have been doing, moving a lot of drugs in school, doing lots of money, partying every day, yeah."

Jackie met her boyfriend, who was gang-involved, when she moved to Winnipeg at eighteen. Jackie started running with the gang and selling drugs for them. "When it came to partying and drinking, it was fun at first and then I got raped and it wasn't fun no more." Jackie explained what happened:

> It was at this party. We were drinking. You know those big bottles of Texas Micky's? Yeah. We had that there and we were partying. And then I remember telling my boyfriend, I said, "I'm going to go to sleep." I told him, "Watch me, okay. Don't leave me there." And what do you know, he leaves me there. They told him I went home and so he went home looking for me. But I guess he was so drunk that he just crawled in through the window and passed out. And I was in that room and I kept opening my eyes and I'd see different guys. And when I woke up I was naked.

Jackie ended up getting pregnant from the rape, but she "kept it a secret." As a result, she said, "Nothing was ever done about it. But I walked away from them. I walked away from that gang. And they just left me alone." The gang did not leave Jackie's boyfriend alone: "They beat the shit out of him and almost killed him. That's how he got out. And they burnt off his tattoos with a blow torch."

Some of the women encountered the "patriarchal bargain" that Jody Miller (2001) writes about: the construction of a gendered gang identity that involves adopting the masculine constructs of gang values. In Mary's case, that meant engaging in violence with other girls who were gang-involved, stealing from sex trade workers, and serving as a front for home invasions:

> We would jump other girls.... If there was somebody walking around with a black rag on their head or something we'd beat up that girl. Or if there was a girl that needed to be jumped in, we would jump her in. Or if we were to jack hookers, we would jack hookers. Or we set up — if they needed a girl for a robbery we'd set up a robbery thing. For one example, this one girl went to this drug dealer's house and pretended she was getting drugs off him. And her bro's rushed her inside the house pretending they were just home-invading that house. But really she was just the person to knock on the door to see if —
>
> [To get the door open.]
>
> Yeah. See, stuff like that. Just really bad stuff that now when I think of it, you would have went down for a lot of crazy-ass charges, man.

While many of the women were exposed to the hypermasculinity per-formed by the street-gang members, not all of them were subject to the "emphasized femininity" that Grekul and LaRocque (2011) found in their research. Grace's story is a case in point.

Grace's Story

Grace started "chilling out" with gang members when she was six years old. They would break into the school on her reserve and set houses on fire. Grace said, "My brother kind of forced me to do that stuff."

[So why do you think he forced you to do it?]

Because he told me that he always grew up with girls, 'cause there's my grandma and his sisters. He wanted a brother and then he picked me, I guess, he picked me.

[You were to be the brother?]

'Cause he didn't have any brothers.

Part of "being the brother" meant that Grace learned from a young age that "crying's for bitches." She also learned from her brother to abide by other maxims. "You don't charge people" when they assault you, and "If someone looks at you wrong, if someone says something wrong, does anything wrong to you, then just get them." Living by those maxims when she was young got Grace into a lot of trouble. It also led her into the care of CFS because her grandmother couldn't control her. When she was twelve Grace was moved to Winnipeg. "The gang that I was chilling out with on my reserve, I guess one of my cousins called somebody [in a gang] in Winnipeg, told them to take care of me." In return for being taken care of, Grace said she "had to sell, just sell stuff for them." Her brother's gender tutoring appeared to have paid off: "'Cause I was a tomboy and they didn't want sex or anything from me. 'Cause I was a little boy and my cousin told them not to fuck with me."

When this same cousin patched over to another gang, Grace was told not to have any more contact with him.

I didn't talk to him for a while and then finally he's like, "Fuck, Grace, you know I love you. I took care of you when you were a kid and whatever. If it wasn't for me you wouldn't even know those guys in Winnipeg." And then I just said, "Okay, fuck it. It's my cousin. Why am I trying to choose people that I didn't even grow up with over him? He's my blood." So I started talking to him and then this one guy started creeping through my Facebook and shit. And then he found those inboxes about me talking to my cousin. And we were just talking about my family and stuff. And I got in trouble for that. And then I got punched out.

After receiving a beating and being expelled ("punched out") from her gang, Grace ended up joining her cousin's gang. She was told that if she wanted to "chill" with them she would have to have her previous gang tattoo burned off: "I got it burned five times by five different guys for five seconds. And that was just for respect…. It looked so gross afterwards, man. You could see the little layers of skin and stuff…. It took four or five months to heal."

The gang life involved a lot of drugs and partying. Grace had been introduced to smoking pot when she was seven years old, but "crack and coke, I was told not to ever do that. That's how the gang was. You weren't supposed to do that or you'd get punched out. And meth, I wouldn't touch that shit 'cause I seen my sister on that shit. All that hard stuff, I never did that hard stuff. I'd just drink and take pills [Xanax, Restoril, Gabapentin]."

Grace talked about what happened at one of the gang parties:

> We were having a big party. It was a big [name of gang] party. And then I went to the washroom and then all of a sudden I heard some bitch scream in her room. I was like, "What the fuck?" So I went to her room. And I guess that chick that I left there [in the basement], she was getting raped by some guy. And I was like, "What the fuck!" That's all I said was "What the fuck!" And then a bunch of people came running into the room. And then that one guy he said "Fuckin' Grace, get him! Get him!" So I fuckin' did 'cause I was told to do what you were told, man, so I did.
>
> And then I got handed knives and stuff and I started stabbing him. Someone handed me the blades, the hot knives, and then I started burning him. And then I just kept stabbing him and stabbing him and then there was just blood everywhere.... And then everyone started punching him out.

When asked where her capacity for violence comes from, Grace replied: "That's just how I was taught, man." She also commented:

> I know where my anger comes from. It comes from, I got sexually abused by my mom's common law, whatever, one of her baby's dads, when I was a little kid. But no one believed me, man. My grandma didn't believe me 'cause all the time we were always told, "You're a liar, you're lying all the time." And then my grandma used to hit me, too. I used to get punched out by her. Well, not punched out, just hit with sticks, with anything, man, anything she could reach for. Over stupid stuff, too. And then my brothers, I used to get terrorized and tortured by them before, all the time. I was not allowed to hang out with girls.

Grace's older brother ended up serving a federal sentence. "He just got out. I think that jail changed him too 'cause he's trying to be, he's trying to preach to me, man. He's trying to tell me to smarten up. I got a bunch of letters from him telling me to smarten up. He's telling me now, 'Just cry. Let it out. Just be a woman. Don't try to be a boy anymore. Fuck that shit. You're a girl, be a girl.'" But Grace figures that she "can't be a girl. I'm not used to it."

"Baby Daddies"

While exposure to the violence inherent in the sex and drug trades and the gang life added to the women's trauma experiences as teenagers, compounding those experiences was their sexual vulnerability. Several of the women experienced sexual intercourse at an early age, and under troubling circumstances. Doreen was just thirteen the first time she had sex.

> I lost my virginity to a twenty-five-year-old. And I didn't even remember. I just snapped out of a blackout [at] a party my brother took me to.
>
> [And you drank a lot?]
>
> Yeah. I drank quite a bit, I guess. And I blacked out and I came to and this guy was just doing his thing and I was like, "What the hell?" And I remember it hurt. It really hurt lots. And after that it was like, "Okay, well, since I can do this I might as well just keep doing it." 'Cause I thought that that's the way it made me feel better about myself.

Annette also became sexually active when she was thirteen. "Once I did have sex for the first time I started being promiscuous with a lot of different guys."

Sexual activity at such a young age put the women at risk of early pregnancies. Data from the 2006 Census show that 8 percent of Indigenous teenage girls ages fifteen to nineteen were parents compared to 1.3 percent of their non-Indigenous counterparts (O'Donnell and Wallace 2011: 20). Manitoba has the highest rate of teen pregnancy among all provinces; most of those teen parents are poor, and at least half are Indigenous (O'Donnell and Wallace 2011; Taylor 2011). Several of the women I spoke to bore children at an age even younger than fifteen. Heather left school in Grade 7 and Melody in Grade 8 because of their pregnancies; Sarah had the first of her nine children when she was only fourteen years old.

Pregnancy at such an early age set the women on a path of relationships with several different "baby daddies." Cyndi had her first child when she was fourteen. Now in her late twenties, she has five children from four different fathers. "Okay, to be honest, I don't think I was ever in a relationship. I think I was just having sex with these people. My second and third child have the same dad. I don't know. We weren't ever really together. I can't say we were actually a couple. We were mostly just sleeping together, I guess you could say."

Unprepared to look after their children when they were still children themselves, the women often had little choice but to have their babies raised by relatives or taken into care by the child welfare system. Heather's children are in foster care. She had six of them with four different fathers. "All my children live in nice areas with normal people [chuckles]." Just as CFS played a role in their own childhoods, the agency has intervened in their children's lives — and the cycle of being taken into care continues.

Along with facing the severe difficulties of bearing children at such an early age, many of the women found themselves in abusive relationships with the fathers. While Tannis was prescribed birth-control pills as a teenager, she only took the pills for a week because, as she said, "I was trying to get pregnant…. I just wanted to have a baby." Her baby's dad, she said, "would beat me up all the time. In front of my daughter, too. Even when I was pregnant. He punched me in the stomach when I was six months pregnant." Tannis was with him for four years, and "it was abusive the whole time." "It got so bad with me and him fighting I had to lock myself in the room and jump out the window and run away, 'cause he was trying to break down the door, trying to fight me. It was scary."

Cheryl's partner kicked her in the stomach when she was eight months pregnant. "I didn't charge him or anything, I didn't charge him for the abuse he put me through. I always had bruises, I always had black eyes…. I thought I could help him, change him."

Brenda, now in her forties, has eight children with four different fathers. She had her first child at age seventeen. Her first partner, she said, "beat me when I was pregnant. He'd try to throw me down the stairs and do whatever he could to make me have a miscarriage, try to kick me in the stomach and everything. He hit me with — you know those big heavy phones, those old phones that they used to have? He hit me with it in the head one time." Brenda's breaking point occurred shortly after her first daughter was born:

> I was cooking for him and she started crying. She was only one month old. She wanted to eat and I had her on the love seat. And so I turned the stove off, I was cooking him supper. And he got

mad and you know how thick the yellow pages used to be? He threw it towards the couch where she was sleeping. And that's when I snapped. I started stabbing him. He was running out the door and I was still going after him when he was running, running away from me.

Brenda said, "I just figured he can do what he wanted to me but not to my baby.... As long as my baby was safe, that's all I cared about."

Much like the experiences of the original *Women in Trouble* cohort, the physical abuse the women encountered from their intimate partners — black eyes, broken bones, bruises — stemmed from the male sense of ownership or possessiveness. The father of Bernice's baby was not there at the time and thought she was cheating on him when she was pregnant. She said she wasn't. "And, yeah, he started domesticating me weeks after I had my baby. He started beating me up pretty bad.... It got really bad where I had to go to the hospital. And he broke my jaw and he did my face pretty good. He didn't want people to date me, I guess."

Annette met her baby's dad when she was fourteen: "I guess why I made him the centre of my world is because [of] the neglect I got from my dad growing up, right. My dad was never there. And so I guess that's why I clung to him right away." But her boyfriend got jealous, to the point of ripping up pictures of her favourite rap artist. "So that was a warning sign, but I didn't look at his warning signs, right. I was like, 'Oh my god, this guy really likes me. Holy shit, okay.'" The relationship became more abusive. As Annette described it, "I never fought back for a long time, I was always the one getting abused. I was never the aggressor for a while."

TRAUMA IN ADULTHOOD

Abuse continued to colour the women's relationships as adults, adding yet another layer of trauma.

Jody found herself in an abusive relationship when she was nineteen. Her partner was affiliated with a biker gang and sold drugs. He "had lots of nice things and lots of money." Jody said she "never really knew anything, exactly what he was selling or how much because he would kind of keep that secretive and go on his own. But I wasn't stupid. I knew something, yeah." With the profits earned from the drug trade, Jody said, "I'd always get whatever I wanted. But I was never happy." Her partner was "really abusive and controlling."

Even if I looked, if we were driving, I was in the passenger seat, if I would even look and there was a guy in the car next to me, he would smash my head into the window. I couldn't even have a cellphone or Facebook. I couldn't really have friends. He'd get even jealous of my girlfriends. And I never could go out or we were always together 24/7. He was just controlling and insecure and manipulative. And he wouldn't let me have my own money or be independent at all. He would make me depend on him and he would pay for everything.

For Jody, it was "like walking on eggshells — always. I didn't feel really good about myself. I cared about him but — I wanted to leave." But leaving him, she said, would have been difficult because she would have had to start all over again. "I was so used to having things a certain way, and I felt like it was hard to start over." While Jody did have jobs, her partner would show up at her workplace "five times a day thinking I'm doing something bad, you know what I mean. So it [the job] would never last. Or he'd be like, 'You don't need to work. I'll take care of you,' you know." Jody didn't see the relationship as abusive in the beginning. "I just thought he was trying to protect me or something." The relationship lasted for five years; it ended when her partner was sent to jail on weapons charges after the police raided their house and found two guns.

Cyndi found herself in a troubled relationship in her early twenties: "Little did I know that he was extremely abusive." The abuse started "a few months into our relationship. And he would buy me stuff after. And he would take it away, though, and break it on me, rip it up or something, you know, depending on what he bought me …. And then the violence started getting a little bit more escalated and whatever and it got to a point where I was coming home black and blue." Cyndi's sisters would tell her to "just leave him," but she would say, "'No, I ain't going to leave him,' you know, like, 'It'll stop, it'll change.'" She had never been through anything like this before, what she described as the "cycle of violence … I'd never been beaten or hit or anything for no reason, yeah, or for even trying to please someone, you know." When Cyndi became pregnant she finally found the wherewithal to seek help from a women's transition centre.

Like Cyndi, other women also eventually found the courage to leave their abusive relationships.

Jennifer's Story

Jennifer met her partner at a party when she was twenty. She wasn't used to drinking but had some drinks. "I ended up having intercourse with this guy. And he was thirty-three, so we were far apart in age. And I got pregnant that one session [chuckles]. That's all it takes. I always hear people say that but I've learned it from experience." The two ended up living together and had a second child.

> He ended up getting abusive to me, started beating me up and being controlling. And he drank a lot and did coke and I wasn't. And I told him I didn't want that kind of life and that. And then I started hearing that's why him and his wife broke up was because of how controlling he was and that. And I hid it for a long time. I didn't tell anyone. I was embarrassed for people to know that I was being beaten and abused.

The turning point for Jennifer occurred late one night. "My son woke up and he came walking in the room and seen me getting beat up. And he just yelled, 'Stop.' He's like, 'Stop hitting my mommy.... Don't hit my mom 'cause I'm going to be a man someday.'" When her son said that, Jennifer started crying. "I wasn't crying while he was beating me up, but once I heard my son say that I started crying." She grabbed her son and wrapped him in her arms.

When her partner left the house, Jennifer dressed the children and fled to her parents' house. Thinking back, she remarked:

> I don't think I was in love with him. I don't know. Maybe it was because he beat me or — I think it was just he kind of owned me. I was scared to leave, you know, scared for him to do something to me or take my daughter or something like that. I always had so many reasons not to leave. But really I could have just left. There's lots of places out there that could have kept me safe. But I was young and scared so I just took the beatings. And, I don't know, I think what made me realize [I should leave] was when I heard my son say that. 'Cause for a little guy to say that and has never seen somebody, has never been around violence or anything, I don't know where he got that from. But he said it.

Maureen's Story

Maureen got together with her partner when she was nineteen. "It took him three weeks before he hit me the first time." Maureen stayed in the relationship for three and one-half years. "I don't know why I stayed. I don't even have a good reason for that. 'Cause I knew what was going to happen. I knew that basically I was telling him that it was okay. The first second I told him, you know, 'Oh, it's okay. I forgive you,' I was basically telling him that he can get away with doing whatever he wanted to me, right."

To avoid getting beaten, Maureen stopped drinking alcohol. "'Cause we used to go out together but if we went out and drank together, I would have to talk my way out of him punching me out. So I stopped drinking, you know, even went to that extent. He would just get so angry. He was on steroids and nothing, nothing would set him off." The physical violence from her partner was often coupled with sexual violence:

> After a while he just became so ugly to me. That person that he was, was so ugly. So I didn't want to have sex with him anymore. And then he would force himself on me anyways. He would just have his way with me. It didn't matter if I was crying or anything, you know, he'd punch me out and then he'd want to have sex. Or if I didn't want to have sex he'd punch me out 'cause I didn't want to have sex. That's what most of my beatings came from, from him. He would choke me out and just, he was a really vicious man.

Maureen recalled three things that happened within the space of a week that led her to make the decision to leave the relationship. The first was a serious beating: "He punched me so hard in the back of the neck that my vision blurred white, you know." For two weeks she couldn't even turn her head around. "I had to literally turn in a circle if I wanted to look, you know. I couldn't move. And that's when I realized he's going to hurt me really bad, he really will paralyze me or he's going to really do something to me." The second thing involved their three-year-old daughter. "I told my daughter to go give daddy a kiss goodnight and she grabbed me by the leg and she told me, 'Mommy I'm scared of my daddy.' And it broke my heart." The third thing had to do with Maureen's father. "He had hit every woman his whole life, you know, well, my whole life. Any woman I've ever seen him with he's hit." Things changed, though, when her father became involved with a particular woman. Then, Maureen said, "He never even raised his voice to her. And that was the first time I could see somebody tell my dad to shut up and him not haul off and backhand her. He never even yelled at her." Maureen realized that "It was *her*" — it was this new woman — "she made him feel like that, she made him understand, he didn't want her to see him in that sense, you know." She also realized that "no matter what I ever did I was never going to be that person" for her own partner. "I just wasn't what he wanted, you know. And it had nothing to do with me or the person I was 'cause I was still an amazing woman, you know. I'm a good woman, I take care. It's him. And he's going to be miserable until he gets the help that he needs."

Maureen ended up leaving the relationship with only the clothes on her back. "I left in the middle of the night and jumped out the window … and took off with nowhere to go." She made the difficult decision to leave her daughter behind with her mother-in-law. As she explained, "His mother was able to provide her the stability that I wasn't."

Carol's Story (cont'd)

Carol married a man from another First Nations community when she was twenty years old. It was an arranged marriage, orchestrated by the parents. "I'd heard of him and I seen him, but I didn't know him." On her wedding day she "was literally dragged down the aisle. My auntie gave me a Valium 'cause I wouldn't put on the dress, the wedding dress."

After they were married Carol and her husband lived with his parents in their reserve community. "So they always made sure that I was in the house. That's the story of my life [chuckles]." Carol was asked to help with the domestic work. "And I would 'cause I was taught to respect elders and that." She was not allowed to go visiting on her husband's reserve. She explained, "I was afraid to do anything. And so I just stayed in the house and took care of my kids. And then he started beating me when he was a band constable."

One winter evening, Carol said, "He strangled me and almost killed me." She took a Ski-Doo and "tried to escape" back to her home community. The Ski-Doo broke down, but Carol's father happened by on the winter road and found her. "I was so happy to see him. He just grabbed me and hugged me and took off his jacket 'cause I had frostbites on me. I felt so relieved. Then he just took me back to his house." When Carol disclosed to her parents about the abuse in her marriage, her mother told her that "it happens in every relationship" and that she should just "take it and not say anything about it. Not to embarrass her, not to shame her." Divorce was also out of the question because it was against her mother's Roman Catholic religion. Carol went back to her husband's reserve.

During a trip to Winnipeg, Carol came across pamphlets about domestic violence. "So that's where I got my information. And I secretly went, I tried to charge him." But Carol said that her husband was "friends with the RCMP" because he was a band constable. "So I was the one they took away. And I was arrested. I was charged." She tried to tell the officers about the abuse, but "they kind of just turned their back on me and not listening to me." They told her that her husband "wouldn't do that." Carol told her father about the most recent abuse, "and he got mad." Her father had her released from custody. But her mother told her she had to go back to her husband. "And I didn't want to." But when her husband showed up at her parents' house, Carol believed that "as a wife and as a Roman Catholic, I had to go back."

The abuse continued, but it became more emotional and verbal in nature. The RCMP came to the house, and they threatened to arrest Carol, "because I wasn't supposed to be near him or something. But he's the one who came and got me." When the officers responded with "But you came along with him," Carol replied: "But I had to. I didn't have no choice." And they said, "No, you have choices." She said, "Tell me what they are. Then I want to go to jail then." Her husband stepped in and said, "No, you're not taking her anywhere." "The men talked and, Carol said, "all I knew is that I was allowed to stay." A month or two later Carol appeared before a judge. "And she told me that, 'Oh, your husband is a band constable. We could charge you for assaulting a band constable.' And I said, 'Excuse me?' And then I wasn't understanding what was going on. And then all of a sudden everything was dropped. And then, yeah, I was to go home with my husband." Carol's husband responded to the legal decision by telling her: "See. I control you." Carol's response: "I didn't feel like a person. I felt like a slave."

When Carol's husband left the reserve for a month of police training she was happy, "'cause I had the house to myself." While the couple had moved into their own house on the reserve, Carol was still being closely monitored by her husband's family. "I knew I was being watched." When she left the reserve to attend a medical appointment in a northern town, she brought back some provisions that they didn't have in her community, "groceries and stuff like that." Her husband had left her with no resources during his absence. "I was to go on welfare." Her husband's family then came and took her groceries. "They just took it. And I was left with only so much." Her in-laws even took her stove. "Because I guess they knew that I didn't know how to stand up for myself and things like that. They would basically just walk all over me." Carol asked the manager at the reserve store for some credit so that she could buy food. "He said, 'Okay, I understand.'

And he was nice about it." But the band office called to ask her, "What are you doing going to the store begging for food?" She was also accused of selling her stove for money.

Carol later travelled to Winnipeg to attend her husband's graduation from police training. Her aunt was also in attendance, and Carol told her about the abuse. Her aunt said, "You don't have to stay in the relationship," and found her an apartment in Winnipeg and arranged for social assistance. They also saw a lawyer to arrange for custody of her two children. As Carol put it, "All I had to do was just start over." She recalled:

> I was happy for once in my life. But then there's times where I'm so used to being told what to do, I didn't know what to do? I don't know if that makes sense.
>
> [Yeah. To be independent.]
>
> Yeah. But I knew what needed to be done, you know, what I needed. Needed food and I needed furniture and beddings and stuff like that, that was provided for the kids. And then I, so I just, I felt like I was walking on eggshells before. But now I just felt free. I just, I was so happy. I cried for days. But I was scared at the same time too. Terrified. I was petrified. But I was happy.

At that point Carol was twenty-five years old — it was seventeen years before we met at the WCC. Thinking back on that time in her life, Carol recalled: "Sometimes I wondered if I could do it, if I can do it. And I'd just be lost. I'd be so lonely. But then — I didn't want my kids to grow up in fear like I did. I enjoyed that smile on them. And then I think back on the way I grew up as a child and I don't want that. I don't want them to live like that."

Women's Violence

Feminists have argued that violence is gendered; it is something that men do not only to other men but also to women (Brownmiller 1975; MacKinnon 1983; Dobash and Dobash 1992). Patriarchy — a structure and an ideology that privileges men — is used as a template for understanding the unequal power and resources available to men and women. In this respect, male violence against women is understood as a manifestation of patriarchy, of the power that men exercise over women. Nevertheless, while the concept of patriarchy allows us to understand some of the pervasive patterns of male violence in society, we should not conclude that women are bereft of power or somehow immune to engaging in violence of their own. This is especially so given the cultural messages that permeate our society, messages that herald violence as resource to be used to resolve life's problems.

Indeed, the women were not always the only ones to get hurt when fighting occurred in their intimate relationships. Several of the women talked about their own use of violence in their relationships. Avery described herself as an "angry teenager," and spoke of how "None of my boyfriends hit me. I was the one that hit two of my boyfriends." She said that she had learned to control her anger. "I've had a few years' experience with my anger so I learned my lesson. I finally don't go to rage right away. I actually get, I calm myself down and I go for a walk."

Brenda ended up in a second relationship with an abusive partner. "He'd beat me. I'd walk around with black eyes, too." But she said, "I started fighting back." When asked whether that helped, she replied: "Eventually he, yeah, he started, he wouldn't, eventually he quit. He wouldn't hit me as often. 'Cause he knew that I'd fight back."

In her late thirties, Alyson has been in a relationship with the father of her ten children for eighteen years. She described her partner as "very possessive." The relationship was "violent a lot in the beginning. But not anymore because he can't beat me no more. I can beat him. If I wanted to I could really give him a good licking." Alyson started fighting back eight years ago, "'cause I was getting sick of it. Just nothing hurt me anymore. The pain didn't hurt, 'cause I knew it only hurts for a while. Yeah, the physical pain only hurts for a while." She also learned to deal with the emotional pain: "I learned to shut everything out."

Violence is not confined to heterosexual relationships. Recognition of violence in same-sex relationships would seem to belie the feminist claim that male violence against women is rooted in the patriarchal nature of our society. In other words, to point to how "women do it too" undermines the feminist view of violence as inherently gendered as "male." In her research on violence in lesbian relationships, Janice Ristock (2002) argues for the importance of considering the social context in which violence occurs. She suggests that a range of contextual factors surrounds abusive relationships, including "contexts in which violence is normalized. These can include using drugs and alcohol, having a history of previous abuse, and experiencing a lifetime of abuse in a context of poverty and racism" (p. 57). At bottom, Ristock places her emphasis on the social inequities that put people at risk of violence.

Three of the women I spoke to were in same-sex relationships that became violent. Their experiences reflect the social contexts of such violence.

Margaret recalled, "Growing up, it was stressful." Margaret's father was abusive towards her mother. After her parents separated, she lived with her mother and grandparents. Her grandparents were residential school survivors, which had an effect on their child-raising. According to Margaret, "The way my mom was raised, they lacked that affection. I mean, they would care for each other, they were always there feeding each other, yada yada, all that, right. But they didn't really give each other that affection.... Scared to get close to each other or whatever." Margaret moved to the city to live with her father when she was twelve years old. At fourteen she began a relationship with an older girl. It was her first time being in a relationship. According to Margaret, the relationship, which lasted for two and a half years, was abusive:

> Well, she would just, like, lie all the time. It would go both ways, right. A lot of cheating.... And she was really, like jealous, jealous and controlling. So it was hard for me to leave. And when a couple of times she said she would kill herself if I left or whatever. And this time I did leave her and ... she did try to do that to herself [try to kill herself]. So it was really stressful.

Maxine was in a relationship with another girl from ages fourteen to eighteen. "And it was a really abusive relationship, both ways.... We'd fight each other and we'd whip each other with stuff, throw stuff at each other. I don't know. We stabbed each other. It was not even a good relationship."

Christine had been in a series of abusive relationships with men.

> I said, "The heck with this. I'm so sick of men. It's bullshit. You know, all the abuse, the cheating, the lying. You know, I'm so sick of it." I was like, "I'm going to be gay." [laughs] ... I was just, I need something different. I still want, I'm the type of person I need somebody. I don't like to be alone. I need a partner, a companion, you know, a good close person I can talk to and, you know, bond with.

Christine started a relationship with a long-time girlfriend. While she thinks it was a good relationship for her, it also had its troubles: "We do fight each other when we're both drunk. That's the only time we don't get along is when we drink together.... Because we drink to a point where we're fighting each other, we're lashing out. Because there's times she cheated on me, then I cheated on her. So the trust is obviously not there right now." The relationship would only work, she said, if they didn't drink.

The violence that occurs in same-sex relationships, then, mirrors what women encounter in heterosexual relationships, including jealousy and possessiveness and conflicts fuelled by alcohol. Moreover, just as in their heterosexual relationships, the women bring with them their previous histories of abuse and exposure to violence. Given the normalization of violence in their lives, violence can, not surprisingly, also colour their same-sex relationships.

THE IMPACT OF TRAUMA

The stories of these women's lives indicate how trauma became a life-defining experience. Several of the women talked about the long-term impact of their trauma experiences. Maxine had a persistent problem with insomnia, which started when she was ten years old. "Maybe because when I was getting bothered by my mom's boyfriends, that they'd only come in there when I was sleeping. And I think maybe that's what triggered it, where I had to be up and they would leave me alone."

Jackie said her experience of being molested by her uncle when she was eight years old was "what made me promiscuous. I'm very promiscuous with men. And I'm scared to be alone. I don't know, it's just, I have to lean on, I have to always have a guy with me or something, you know. I always have to have a male figure with me."

For many of the women, experiences of childhood trauma left them feeling unable to trust men. As Corrine commented, "Growing up I didn't feel like I could be with somebody after, you know, all the stuff that happened to me. I felt gross, and even though I wasn't 'hurt hurt' but I still kind of, I was still traumatized, right, about being touched and stuff. And I just felt, I don't know — I was scared, I guess I'll say. I was scared to be with somebody." Maxine also had difficulty trusting men: "I was always aggressive towards men. And I think being sexually abused, maybe that was part of it, not trusting men and thinking all men are going to be like this." Harmony was more forthright in her attitude towards men: "I think I've been abused by every single man who has been in my life.... I have this *hate* towards men.... I have this thing towards men where I just don't like it."

Ashley, in her early twenties, had several experiences of sexual trauma. She was groped by an older man when she was twelve and then violently raped when she was fifteen. "And then when I was seventeen my mom was having a party and then this guy just put his hands in my shirt and started grabbing my boobs. And then I couldn't even do anything about it. And I was just messed up. And he'd given me drugs and stuff." Even though all of her perpetrators were criminally charged and convicted, the experiences continued to haunt her.

> Till this day I still have feelings of, from that guy touching my boobs. 'Cause he was a really repulsive looking guy. And I have this thing where I feel like his hand is on me and I can't take it off. And it's a really sick feeling I have. And it's — I hate it. And there's nothing I can do about it. I can't take it off. It's really weird. Yeah, sometimes I cry about it. Yeah. But he took something there. It's weird, yeah.

> And the whole rape thing, that was my first time ever having to go through intimacy. And it was horrible. So now I can't have intimacy with guys. I start resenting them and I start getting mad at them. "This is all you want" or, you know, sex is not what it's supposed to be for me. So it's really hard for me to maintain a relationship.

Ashley had never had a long-term relationship: "That's something I really want but I can't. Every time I try, it just doesn't work out, you know. And I can't. It's like I'm pretending to be like everything is okay and normal in the relationship. But it's actually, on the inside, I'm not. I don't know what the hell this is." When Ashley drinks alcohol, things become easier.

> I don't have to feel uncomfortable when I'm drinking or I don't have to feel weird about a guy touching me. It feels more like I'm not scared. And so I think that's why I drink a lot because I starve for that, for that kind of affection, that kind of intimacy…. It's easier for me to be with people when I'm drinking. 'Cause everything feels okay when I drink. And it's the only way I know how to do it. Otherwise when I'm sober it's really uncomfortable for me. I'm just really a different person.

Turning to alcohol and drugs was also used by the women as a coping strategy to manage the trauma of loss.

THE TRAUMA OF LOSS

Indigenous people have a lower life expectancy than do other Canadians. In Manitoba, First Nations males have a life expectancy of 68.4 years compared to 76.1 years for all other Manitoba males; First Nations females have a life expectancy of 73.2 years compared to 81.4 years for all other Manitoba females (Brownell, Fransoo, and Martens 2015: 40). The premature mortality rate for the First Nations population in Manitoba has also been found to be double the rest of the province; the prevalence of diabetes was over four times higher, and hospitalizations for injury were almost four times as high for the First Nations population compared to other Manitobans (p. 41). Many of the women I spoke to had lost parents, grandparents, and other relatives to diseases such as diabetes and heart failure. Troubles with alcohol had also led to early deaths due to cirrhosis of the liver and other medical complications. As well, the high rates of youth suicide in many Indigenous communities had touched their lives; several lost siblings and cousins at an early age. Another contributing factor generating the trauma of loss is the normalization of violence. Partying, drugging and drinking, and the gang lifestyle put people at risk of an early and tragic death. Women involved in the sex trade are also at risk of violence and death, as attested by the numbers of missing and murdered Indigenous women and girls in Canada (some of whom worked in the sex trade).

In addition to the trauma resulting from abuse, therefore, many of the women were dealing with the trauma of the loss of their loved ones. In most cases, they turned to drugging and drinking as a coping strategy. As Gabor Maté (2008: 193) notes, individuals who have encountered trauma in their lives often use drugs or alcohol as a way to "self-medicate to soothe their emotional pain." He also states: "Addiction is a deeply ingrained response to stress, an attempt to cope with it through self-soothing. Maladaptive in the long term, it is highly effective in the short term" (p. 198).

Jackie lost her mother to suicide eleven years before I spoke to her. According to Jackie, her mother "met this guy that was younger than her and she caught him cheating on her with this other woman in her house and she died of a broken heart." Jackie recounted that harrowing experience:

> I was the last one to find out. It was really devastating. I remember going in the North End off Flora and Robinson, The Developments, I remember pulling up there. My friend drove me there and they're yelling to go around. And I just ran through that tape, ran through the cops, ran upstairs. And my mom was laying right there — right in the corner — and she was, it looked like she was sleeping. And she wasn't wearing her glasses. 'Cause she always complains without her glasses, right, that she gets headaches and stuff. And then I saw her there and I was telling them, "Pump her stomach. What

the hell's wrong? Why are you guys just standing around?" And that one cop just picked me up and carried me out the door. And then it was like my whole life flashed before my eyes. It felt like a dream, a bad dream.

Since her mother's death, Jackie said, "I've been drinking a lot. A lot. I drank every day."

Janice, now in her early forties, was twenty-one when she suffered her first significant loss, her grandmother.

She had a huge impact on my life. I'd go to her for guidance. She was my best friend. Everything. She was everything to me. I don't want to say she was more important than my mom, but she was up there.... And when I lost her my whole world just fell apart.... I didn't even want to live anymore. I was just so depressed. And somebody had introduced me to cocaine. I started snorting it. And a month later I was banging it. So it just made me forget about stuff. It made me feel good.

Janice encountered other significant losses. In 2005 her sister died, and in 2008 she lost her brother. In 2011 Janice's husband of nineteen years died unexpectedly after a surgical procedure. "Our marriage was pretty solid. It was good. I mean, I always had his back, he always had mine. We loved each other. He was the love of my life, right." Janice again turned to drugs (this time, crack cocaine) to deal with her pain. Janice said that when people ask her, "Are you ready for a relationship?" her response is always:

Absolutely not. I won't do that again. I'll never do that again. Why? Because I'll never put myself through that much pain again of losing somebody. And I'll never do that to somebody else by dying, you know. I don't want somebody else to go through the pain I went through. It was that great. It was a lot of pain involved in that. So I pretty much, I got lost myself.

As a coping strategy to deal with the pain associated with their losses, drugging and drinking became a common response for other women. As Christine commented: "The only time I hit rock bottom is when I lose someone close to me, when death comes or a family tragic situation comes. So my way of dealing with pain is to get high so I don't have to cry and block everything out." Maxine lost a cousin to suicide when she was fourteen.

"And he was really close to me. And I took it really hard. And I just gave up on everything. I started using drugs and drinking a lot."

Jessica had "seen a lot of things," including witnessing her cousin being fatally stabbed with a knife by her boyfriend when she was just seventeen; "I seen her get murdered, brutally." While Jessica said she "just learned to get over stuff," the images continued to haunt her: "Sometimes I think about it every day. I think about all those things every day…. I still can picture those things." Not long after her cousin was murdered, Jessica became a regular drug user, injecting crystal meth.

Margaret lost her dad when she was sixteen and her sister to a drug overdose when she was seventeen. They were the only two in the family that she felt she could talk to, "so it was really hard." Margaret too dealt with her losses by turning to drugs: "I stopped caring, right. I used to care a lot about everyone and everything. And then I just stopped caring and, yeah, I turned to drugs. And it didn't really help."

Mary's story illustrates the multiple losses that many of the women encountered. Mary described herself as a "rebellious teenager." Her rebellion included becoming immersed in the gang life. Mary met the "love of her life" when she was eighteen. He too was involved in the gang life. When she met him, she said, "I was — I didn't think there was a love like that. I was so in love. I was so in love." They were together for four years. "When we got together he loved me. I had nothing to worry about with him. He didn't cheat on me. He didn't hit me. He told me he loved me every day. He told me I was pretty every day." But the gang life brought with it an exposure to violence. Tragically, Mary's partner was murdered by gang members.

Her partner's death was not the only loss Mary experienced. As she put it, "Death has been all around me for the past year." Within the space of five months she also lost her father and a cousin. Mary said that her dad's drinking was what killed him: "He had cirrhosis of the liver. And he chose not to stop drinking. And we slowly watched him — is perish the word? Slowly watched him, yeah." Soon after her father's death, Mary's sixteen-year-old cousin overdosed on Benetol patches. To deal with her losses, Mary said she "ran from everything — all the pain, all the hurt, the depression, my family. And I went to the family I had known for the past four years, the gang member family. And they introduced me to this drug called crystal meth…. And I used it as a crutch to drown all the pain." Mary explained how the drugs helped her to cope with her losses: "When I was on drugs I would remember but I'd be high as fuck, you know what I mean…. I wouldn't feel no pain. I had no pain. I didn't care about myself. I didn't care about my daughter. I didn't care about the family that was grieving all this loss we just had."

Loss of Children

In addition to grieving the loss of their partners, family members, and friends, many of the women were also dealing with the trauma of losing custody of their children. Drugging and drinking became their way of coping with that loss.

Lori said she had to give up her kids because of her partner's behaviour. After one occasion when he threw her against a wall, breaking her ribs, she took her kids to her mother's place. "I was so heartbroken that I couldn't have my kids. I was so upset that it wasn't fair that I had to give up my kids because of his behaviour. But it was safer for them with my mom. All he was going to do was follow me. And I've moved so many times trying to avoid him." After that happened, Lori said that she "broke and started using."

When Bernice and her partner were in the process of breaking up, he called CFS on her and the children were taken away. "I started doing coke every day. I didn't even want to go to the visits. I just stopped.... I feel really guilty. And if I see them I'm not going to let, I wouldn't want to let them go, you know. It's going to hurt. [Crying] And it's hard, you know. As much as I miss them I just can't."

Wanda had started using drugs when she was twelve years old, first weed, then pills, alcohol and ecstasy, and then crack, cocaine, and meth. When her partner phoned CFS and had her son taken away, she "just didn't care anymore. I just gave up on everything."

> Before I liked them [drugs] because I thought they were fine and it was cool. And then now I just, I was doing them just to take my pain and hurt away from my son being taken away from me and having to deal with the system. So it was just for me to run away from everything and not feel no pain or have no feelings. Just to be constantly high and numb the pain — high, drunk, or fucked up, anything that I could get my hands on just as long as I wasn't sober.

THE TROUBLE WITH NORMAL

Each woman's story is unique, given its texture and form according to how a woman constructs her own biography and what she is prepared to share at the moment of its telling. Still, taken together the women's stories contain important commonalities — which, in large measure, stem from their shared social conditions. They are conditions that generated considerable trauma in their lives.

While some of the women shared memories of loving and supportive relationships with their caregivers as they were growing up, many more told traumatic stories of the hardships and neglect they encountered as children — stories that are a far cry from the idealized version of the safe and secure childhood wanted for any child. Many of the women also grew up in households in which drugging and drinking and violence became all too common occurrences. In that respect, it would be an easy step to simply lay blame on their caregivers for the trauma that invaded the women's lives as children. Similarly, it would be easy to hold each woman accountable for the choices and decisions made in dealing with her troubles as she grew older — involvement in the sex and drug trades and the gang life, choosing partners who turned out to be abusive, turning to drugs and alcohol as coping strategies to deal with the traumas of abuse and loss. After all, individuals are not without their own power or agency.

Yet once we place the women's stories in their broader social context, it is not enough to simply rest blame on them as individuals. Wider systemic processes are at work, and they operate to limit and constrain the choices or options available to manage the troubles — and the trauma — that the women encountered in their lives. As British criminologist Pat Carlen (1988: 14) so aptly put it, "Women set about making their lives within conditions that have certainly not been of their own choosing."

Settler colonialism is a systemic process that continues to wreak havoc on Indigenous communities, not only in terms of the intergenerational impact of the residential school system (starkly evident in the women's narratives) but also in terms of the collective trauma and corresponding breakdown of communality as members endeavour to manage the economic marginalization and social exclusion generated by that process. Similarly, capitalist globalization and neo-liberal economic restructuring have exacerbated the complex poverty found in inner-city spaces, creating the conditions for the sex and drug trades and street gangs to flourish — and setting the stage for more trauma. Then too, the women's lives are gendered. Many of the troubles that they face — abuse in their intimate relationships, pregnancy and the demands of mothering, exploitation in the sex trade — they encountered *as* women and *because* they are women living in a patriarchal society. The women's lives, and the choices and decisions made, have been deeply influenced by these systemic processes. These intersecting structural or systemic inequalities — of race, class, and gender — are at the root of the women's lived experience of trauma.

Given the impact of these social conditions on the women's daily lives, "normal" has taken on troublesome proportions. As many of the women recounted, being exposed to the trauma of abuse and to drugging and drinking from a young age came to constitute their "normal." So too has the trauma of loss. Heather aptly sums up what that "normal," that lived experience of trauma, involved:

> I've had so many friends and family die just in the twenty-two months that I've been here. And I've had even more die before I even got to this place. This is my first time in jail. I've had people come in the house bleeding, stabbed up, shot, beat up. I've seen so much stuff it's unbelievable. I've been in drug raids. I've been in gang raids. Even as a small child I've stopped my uncles from beating up their girlfriends. I've put myself in front of knives and guns and I've had guns pulled and knives pulled. And it's a very traumatic lifestyle ... [and so] I understand my anxiety [laughs].

While the women share commonalities in their race, class, and gender positioning, they also all hold in common another important feature of life: all of them have been accused (for those on remand) or convicted of criminal offences and were being held in custody as a result. Involvement with the criminal justice system becomes yet another layer of their lived experience of trauma.

CHAPTER FIVE

INVOLVEMENT WITH THE CRIMINAL JUSTICE SYSTEM

In popular thought crime is a relatively straightforward matter confined to the actions of wrongdoers or offenders. Legal codes and official statistics promote this understanding. The codes and statistics alike break crime down into discrete categories (against persons, against property) and delineate specific offences (assaults, robberies, theft) for which people are charged and held accountable by the criminal justice system.

At the same time, society promotes the criminal justice system as a fairly well-oiled machine dispensing justice, with clearly delineated roles for each of the legal actors. The police are crime fighters whose job is to investigate and apprehend suspects. Crown attorneys, acting on behalf of the state, take on the role of pursuing charges by meeting the burden of proof and establishing the guilt of the accused "beyond a reasonable doubt." Defence lawyers not only ensure that the Crown proves its case beyond that "reasonable doubt" but also see that the investigation and prosecution of the offence does not violate the accused's rights. Judges serve to determine the guilt or innocence of the accused and, if the finding is guilty, apply the appropriate punishment. This way of framing crime and the work of the criminal justice system easily leads to the view that the individuals who are the focus of criminal justice intervention constitute the "criminal Other." They are separate and apart from the "rest of us," the law-abiding.

For the most part these popular constructions of crime and the criminal justice system tend to be taken for granted. What happens, though, when we take up a different starting place — a place that begins by acknowledging that crime is a social construction that varies over time and place? As Wendy Chan and Kiran Mirchandani (2002: 14) note, "Definitions of crime and categories of criminality are neither fixed nor natural." Stuart Hall and his colleagues (1978: 188) make a similar point: crime is not a "given, self-evident, ahistorical, and unproblematic category." In this sense, crime cannot be separated from the social context in which it occurs; it is "differently *defined* (in both official and lay ideologies) at different periods; and this reflects not only changing attitudes amongst different sectors of the populations to crime, as well as real historical changes in the social organization of criminal activity, but also the shifting *application* of the category itself" (Hall et al. 1978: 189).

The recognition of crime as a social construction directs our attention to the act of criminalization. This process involves the exercise of a particular form of power: the "power to criminalize" or "to turn a person into a criminal" (Comack and Balfour 2004: 9). At its core the goal of criminalization is "to target those activities of groups that authorities deem it necessary to control, thus making the process inherently political" (Chan and Mirchandani 2002: 15). For instance, criminologists have long noted that the criminal justice system devotes far more resources to policing the poor and marginalized in society than it does to controlling the harmful activities of the wealthy and their corporations (Snider 2006, 2015; Reiman and Leighton 2016). Surely crimes promulgated "in the suites" of large corporations (price-fixing, tax evasion, environmental pollution, workplace injury and death) produce great harm in lives lost and financial costs incurred. Yet as actions they receive far less attention from the justice system than do events that occur "in the streets" (assaults, robbery, theft). One result of this focus is that measures taken to control and contain the threat posed by crime have resulted in the construction of particular groups as troublesome "problem populations" (Spitzer 1975) and particular spaces — such as inner-city neighbourhoods — as dangerous and disorderly. Accordingly, police focus their attention and resources on surveilling these particular groups and spaces.

In his research David Sudnow (1968; see also Worrall 1990) uses the concept of "normal crime" to examine the criminalization process. He argues that over time criminal justice actors (police, lawyers, and judges) develop proverbial characterizations of offences that encompass features that go beyond the statutory conception of an offence. These features include the typical manner in which offences are committed, the social characteristics of the persons who regularly commit them, the settings in which they occur, and the type of victim who tends to be involved. In the course of their work, criminal justice actors come to learn how to speak knowledgeably about different types of offenders and "to attribute to them personal biographies, modes of usual criminal activity, criminal histories, psychological characteristics, and social backgrounds" (p. 162). Following this approach, rather than encountering corporate embezzlers or environmental polluters, actors in the criminal justice system are most likely to meet up with people whose lives are characterized by poverty, addiction, and violence. For these actors the features and settings in which these individuals move therefore become the locus of "normal crime."

Understanding crime as a social construction and criminalization as an inherently political enterprise has implications for how we approach the women's involvement with the criminal justice system. Rather than being a straightforward matter, crime needs to be acknowledged as a messy and complicated affair. The offences for which individuals are deemed to be criminal are the end result of a lengthy process of detection, apprehension, accusation, judgment, and conviction. They represent the "official version" of a person's actions and behaviours. In the process of making these determinations, the criminal justice system imposes a particular understanding onto events. As Carol Smart (1989: 11) describes it:

> Everyday experiences are of little interest in terms of their meaning for individuals. Rather these experiences must be translated into another form in order to become legal issues and before they can be processed through the legal system.... So the legal process translates everyday experience into legal relevances, it excludes a great deal that might be relevant to the parties, and it makes its judgement on the scripted or tailored account.

In this respect, crime categories become part of what Smart calls law's "claim to truth" about events. But this scripted or tailored account represents only one way of making sense of social life. The women's accounts, their own "claims to truth," provide a quite different entry point.

From the standpoint of the person accused of a criminal offence, involvement with the criminal justice system may feel not so much like being handled by a well-oiled machine, but more like being caught in a net — a net that entraps and confines them, not only in limiting their freedom by means of arrest and incarceration but also in imposing restrictive conditions if they are to be released on bail pending their court date. Failure to abide by those restrictive conditions draws the person further into the criminal justice net; the court can add administration of justice charges to the initial charges and the person can be taken into remand custody.

Rather than accepting law's "official version," therefore, we need to attend to the social contexts in which the women's law violations occur and the often complicated situations that produce their criminal charges and draw them into the criminal justice net. Tannis's story of what happened on her birthday showcases the importance of this approach.

"THE SHITTIEST BIRTHDAY EVER"

Tannis was intent on celebrating her twenty-second birthday — but she got more than she bargained for. That afternoon Tannis had met up with a male friend. After she told him, "It's my birthday. I wanna go drink," the two headed off to a hotel where they joined with another couple.

At some point Tannis's friend began arguing with her and putting her down. "All of a sudden," she said, he "started getting mad at me and saying that I was checking out these guys or something. He was starting to get jealous and then he started arguing with me, calling me a 'scally' and calling me down. And I said 'Don't call me that.' And, you know, it was my birthday and he was trying to bring me down. I said, 'Whatever.' I said, 'Don't call me that.'"

Tannis's friend and the other man left, leaving Tannis and the other woman behind. With the other woman crying, Tannis calmed her down, telling her, "It's my birthday. Let's go do something. Let's go have fun." The two women headed off to another bar, but were denied service because they didn't have their IDs with them. A man at the bar gave them $20, saying, "Go buy you guys something somewhere else." So they stopped at a vendor to pick up some alcohol and headed to Tannis's nearby apartment.

As they went up in the elevator, another female resident of the apartment block started calling them "fucking bitches." Tannis's companion responded by grabbing the resident's cellphone and punching her in the face. After that Tannis and her friend proceeded to the apartment and began drinking. The police arrived soon afterward. "I opened my door and then the cops just busted their selves, let themselves in. I didn't even let them in. They just moved me out of the way. And then I said, 'Do you have a search warrant?' And they were like, 'Shut the fuck up.' And I said, 'Holy.'"

The police searched the apartment and found the other woman hiding in the bathroom. They also found hot knives on the stove. One of the officers asked Tannis, "What's this?" She replied, "That's to smoke. That's blades." "What for?" asked the officer. "To get high," said Tannis. "He didn't say nothing. And then they were like, 'Okay, wait.'" The police then arrested her friend for assaulting the resident in the elevator. "And the cops took her and the next thing you know I was by myself again. I was by myself in my apartment and it was ten o'clock at night."

Not wanting to be alone on her birthday, Tannis dressed up and headed out to a friend's house down the street. By then it was almost midnight. As she was walking towards her friend's place, a man in a white truck pulled over and asked Tannis, "Do you want to go for a drink?" Tannis jumped in the truck and told him it was her birthday. The man drove to a vendor and bought Tannis three cans of beer.

The two drove around for a while. "Then all of a sudden he started going towards the outskirts of Winnipeg." Tannis asked him, "What are you doing driving this way to the outskirts?" He replied, "Oh well, what do you think I bought you the beer for?" Tannis told him, "I ain't a hooker. I don't work the streets." She asked him to take her back to the city centre. Instead, the man pulled over to the side of the road and shut off the engine. "And then I was getting scared and then he took off his seatbelt and he came towards me. And then I had a knife in my pocket, 'cause I always carry knives just in case something like that happens to me. 'Cause Winnipeg's dangerous." Tannis pulled out her knife and said, "Can you take me back to Winnipeg. I'm not comfortable."

The man took the keys out of the ignition and left the truck. "And then he went to the back of his truck and he grabbed this long wooden stick. And then he came towards my side, the passenger, and he opened the door and he says, 'Where's that knife?' And then I said, 'I don't have that knife. I threw it. It's gone.' And then he started whipping me with that stick hard. And I was going like this [motions], with my, trying to block him from hitting me. And I was crying, and I was like, 'Leave me alone.' I was so scared. I thought he was going to kill me or something."

The man then threw Tannis out of the truck and drove off. She lost her shoes and other belongings in the process. It took her twenty minutes to walk back to the city, where she made her way to a bus stop and caught the last bus. "I jumped on that bus and then the bus driver, I didn't have no money or nothing and then the bus driver, he seen me with no shoes on, my hair all messy, and I said, 'Can I jump on?' And he said, 'Yeah.'" The bus driver dropped Tannis off close to her apartment.

Walking towards her apartment block, Tannis came across six young men. One of the young men started laughing at Tannis because of the way she looked, all messed up and barefooted. When she told him, "Fuck you. Don't laugh at me," the young man gave her a "shot in the face." "And then I was just gushing out blood and my whole mouth was just bloody, man." When

Tannis arrived at her apartment block, the security guard took one look at her and asked "What happened?" She explained her situation, including how in all the scuffle she had somehow lost her apartment keys. The guard arranged for a locksmith to come and open her door for her. By then it was two o'clock in the morning.

Tannis was cleaning herself up when there was a knock on the apartment door. It was a man she had met the previous day. She had told him, "I'm going to have some drinks at my place [tomorrow]. It's my birthday. You should come drink." So here he was at her door at two-thirty in the morning. Tannis invited him inside and they had a few drinks.

A half-hour later, the man who had abandoned Tannis at the bar earlier in the evening showed up at her door. Tannis grew angry at him and "started smashing shit" in her apartment. "I said, 'Fuck you, [his name].' I was swearing at him. I was like, 'Look what happened to me…. Where the hell were you? All of a sudden you're trying to come here now?' … I was so mad. It was the shittiest birthday ever."

The guy who had come at two-thirty then left the apartment, and Tannis's friend tried to calm her down. When Tannis went to sit down, she spotted a bloody methadone needle on her bed. Outraged that the visitor had "brought a meth needle" to her place, Tannis grabbed a dustpan and broom and used them to throw the needle out her apartment window. Five minutes later, that man showed up again at her door, looking for his needle. Tannis "started giving him shit." She got so mad at him she pulled out a knife. Her friend also had a knife and "started shanking that guy up in the face. And then all of a sudden that guy was screaming for help and he's like 'Aghh' and then he's all bloody and there was blood gushing all over. And then I just let go of that guy. I was so shocked. I didn't mean to do that. I didn't tell [her friend], 'Stab this guy.' I didn't tell him to do that. I just called him for help because that guy was arguing and trying to say shit and then I said, 'Leave,' and he wasn't trying to leave."

The visitor fled the apartment screaming "like he was gonna die or something." Tannis tried to clean up the blood. The police arrived shortly afterward and charged Tannis and her friend with robbery with a weapon. Her friend volunteered to "take the rap for everything," but Tannis felt that she should "do my time too." When she went to court the charge was reduced to assault with a weapon. Her lawyer struck a plea bargain with the Crown and Tannis ended up receiving a sentence of nine months' incarceration in return for a guilty plea. As Tannis summed it up, "That was a crazy day. I know that's one day I won't ever forget [chuckles]."

Tannis's birthday story exemplifies what feminist criminologists refer to as the "blurred boundaries" between victim and offender, a term that calls into question the tendency to see the identities of "victim" and "offender" as separate and distinct (Comack 2014; Daly and Maher 1998; Faith 1993). Earlier in the evening, Tannis was arguably the victim of forcible confinement and assault in the man's truck, and of assault on the street outside her apartment building by the young man. By the end of the evening, she had been transformed into the offender for the assault against the man who had come to visit her in the middle of the night.

Her story also exemplifies the social construction of crime. When the police officers entered her apartment earlier in the evening, they could have exercised their discretion and charged Tannis with drug possession, given the presence of the hot knives on the stove. Instead, they ignored that evidence and proceeded to arrest her female acquaintance for assaulting the resident of the apartment building. Later that same night, when police returned again, they chose to arrest both Tannis and her friend and charge them with robbery with a weapon (ostensibly on the basis of a claim made by the male acquaintance that he had been robbed of his possessions).

Also evident in Tannis's story is how the legal process "translates everyday experience into legal relevances" and "makes its judgement on the scripted or tailored account" (Smart 1989: 11). Tannis was most likely not provided the opportunity to tell her full story in the courtroom. Instead, the justice system reduced the complicated events of that night to a single legal issue: her culpability in assaulting the male acquaintance. Deemed guilty of the offence, Tannis found herself with a nine-month sentence.

Like Tannis, all of the women I spoke to at the WCC were accused (for those on remand) or convicted of a criminal offence — everything from manslaughter, aggravated assault, robbery, and intent to traffic in drugs to violations of their bail conditions (for example, keeping a curfew, abstaining from drugs and alcohol, and keeping the peace and being of good behaviour). As Tannis's story exemplifies, much more went on than indicated by these crime categories.

LOCATING THE WOMEN'S LAW VIOLATIONS

Locating the women's law violations in the context of their everyday experiences means that, for one, rather than constructing them as the "criminal Other" we come to recognize that they are in many ways no different than the "rest of us." The women I met with at the WCC are daughters, sisters, girlfriends, wives, and mothers, and they share the experiences of women collectively. Given that crime is the outcome of a process of criminalization, it makes more sense to think not in terms of "criminal" women but of "criminalized" women (Laberge 1991). For another, the social contexts in which women's law violations occur indicate that those violations are an outgrowth of everyday problems, conflicts, and dilemmas. For so many of the women at the WCC, trauma was a key component of that lived experience. Getting caught in the criminal justice net only compounded that trauma.

Problems: Lynne's Story

In her late twenties, Lynne has two children, ages six and seven. While she spent her early years living in the city with her mom and grandparents, she moved to her reserve community when she was fifteen. That's where she met the father of her kids. "At first it was okay and then there was a lot of mental abuse in that relationship. And he hit me a couple of times, like physical abuse. But that didn't start 'til, I think, after my son was born.... I think I was about eighteen." Lynne said the abuse occurred because her partner would "get jealous."

Their relationship lasted ten years. Around the time they were breaking up, Lynne's house on the reserve burned to the ground due to an electrical fire. "And Housing wouldn't give me another house, they didn't put me in another. So I basically got kicked out of my reserve [with them] saying, 'You know what? There's a lot of resources in Winnipeg. Go to Winnipeg to get help yourself.' That was my band's idea. *My own band.*" Lacking other options, Lynne moved to the city with her two children.

When asked what that move was like for her, she replied: "It was *shitty.* 'Cause my family said, 'Oh, come live here, come live here, we'll help you get on your feet' and all that other kind of stuff. But that's when I started doing drugs. 'Cause they were all doing drugs." Lynne explained that most of her family members were "struggling with their own addictions.... Growing up, that's all my family ever did."

Moving to the city exposed Lynne to the drug scene and violence. While living with a cousin, she was assaulted by her cousin's boyfriend. Her cousin responded to the incident by telling Lynne to leave. "And even though I paid money for rent, even though I put money in the groceries towards me and my kids, she still kicked me and my kids out anyway." Lynne went to stay at the house of another cousin and her partner, giving them a bit of money for rent, "so me and my kids would be okay."

And then — they have four kids together so I said, "You know what, you guys go out. You guys are letting me stay here, you guys go out and be alone, go have your time together. I'll sit here with all the kids." And then they came back drunk and he was trying to fight her and then I was kind of like stopping him, like, "No. Don't hit my cousin. Don't be like that." ... So I think she ended up going and blacking out, because she ended up trying to fight me because I was trying to kick him out because he was trying to fight her. So it got like a triangle where, and then I ended up getting beat up pretty bad.... And then he kicked me out. I just left. I was like, "Whatever." I remember walking out full of blood. I was literally covered in blood. It looked like somebody got murdered in that house 'cause I bled everywhere, from my nose and my head.

Now homeless, Lynne tried to get help from a women's shelter, but she didn't qualify to stay there because she wasn't in an abusive relationship. Lynne had left her children with her mother at her cousin's place. "My mom was staying over there with my kids and she was watching my kids and then after the whole fight and everything my cousin phoned CFS, saying that I had abandoned my kids. But meanwhile I was trying to get into shelters. And that's when I started selling drugs."

Lynne's decision to sell drugs was founded on the thinking, she said, that "I'm going to make money fast and then get a place, going to get my kids back and stop, once I have enough money." It was also a solution to her homelessness.

If I sold drugs then that means I'm going to be up all night at a shack all night. I'm not going to be outside. I'm not going to have to worry about sleeping in some park somewhere or trying to figure out where I'm going to sleep. 'Cause I've done that. I've had to sleep in stairwells. It sounds so bad but I had to sleep in stairwells, the outside stairwells, you know, you go into an apartment block and you see the stairs going up? I had to go all the way to the top and kind of huddle in a corner somewhere and sleep like that.

Lynne took the initiative in finding employment by connecting with a street-gang leader and setting herself up to "sit" through the night in a "crack shack," a designated house where the people living there get free drugs in return for letting the place be used as a drug-selling point. As Lynne tells the story, she went up to a guy and said, "Listen, I heard you're looking for workers."

> I came up to him and I said, "I'll be a good part of your team. I'm a good worker. I don't take shit from nobody. I could find you new spots instead of me just going to sit in the spots you already have set up." I told him, "I can be a good hunter for you 'cause I can find spots all over the West Side, all over the North Side, and I can do all this for you and [we] could make good money together." And then he said, "Okay, well, I'll give you a chance." So I was like, "Fine, then." And then he just gave me a big bag [of drugs] and said, "Where are you going to sit?"

Lynne suggested a number of different spots, and the man picked one of them. It was one she was hoping for, she said, "because I kind of knew the people that lived there," though not all that well: "They were just people that did drugs. So I'd just give them free drugs and I'd just sit there all night."

Working in the crack shack meant putting in long hours. "I'd be working sixteen hours and I'd get a couple of hours' sleep, then I'd have to wake up and do it all over again." Customers would come and go, and Lynne would "just sit in a room and make money." She "got really good at it," so much so that she was taking business away from another street-gang crew.

> It was to the point where people all over the West Side were coming to me. They were coming to me and they weren't going to the other guys anymore. They were coming to me 'cause I was nice to them. I would treat the working girls with respect. I wouldn't be, like, "Oh, you're just a customer." … If they were hungry I'd make sure they'd eat. I would take care of them. I'd be like, "You know what, go have a shower," you know, "Go freshen up so you're not so jittery." And I took care of those girls. And that's what the competition didn't do. And it got to the point where they weren't making no money and I was making all the money. And that's when it got dangerous.

Lynne's competition "didn't like it and they started sending guys after me."

> They came after me in the house. They didn't know it was me at first. They were looking for men that were selling drugs. They didn't know it was a female. So I seen all these guys come in the house and leave. And then they came back three other times. They still

didn't know. There were like, "Where are these guys?" And they didn't tell the guys that it was me. So then they kind of just left me alone. And they found it was me and that's when they came with guns and stuff.

[That must have been really scary.]

It was really scary. 'Cause the one time that they came there, I was in the room and they didn't even go in the room, but I could hear them talking about me. And I was scared that they were going to come in the room. I was really scared. The door was open this much and I could see people, all these guys, moving around the house. I'm like, "Oh my god. They're going to come in here and they're going to kill me." And I sat there and I kept looking out there and I could hear them, "Oh, where the F is this girl, where the F is this girl, her family's going to get her in a body bag." And they were talking about me and they were — just over me cutting them off, I guess, on some drugs.

Lynne phoned her boss and told him what was happening. "I had the door barricaded and I was in this room and I'm like, couldn't fit out the window 'cause it was a tiny little window where I couldn't fit out of it. So I'm phoning them. I was like, 'Okay, you know what? I'm out [of] here. As soon as I get out of this room, I'm done.' I was like, 'I'm done.'" Members of his street-gang crew then "showed up with all the guns. They kind of went over and beyond and, you know, 'No one's going to come in on our turf,' and no one's going to do this.'" During the conflict one of the rival gang members was shot in the leg.

Afterward, Lynne said, "People made statements against me, saying that I was on the phone and I was arguing with this guy [the one who was shot]." So the police charged her with aggravated assault and several firearm offences. Lynne was held in custody on remand, awaiting her trial. It was her first time in prison. While she had explained to her lawyer what her role in the incident involved, the Crown attorney was asking for five to ten years' incarceration. "According to the Crown, I'm the mastermind behind the whole shooting, that I planned everything, that I got the guys there. It's kind of rough knowing that I'm going to go away for something that, well, I had something to do with kind of — but I didn't plan it."

The police news release and media reports about the shooting — including a mug shot featuring a dishevelled accused — encouraged the construction of Lynne as the "criminal Other." According to the police news release, Lynne and the man who was injured were selling drugs together in the house. The report made no mention of a gang turf war. This official account also missed an important back story, one that showcases Lynne's life problems; in particular, her homelessness and the loss of her children. In that situation, her choice to sell drugs makes her actions more understandable. Lynne believed that she needed to "make money fast" in order to find housing and get her kids back. She could make up to a thousand dollars a day selling drugs — a far cry from what could be earned doing minimum-wage work. While the choice may have seemed reasonable given her circumstances, it exposed Lynne to the risk of violence — and to criminal justice intervention.

Conflicts: Jennifer's Story

Jennifer had been living in a rural community with her boyfriend and her children. She had befriended two young women who also lived there:

> I trusted them so much. I let them in my house all the time. I lent them food. I let the girl babysit my kids 'cause she would need money for cigarettes or something. And I knew they smoked drugs. I knew they drank. And I knew that's why they needed money and that. But I still trusted them. And I knew them for a couple of years, a few years, actually. And the one called me her sister, her street sister because I helped her out so much.

That trust turned out to be misplaced. One time Jennifer left the house for four days. "We came back and our house was *empty*, broken into and empty." The loss was extensive. "We had electronics in every room, 'cause the kids had all their own TVs, all their own games, everything, and iPods and everything. Our whole house was empty. And we had two deep freezers. One was full of moose meat, one was full of store meat. They took the deep freeze of moose meat even. They stole all the food."

Jennifer initially had no idea who would have committed the theft, but eventually found out from the neighbours. "They even told us what kind of vehicle came there, what vehicle they were loading up. And they said, 'We'll show you. We'll show you which house they took everything to.' 'Cause they were watching our house while we were gone." The house turned out to be where the two young women lived.

Jennifer phoned the police to report this information. "We had all this information. We had all these statements. We had all this proof, all this evidence that they did it. But they said they couldn't do anything because they were our friends. They said they couldn't do *nothing*." The neighbours had even phoned the police to report the theft. "And all the cops did was do a drive around. They didn't go to the house. Yet all the windows and lights and doors were open in the house. And they didn't go there and do anything. They just did a drive around. 'Cause even some of the neighbours, the older neighbours, took pictures of them driving around." The police told Jennifer that it was a "setup" — that she had encouraged the young women to break into the house to claim the insurance. "And yet I didn't even have insurance on anything in my house. I didn't have no kind of insurance, no house insurance, no nothing. And I pointed all of that out to them."

Jennifer waited two weeks for the police to take action. Meanwhile, one day she saw the two young women walking down her street, wearing her clothes and shoes. "The only reason I think they did that is 'cause they knew the cops weren't fuckin' doing anything. And I was like, 'That's it!' I was like, 'F.' I said, 'I got to go.' I said, 'I got to go and do something.' I said, 'This is stupid.' I was like, 'They're taunting me.' I was like, 'I just can't lay here and not do anything.' And that's when I went there and beat them up."

Jennifer said she ended up beating up the young women with a bat. "But not even bad, not bad. But it was bad to even do it, you know. I hit one of them in the arm with a bat. I knew not to hit them in the head or anywhere deadly because I didn't want to hurt them really bad. I just kind of wanted to scare them." The young women phoned the police. "The cops came and arrested me *immediately* because I ended up taking justice into my own hands."

When Jennifer appeared in court the next day on two assault charges, she told her story to the judge. Although apprised of the previous break and enter and its role in triggering the assault, the Crown prosecutor was opposed to Jennifer's release, saying that she "had no right to go and do that just because the law enforcement didn't do anything." But the judge disagreed with the Crown's request and released Jennifer on her own recognizance. One of the conditions of Jennifer's release was that she abide by a curfew. She ended up breaching that condition by coming home late on two occasions and was taken into custody. Jennifer pleaded guilty to the charges (for the assaults and the breaches) and was ready to accept a sentence of two years less a day.

When she appeared in court several months later in front of the same judge, however, the judge ordered a *Gladue* report and held over the sentencing for another two months. *Gladue* reports were developed in response to the inclusion of section 718.2(e) in the Criminal Code, which provides that "all available sanctions other than imprisonment that are reasonable in the circumstances should be considered for all offenders, with particular attention to the circumstances of aboriginal offenders." The provision — passed in 1996 and affirmed by the Supreme Court in the *Gladue* (1999) case — is designed to address the overincarceration of Indigenous people and acknowledges systemic racism and the way in which it disadvantages Indigenous people. In compiling a *Gladue* report, the intention is to provide information "to understand and locate the accused's background in the context of systemic factors facing Aboriginal people generally" (Milward and Parkes 2014: 124). In the meantime, Jennifer remained in custody at the WCC.

Jennifer's story exemplifies how women's law violations sometimes emerge out of conflicts; in this case, a conflict between Jennifer and the two young women who stole her family's belongings. Adding to the situation was the apparent reluctance of the police to take action in resolving the conflict. Feeling betrayed by two young women she thought she could trust, and frustrated by the lack of police response, Jennifer resolved to take the law into her own hands and dispense a kind of street justice.

As in Tannis's story, here the boundary between "victim" and "offender" is again blurred, because Jennifer was both a victim (of a break and enter) and an offender (by committing assault). It would appear that the judge was mindful of this blurred boundary, releasing Jennifer on her own recognizance and then later ordering a *Gladue* report.

Jennifer was apprehensive about having a *Gladue* report done. "One of my caseworkers here told me to do it and she said I'll probably get really emotional 'cause they'll ask me lots of questions, not just about, like, around these charges, they'll ask me about stuff that happened to me in my life." For Jennifer, the "hardest thing" for her would be to talk about the physical and sexual abuse she had experienced as both a child (at the hands of her father) and an adult (at the hands of her intimate partner).

Dilemmas: Lori's Story

Lori had struggled with mental health issues for most of her life, and had been diagnosed with several mental disorders: "I've heard voices since I was a kid. I think bipolar just runs in the family. And then I have Post-Traumatic Stress Disorder." Her mental health was compromised by the physical and sexual abuse she experienced at the hands of her stepfather at a young age.

Encountering abuse in her relationships with intimate partners exacerbated her mental health issues. One of her coping strategies was to turn to street drugs.

Lori was introduced to drugs as a teenager and started using again after she left her children with her mother to escape an abusive relationship. While turning to drugs was a way of coping with that loss, it also put her in a vulnerable situation. She found herself on the way to Manitoba with a man she had met in another province. "I was apparently awake for three weeks, agreed to date the guy that I came out here with, and I didn't like him like that. I'd spent an entire month telling him, 'No, I'm not going to date you.' And I agreed to date him, ended up in a truck with his dad. 'Cause his dad came to pick him up to clean his ass up."

The family lived "in the middle of nowhere…. No way in, no way out except for the truck that his dad drives." Lori was trapped there for three months. "Every time I tried to leave my stuff would get taken away from me. It was like basically I was a prisoner. I didn't like it." Complicating matters further, Lori couldn't get access to the medications she normally took to control her mental health issues. "'Cause I couldn't make it from out in the country where [name] and everybody lived to [the town] to go see my psychiatrist. We just, there was no in and out at that time. And I couldn't walk it 'cause it was still winter." When Lori and the man she was living with "started fighting really bad," one of his friends — whom she had struck up a friendship with — came and picked her up. "And then I got out and I got put into an even worse situation."

Lori ended up in a relationship with the friend, who was a heroin addict. "But the people he was living with were even worse…. His best friend who he was living with is a psychopath. When he talks about sleeping with women he talks about mutilating them, okay. And my boyfriend was too high to realize all the f'd-up-ness that was going on in this house." Lori made plans to leave the house once she got her disability cheque. She and her boyfriend gave a friend a ride to Winnipeg, "And he ended up stealing all of my money."

> I went into McDonald's, left my wallet on the centre console. My boyfriend's having a smoke, right, and he steals five hundred dollars out of my wallet…. All of my money. We went and drove, dropped him off, found out he stole my money, tried driving all around Winnipeg looking for him, couldn't find him, then we left and went back to the house.

When they arrived back at the house, her boyfriend's roommates "were screaming and yelling, saying they're going to kick me out onto the curb, they want their money, I have this long to get it." One of the men approached her, saying, "Lori, I know what we're going to do. We're going to rob a store and you're going to help me. You're going to do it." Lori said, "He keeps repeating, and I'm scared of him. I have Post-Traumatic Stress Disorder from being hurt by people who have all of the same symptoms of it as he does. So I'm like, 'Okay, okay, I'll help you, right. Just don't hurt me.'" Lori had reason to be fearful of the man:

> I was petrified, petrified of him. Like, he would come into the bathroom while I'm showering. He would come into the bathroom while I'm going to the bathroom. He would try and come into the bedroom that I was renting while I was changing. He would try and come in there while I was sleeping by myself. My boyfriend would have to chase him away.

The man then went out back and sawed off a twelve-gauge shotgun, stuffing it into a rucksack. "He's like, 'Come on, Lori. We're going to ask [her boyfriend] for a ride. Don't you fuckin' tell him anything.'" Lori, meanwhile, is "panicked because I know all the signs of a serious predator." The three of them got in the car and drove to the city. Lori's boyfriend was not aware of what was going on. "I'm just sitting there quiet. He thinks I'm still upset about the money being stolen. He doesn't know that I'm upset because I'm about to do something *horrid*." Around eleven o'clock at night they parked the car a few blocks from a 7-11 store. The boyfriend stayed in the car.

> So we jump out, we walk up to the 7-11, we stop in the alley before it, he tells me "Lori, you're going to hold the gun 'cause you're going to be the one in less trouble. That way you won't say nothing. That's what you're going to do. You have no choice." "Okay, okay." And I take it and I put the sawed-off down my sweatpants and up in my sweater. We go in. I'm panicking. I'm shaking 'cause I've never done this before. I have no fuckin', the voices are telling me I'm going to get hurt if I don't fuckin' do it. He's telling me I'm going to get hurt if I don't fuckin' do it. So I was just like, "Oh my god, self-preservation."

When they guy in charge of all this wasn't looking, Lori managed to unload the gun.

I'm not gonna hurt nobody. There is no way in hell he can expect me to hurt somebody. You're already expecting me to scare the hell out of somebody, why the hell would I fuckin' hurt them? So my only intention in all this is it's going to happen no matter what I do, I've got to make sure that nobody gets hurt. I don't care about me getting through it. What I care about is nobody innocent getting hurt. Yes, I'm innocent, too. I'm being threatened into it but, you know what, that's the cards I was dealt. I just want to make sure nobody else gets hurt 'cause I'm already going to get hurt anyway.

Lori figured she had two choices: "I'm going to either: (a) end up in the justice system or (b) I'm going to get smashed out by a guy who is not scared to hit women. He's hit his mother. He's hit his grandma before. I fuckin' watched it. So I have every reason to be scared of him, *every* reason." So the two of them entered the 7-11 and proceeded to rob it.

I'm the one with the gun. I made sure. He went to go kick buddy [the store clerk] that was involved and I said, "Don't hurt him" and pointed towards him. I'm like, "Don't touch him." I'm like, "Come on. Let's go, [his name]. Let's go." And I said his name. I said his name on purpose 'cause I was hoping it would help lead, I walked out of that 7-11 and walked down the street to where I was going, hoping the police would come. But they didn't. They didn't come on time. Got in the car, drove away and [the boyfriend] didn't know the difference until the next day.

The police eventually apprehended all three of the car's occupants. Lori noted, "The guy who robbed me is the guy who went to the cops." He had seen the picture of her accomplice in the news reports, "so he assumed that the girl that was with him was me." While this was Lori's first offence, she was denied bail and to that point had remained in custody eight months pending her trial. She was expecting to receive a sentence of between four and ten years' incarceration.

Committing armed robbery is a serious matter. While the circumstances that led to Lori's crime were certainly no excuse for her actions, the background details help to explain the reasons for her involvement in the offence. They also shed light on the issue of choice. After her money was stolen, and under pressure from roommates to pay her rent, Lori faced a dilemma: should she go along with what the male acquaintance was pressuring her to do, or resist that pressure and risk getting "smashed out by a guy who is not scared to hit women"? For the sake of her own "self-preservation," Lori chose to go along with the acquaintance, doing what she could to reduce the risk of others getting hurt in the process. All the while, she was dealing with the cumulative impact of former traumas in her life. As she remarked:

> If I hadn't been abused when I was younger and I didn't have the Post-Traumatic Stress Disorder or if I'd even been medicated for it, this wouldn't have happened. Because my previous experiences of being hurt by men did constitute my decision-making. When he triggered my PTSD I wanted nothing more than to make sure it didn't happen again. I was so scared of being hurt again that I was willing to do anything to make that fear go away.

Lori also spoke to the issue of her state of mind and ability to assume responsibility during the crime:

> The fact that I'm going to be punished for keeping myself safe when it was his idea, his everything. And I'm in trouble because I couldn't, I wasn't medicated. I couldn't make the proper decision. I was incapable of making proper decisions at that point in time. 'Cause I wasn't on medication. I was still coming off the drugs. I was in no way, shape, or form capable of making sound decisions.

Despite her mental health issues — and the limited choices she believed she had at the time — Lori was facing a lengthy prison term.

ATTENDING TO SOCIAL CONTEXTS

Crimes such as assault and robbery are serious offences, and individuals who engage in such harmful actions are to be held accountable for their behaviour. Indeed, a key premise of our criminal justice system is that it is designed to punish "those who have freely chosen, as autonomous individuals, to commit crime" (Parkes and Cunliffe 2015: 227). In accounting for the criminal charges in these cases, law fashions a scripted account based on individual culpability and blameworthiness.

Yet the law violations of the women I spoke to clearly occurred in a more complex social context; and an examination of this context indicates that much more is going on than indicated by simple crime categories such as assault and robbery. Behind these criminal charges is a set of events; and these events sometimes involve harsh everyday problems — such as having to decide what to do when you've nowhere to live and need money to support yourself and your kids. Sometimes the events involve personal conflicts — for example, when someone you thought you could trust steals all of your belongings. Sometimes they involve a serious dilemma that offers no ready solution — as, for instance, in being pressured to commit a criminal offence and having to comply out of fear for what will happen if you don't.

In managing these situations, the women I spoke to did make choices, but those choices were not always "freely chosen." More often than not, their choices were limited or constrained by their past and current social circumstances. Lori, for instance, had a history of trauma experiences. Finding herself under pressure to commit armed robbery, she was well aware that she was "incapable of making proper decisions at that point in time." The choices made by each woman, therefore, were informed by their own histories, including the trauma trails that had shaped the course of their lives.

DRUGGING AND DRINKING

The stories of some of the women revealed a direct connection between trauma experiences and their involvement with the criminal justice system. Ashley, for instance, had been charged with assaulting a police officer. She said that when she was tackled by the officer, her natural defence was to fight back. "'Cause that's what happened when I was being raped. I was trying to fight back. And then they were doing that to me so I just, that's just the only way I knew how to react. And, yeah, so I ended up getting charged for assaulting a police officer."

Routinely, however, the connections between the women's trauma experiences and their involvement with the criminal justice system were more indirect, mediated by their use of drugs and/or alcohol. Turning to drugs and alcohol offered a way of coping with their trauma experiences — an easy move given the prevalence of street drugs in Winnipeg's inner city and the ready availability of alcohol. But this coping strategy increased the risk of criminal justice intervention into their lives.

In some cases, the women were either so high on drugs or blacked out on alcohol that they had no recollection of the events that plunged them into the criminal justice net. When Margaret's sister and father died, she turned to drugs to cope with her loss. "I was doing a ton of different types of drugs. And that led to these charges." Margaret ended up being convicted on two robbery charges and a break and enter. She told me:

I'm trying to remember what the [police] report said. 'Cause I, honestly, I barely remember what happened. I just remember blacking out and being on the ground at gunpoint and then blacking out and then coming to in the police station. I don't remember which police station it was. And then coming to and then waking up in jail.

In her first time in jail Margaret served twenty-nine months on remand and received an additional nineteen months on sentencing.

Melody, who said she turned to drugs and alcohol as a way to "numb" herself, stated, "When I drink I think that's when I fight out on the street, when I'm drinking." Melody had gone through several aggravated assault charges, but she said that she did not remember any of them. Christine got drunk to the point of blackout and ended up robbing a gas station. "I didn't even know until the next day. I woke up. I'm like, 'What the fuck did I do? Why am I locked up?' And they told me, 'You're here on robbery.' I said, 'Oh my god. No way!'"

Jessica had a string of charges: theft, possession of stolen goods, robberies, home invasion, break and enter, and assault. All of them were related to her use of drugs. Jessica said, "I don't even know why I did all those things. I'm not even like that when I'm sober." For her most recent charges Jessica commented, "I don't even remember getting arrested. I don't remember coming here."

Corrine's first offence as an adult came about when she was high on pills.

It was in the middle of winter and I was high on pills and I was trying to go home.... And I was so cold. I went into somebody's car just to warm up and I guess I was sitting there and I lit up a cigarette and I just remember smoking a cigarette and ... all I remember is "Why am I in this car? Whose car is this?" I was thinking. And then I just remember the cops pulling me out of the car and I'm like, "What the hell!" And then I went to jail.

Another time Corrine drank while taking pills and had no memory of what happened after that.

I woke up the next day and I was at my mom's house and my jacket was gone and my purse was gone and I'm wondering where my jacket and my purse were. And I woke up with these alcohol bottles in a grocery bag, and I asked, "Whose are these?" And my cousin said "You brang those home last night." And I said, "What the hell." I didn't even have no memory of what I did and I got scared.

Corrine went to a clinic to make sure she was okay, "just in case I had unprotected sex with somebody. 'Cause I didn't know what happened, right. I had no memory so I was just being aware." A few days later, the police showed up at Corrine's apartment and charged her with robbery. Apparently she had gone to a residence looking for her boyfriend, but got the house number wrong. The police told her that "a lady answered" her knock and told her no such person lived there. "And I got violent. I said, 'I know he's here' or whatever. And I went inside." According to the police she took some bottles of alcohol and left. "And I don't even have no, I don't even remember that. In that statement that woman said that I could barely even stand or whatever."

The connections between drug use and criminalization are strong: 94 percent of women in provincial custody and 74 percent of women in federal custody in 2008/09 were assessed as having substance abuse issues (Mahony 2011: 35). Those connections have become a part of the conception of "normal crime" that police officers employ in the course of their work.

"NORMAL CRIME"

Police work involves attending to all manner of problems, conflicts, and dilemmas. In doing so, police employ particular cultural frames of reference that inform their conception of what constitutes "normal crime." As officers go about their daily work these cultural frames come to form the police "storybook" or particular way of seeing their world that develops over time. The stories enable police officers to make decisions "on a moment-to-moment basis, often without a moment's reflection" (Shearing and Ericson 1991: 485). Carol's story provides a clear indication of this practice of framing at work.

Carol's Story (cont'd)

The childhood trauma that Carol experienced growing up in her First Nation community — including physical and emotional abuse from her mother and siblings and being raped by her relatives — continued in her life as she grew older, and especially in the forced marriage to an abusive partner that left her feeling "like a slave." Finding the courage to leave that relationship and move her children to the city, Carol then faced the challenge of having to "just start all over."

When we met, Carol's two youngest children were teenagers. Her daughter had begun moving with a tough crowd and getting into drugs and alcohol. Carol didn't know how to discipline her children. "I didn't know how to say 'no,'" she said. "All I knew is I wanted them happy. I wanted to give them the love I didn't have. And I wanted to give them what I didn't have, the freedom." Not wanting or able to impose discipline, Carol let her teenagers stay out past their curfew. Things "got worse and worse."

Carol's daughter was spending time at a friend's house. Concerned about her doing drugs and drinking, Carol phoned the police for assistance. The police went to the friend's house. "And then they came back out and said, 'You're right there. It's not a place for her. Do you have a place for her to go to?'" Carol had been volunteering at her children's school and the Salvation Army, but felt that she couldn't impose on the people she knew. "I basically didn't want to be a burden to anybody." She also said she "didn't know how to ask." When the police tried to take the daughter back home to Carol, the daughter told them that her mother was abusing her. Carol said, that news "really killed me…. I just felt this flush over my body and just — and I said, 'Oh my god.'" She remembered how she had told her children about being abused herself. That was because her daughter had asked her one day about another family. The daughter had asked, " How could they have hit their children?' and stuff like that," Carol said. "Then I said, 'I was abused. I was. That's something that you don't want to go through.'" Her daughter had asked, "Mom, you would never hit me, right?" And Carol told her, "No. I wouldn't hit you. I can't." The police investigated her daughter's claim, found it not to be true and took her home.

In trying to understand why her teenage daughter would accuse her of being abusive, Carol said she "put two and two together."

> The friends that she hangs out with are in [the] care of Child and Family Services. And I remember my daughter saying something like her friends told her that she'd get money, she'd get lots of clothes, and they'd buy her clothes, she'd live in a really nice house, and stuff like that. But I just told her, I said, "You know that doesn't happen for a lot of people. 'Cause you can be put in the wrong place. And there's stuff that can happen in foster homes" and stuff like that.

After her daughter was returned to her care, Carol said, "Everything would be okay for a while. Then they would start over and over again." It got to the point where she felt "I just couldn't do anything more." Carol had called on

CFS for assistance with her teenagers, but found that "they're not much help." To make matters worse, Carol's son suffered a debilitating health issue. He was hospitalized for a long time, learning to walk and talk again. When they released him from the hospital, Carol said that she "wasn't ready. 'Cause I didn't have a bathroom on the main floor and then I didn't have, I don't know, I just felt that he could fall and whatever. 'Cause he still gets dizzy."

The day her son came home from the hospital, "It was just me and him at the house. So everything was okay at first." But then Carol's daughter arrived home that night, "just drunk as usual with a friend. I didn't know they had a bottle in the house. I didn't know. And they were drinking and then she tries to fight with me." Carol had not been drinking. But she said:

> I was so tired. I was so exhausted that I just didn't have any energy. And then we argued. And I tried to stop her. And then her friend, I just remember her punching me. I don't know what happened. I just, I felt so, I don't know, my head was spinning…. When I'm being yelled at I go into this, I don't know if it makes sense, but I feel like a child again. And I don't do anything. I can't. I don't know how to protect myself. I don't know what to do. I just let it happen. Even when somebody yells at me, I start crying. I feel, I don't know, I just, I just feel like that abused child again…. I get scared. I do what I'm told.

A neighbour who heard the commotion phoned the police. When they arrived Carol said she was "all disoriented. I was just coming back to myself again. I don't know if that makes sense. But I could see myself. It's like watching TV."

Even though she hadn't been drinking, the police thought that Carol was intoxicated — and that she had been the aggressor in the situation. Still disoriented, Carol was put into the back of the police car. "And then it was like, all of a sudden I hear, 'You should be ashamed of hitting your son, your disabled son.' I said, 'What? What's going on? I didn't hit him.' And then, 'No, he's sick. He had a stroke,' I said. And then I said, 'No, my daughter's intoxicated.' And then they found that bottle. And then they thought it was mine. So now I couldn't say anything. They wouldn't listen to me."

Carol asked the officers to call an ambulance to take her son to the hospital because no one was left in the house to look after him. She was transported to the Remand Centre. "I didn't say anything 'cause I didn't know what was going on. And 'cause I didn't know how to speak for myself.

I don't know how to speak for myself. I just kind of let things happen. 'Cause I was always told not to, you know, just to basically, just to follow what goes on, just stay quiet."

Carol was released from the Remand Centre a few days later. In addition to being charged with assault causing bodily harm and failure to provide the necessities of life for a minor, she had bail conditions imposed: a curfew, no contact with her kids, and "abstain from alcohol."

When Carol returned to her home, the door was open. "Somebody had walked in there and taken my stuff. The fridge was empty and the cupboards were empty. And then I just started crying right there." After that experience, Carol said she "grew into depression…. I just stayed in the house. I just cleaned. I just cleaned up the mess that was there. And I just stayed in bed. And I'd turn on the TV just so there'd be a noise."

Carol's children tried to have contact with her after the charges were laid. But with the court's no contact order, Carol was aware that she couldn't even open the door to them. Her children got angry, and she was afraid they would think she didn't want to see them. She also knew that otherwise she would "get in trouble. It's not because I don't want them. I have to follow the law." She contacted the police and CFS to let them know the situation. "They try to tell them but they still come. And I pray and cry. I stand by the door where they're standing. And I just wish I could help them and hug them."

From there "things just got worse." Carol hadn't been drinking much before that time, but she started going to bars with her boyfriend. "'Cause he likes to drink, so I started drinking. I don't like the taste of beer but I drink anyway…. And then I would just drink because he was drinking." Carol said, "It felt good not to be sad — and lonely." Drinking "just felt like it took my mind off things" and helped her to "feel calm," which enabled her to cook meals and begin to take care of herself. Before that she had been just staying in bed, not eating, not doing anything. When she went out with her boyfriend:

> He would get really drunk. I didn't like it. I knew there was something bad going to happen. Sure enough, he would beat me. And I wouldn't want to go with him anymore. Then he would do that cycle [of violence] with me — he's sorry. I don't know, he would caress me, I guess. And then it would be okay for a while and then he'd do it again. And then I started drinking more. I would drink more. Usually I would just drink like four or five beers, but it would take, I'd drink more than that.

Carol was eventually apprehended by police and charged with breaching her bail conditions (no alcohol consumption). She was denied bail and admitted into custody at the WCC.

The incident that brought Carol into the criminal justice net cannot be fully understood without an awareness of her biography and the trauma she endured over the years. Her use of "dissociation" as a coping strategy when confronted with violence in her home springs from that history. As Carol described it, "It's like watching TV." She felt as though she had reverted back to "that abused child" again. Clinicians might well diagnose Carol as suffering from PTSD. The police framing of the incident interpreted her state as a matter of intoxication rather than dissociation.

In policing Winnipeg's inner city, the officers have come to rely on constructions of "normal crime" that are racialized in terms of the social characteristics of the persons who regularly commit crime (Indigenous people) and the settings in which they occur (drinking parties where violence breaks out) (Comack 2012; Comack and Balfour 2004). In the aftermath of the assault by her daughter's friend, Carol was in no position to challenge that framing. Her upbringing had taught her "just to follow what goes on, just stay quiet." Criminal charges and restrictive bail conditions followed.

Carol did her best to abide by those restrictions, including no contact with her children. As she said, "I have to follow the law." But the trauma of losing her children generated a debilitating depression. As a coping strategy, Carol turned to alcohol. In law's terms, that move put Carol in violation of her bail conditions, resulting in her being taken into custody to await her court date.

CAUGHT IN THE CRIMINAL JUSTICE NET

Once caught in the criminal justice net, the women found themselves in an even more precarious situation. Having been accused of committing a criminal offence — of breaking the rules — they were now faced with even more rules governing how they needed to behave if they were to maintain their freedom while out on bail awaiting their day in court.

MAKING BAIL

When initially charged with a criminal offence, an individual can be released by police on a summons or a promise to appear that notifies them of their court date and their obligation to attend. Otherwise, the police detain the person in custody pending a bail hearing. As required by law, accused persons should appear in court within twenty-four hours of their arrest or as soon as reasonably possible thereafter. The Criminal Code provides that a bail hearing should be held within twenty-four hours, but the prosecution can delay the bail hearing for up to three days without the consent of the accused person.

Bail is "a form of guarantee — usually an amount of money — undertaken by the accused or a surety [a person who takes responsibility for them] to guarantee that the person in custody will appear for trial if released." It constitutes "a way to grant freedom to the accused, who, in exchange, agrees to respect certain conditions while awaiting trial" (Renaud 2016: 158). While some criminal offences have a "reverse onus," meaning that it is up to the accused persons to demonstrate that they ought to be released pending their trials, in general the onus is on the Crown prosecutor to "show cause" or demonstrate that detention for trial is necessary. The Bail Reform Act of 1972 placed the onus on the Crown prosecutor to make the case for detention and established the presumption that individuals be released on bail and on the "least onerous form of bail possible" (John Howard Society of Ontario 2013: 7). The law provides for a presumption of release on bail without conditions, but the practice in courts across the country is very different from that. The courts routinely attach conditions — and many of them — to all bail orders.

Section 515(4) of the Criminal Code specifies the conditions that can be imposed in granting bail: report to a peace officer; remain within a territorial jurisdiction; notify the peace officer of any change of address or employment; abstain from communicating with a victim, witness, or other person named in the order; and relinquish a passport. In addition, an accused can be ordered to "comply with any other condition specified in the order that the justice considers necessary to ensure the safety and security of any victim of or witness to the offence." The accused can also be ordered to "comply with such other reasonable conditions specified in the order as the justice considers desirable."

Before imposing any of these conditions, the court "must take the presumption of innocence into account" and "only conditions that are connected to the purpose of bail are permissible. The *Charter* also requires that any conditions imposed be 'reasonable'" (Deshman and Meyers 2014: 18). Nonetheless, "a decision to liberate an accused from custody pending trial (or appeal) does not result in the granting of freedom" (Renaud 2016: 165). Most individuals who are released on bail are bound by stringent conditions. "Other reasonable conditions" that are typically imposed by the court include: keeping the peace and being of good behaviour; attending treatment or counselling; abstaining from drugs and/or alcohol; abiding by a curfew; and a weapons or firearms prohibition.

Researchers have found that many of the conditions routinely imposed during a bail hearing often have little or no relationship to the grounds for detention and facts of the alleged offence. For instance, in their study of bail conditions imposed in Ontario youth court, Nicole Myers and Sunny Dhillon (2013) found that, on average, 9.3 conditions were imposed and over 41 percent of the youth had more than 10 conditions attached to their release order. Some 41 percent of the conditions imposed had no apparent connection to the allegations or grounds for detention and a further 22 percent were only ambiguously connected. "The only conditions that routinely had a clear connection to the grounds for detention and the facts of the alleged offence were those that dealt with prohibiting contact with the victim or the co-accused" (p. 202). Other conditions imposed on the youth — such as, attend school or counselling, be under house arrest or a curfew, and abide by the rules of the home — appeared to emerge from a desire of the Crown and justice of the peace "to control conduct they saw as undesirable rather than as reducing the likelihood of future criminal behaviour" (p. 205). Such considerations run counter to section 11 of the Charter of Rights and Freedoms, which mandates that bail conditions be "reasonable." As Abby Deshman and Nicole Myers (2014: 56) note, "Bail considerations are not remedial, they cannot be used to enhance the rehabilitation of the accused and they must be related to the circumstances of the offence." Moreover, imposing restrictive bail conditions can create a systemic disadvantage for marginalized groups, especially Indigenous people:

> There is a general recognition that the bail system operates in a manner that disadvantages individuals living in poverty and those with mental health or addictions issues. Aboriginal people, who are disproportionately impacted by substance abuse issues, poverty, low educational attainment, social isolation and other forms of marginalization, are being systematically disadvantaged as a result. (Deshman and Myers 2014: 75)

For many Indigenous people, the matter is more complicated than just the restrictive release conditions that are often imposed. One issue is that Indigenous people often have to travel long distances to attend court. A

Manitoba front-line worker explained: "You may have a community that's prepared to support you. They're in Norway House. You got arrested in Winnipeg. The judge goes, 'Ah, it's too far. You're staying here in jail because there's no guarantee we're going to get you back from Norway House for the trial'" (cited in Comack, Fabre, and Burgher 2015: 11). Another issue raised by this front-line worker is the need to have the economic resources to post a surety:

> The courts require somebody to be in court in person to do a surety…. If you live in any one of the fifty communities in Manitoba that isn't connected to Thompson by road, that could be a thousand dollar plane ride, and then you do get the money to go in and the court's adjourned today because the court party didn't make it up or the judge, you know, or it didn't get heard on the docket or whatever. And so the next time, they're not there and the person doesn't get bailed out. (Cited in Comack, Fabre, and Burgher 2015: 11–12)

As well, cash or financial sureties are not as common in Manitoba as in other provinces. "But in some cases you might be asked to do that," especially in terms of equity in a house. "If you are a First Nation person living on a First Nation, you don't own a house. So that's an asset that [for] a lot of people, it's taken away. So that would make it harder as well" (cited in Comack, Fabre, and Burgher 2015: 12). According to this same worker, cultural issues could also be at work:

> A lot of Aboriginal people I know and I've worked with and I've met up North in particular, especially in the smaller communities that are more isolated, are part of a high context culture, which means no direct confrontation, you wouldn't disagree with somebody. You know, speaking up and saying, "No, that's wrong" would be very much against the person's cultural background. It would be just unheard of because it would be causing someone in authority to lose face…. Somebody goes to court, they never say anything. It's their cultural background. You don't disagree. You don't argue. "Well, we're going to give you this and we're going to give you this and we're going to give you this, and can you handle that?" You're not going to disagree. It's a cultural thing. And so that's part of it as well. (Cited in Comack, Fabre and Burgher 2015: 12)

Breaching Release Conditions

If accused persons are found to be in violation of their release conditions — or to have "breached" — they can have their bail rescinded and be taken into custody. As well, they can face further criminal charges for failing to comply with a court order. As specified under s. 515 (6) of the Criminal Code, "Once there is a failure to comply charge, the Crown no longer has to prove why a specific individual should be detained. Instead, the accused has to demonstrate why he or she should be released into the community again" (Deshman and Myers 2014: 63). Facing charges for administration of justice offences is common in Canada. In 2013/14, an administration of justice offence was the most serious charge in 23 percent of all adult criminal court cases completed that year; 43 percent of these charges involved a failure to comply with a court order (Public Safety Canada 2016: 10).

Avery talked about her experience of breaching her release conditions. Her first charge was for shoplifting. "I went to The Bay and I stole some clothes because I needed money and, yeah, I got caught." She was released on her own recognizance but breached the order when she missed her court date. Avery had gone to the courthouse but realized she had gotten "the dates mixed up" and was a week late. She said she "was too nervous to go up to the front desk" and talk to them when she was there. "I've never been in trouble with the law before so I was really nervous to go up and say, 'Hey, I missed court.' And I didn't want to go to jail. I don't know. I should have. I know I should have, but I just, I didn't."

Not long afterward, Avery was partying with her friends. "I got really drunk and I blacked out." She woke up the next morning to find a "SWAT team" with their guns pointed at her. "They brought me into the living room and then they brought out a safe and they started smashing that up. And a cop threatened to punch me in the face because I didn't know the code to the safe." Avery not only didn't know the code to the safe; she also didn't know who was living in the residence. "It's a duplex. So there was other people on the upstairs that I know. But I wasn't with them. I somehow ended up down there."

The police found drugs and weapons at the residence. "The cops are trying to say everything was in my plain sight but there was nothing that was in my plain sight. I didn't see anything." Because she was the only person present in the house when the police raided it, Avery faced thirty-eight charges. She was initially released on bail, and one of the conditions was not to be at the address where the arrest took place — but she went back to retrieve her possessions. "I know I should have asked a friend to go there but … I don't really talk too much to too many people. So plus I didn't think that would happen. I thought I would just be in and out. I don't have ID. I don't have any clothes. I don't have anything now when I get out. I have nothing." When we met, Avery had been in custody for seven months, awaiting her court date.

Deshman and Myers (2014) argue that imposing stringent release conditions means that people are "set up to fail." In their review of Manitoba bail cases, they found that the requirement to abstain from alcohol was imposed in 46 percent of the cases and to abstain from drugs in 41 percent of the cases (Deshman and Myers 2014: 56). Similarly, a study conducted by the John Howard Society of Ontario found that of their bail supervision clients who reported ongoing problems with alcohol, 81 percent were released on a condition that they not consume alcohol. Of the supervision clients who reported having issues with drug use, over 81 percent were required to abstain from drugs while they were on bail (John Howard Society of Ontario 2013: 12). The study also found, "The majority of breaches while under bail supervision were related to a failure to comply with release conditions, rather than committing a new offence or missing a court appearance" (p. 12).

As one Alberta judge remarked, "Ordering an alcoholic not to drink is tantamount to ordering the clinically depressed to just 'cheer up'" (*Omeasoo* 2013 cited in Deshman and Myers 2014: 58). For individuals who have troubles with drugs or alcohol, abstention conditions put them in the position of becoming a criminal if they do have a drink or take drugs, because a failure to comply charge is likely to follow. Breaching their release conditions also means that accused persons are likely to be taken into custody pending their trial date.

PRE-TRIAL DETENTION

Pre-trial detention (or remand) refers to "the temporary detention of accused persons in provincial or territorial custody prior to trial or a finding of guilt" (Correctional Services Program 2017: 4). The decision to hold an accused person in custody pending trial is governed by the Charter of Rights and Freedoms, which states that "Everyone has the right not to be arbitrarily detained or imprisoned" (s. 9) and that any person charged with an offence has the right "to be presumed innocent until proven guilty" and "not to be denied reasonable bail without just cause" (s. 11). Despite these rights, and the presumption of bail without condition in the Criminal Code, many accused people are held in pre-trial detention.

The Criminal Code sets out three grounds under which an accused person can be detained in pre-trial custody. The primary ground is when detention is required to ensure that the accused attends court (s. 515 (10) (a)). The court can take into account a broad range of personal circumstances — a fixed address, employment status, family or marital status, prior record of criminal convictions, and relationships with friends and relatives in the community — in determining the likelihood that an accused will appear for trial (Comack and Balfour 2004: 81). A secondary ground allows for detention when it is necessary "for the protection or safety of the public, including any victim or witness" (s. 515 (10)(b)), including a substantial likelihood that the accused will, if released, commit a criminal offence. Factors associated with secondary grounds include a prior criminal record, whether the accused is already on bail or probation, the type of offence, and whether the accused is addicted to drugs and/or alcohol (Moyer and Basic 2004: 6). A tertiary ground is "if the detention is necessary to maintain confidence in the administration of justice" (s. 515 (10)(c)). The gravity and nature of the offence, the circumstances surrounding its commission (such as whether a firearm was used), and the potential for a lengthy term of imprisonment are factors to be taken into account.

Despite declining crime rates, remand numbers are increasing in Canada — and to the point at which more remanded adults than sentenced adults are now being held in provincial and territorial correctional facilities. Between 2004/05 and 2014/15 the number of adults held in remand on a typical day increased by 39 percent, nearly six times the increase in the sentenced custody population. In 2004/05 the remand population accounted for 51 percent of the custodial population. In 2014/15 on an average day 13,650 adults were being held in provincial or territorial correctional facilities awaiting trial, representing 57 percent of the custodial population (Correctional Services Program 2017: 3, 5). Manitoba has one of the highest remand rates in the country. In 2014/15, 67 percent of adults admitted to provincial custody in Manitoba were being held on remand; Indigenous people represented 70 percent of that population (Correctional Service Program 2017: 14, 7).

Cheryl Webster, Anthony Doob, and Nicole Myers (2009) explain the growing remand population in Canada as a consequence of a culture of "risk aversion" in the criminal justice system. In the same way that the element of "risk" has increasingly come to inform practices and policies in other areas of the criminal justice system, it has influenced the decision to hold accused persons in custody to await their trial. Rather than releasing the person on a summons or promise to appear, police are bringing more cases to court for a bail hearing. These hearings impose more conditions of release, creating a greater potential for administration of justice charges if people are found in breach of those conditions. Added to the mix, cases heard in Toronto bail courts were regularly being adjourned or held over, leading to longer periods in pre-trial detention for accused persons (Webster, Doob, and Meyers 2009).

While Webster, Doob, and Myers (2009) focused their attention on the Ontario courts, the situation varies across the country. Unlike other provinces, Manitoba has a "zero tolerance" approach to breaches of bail conditions (Deshman and Myers 2014: 69; Office of the Auditor General Manitoba 2014: 265). Once found in violation of their bail conditions, individuals are more likely to be taken into custody in Manitoba to await their trial dates. As a Manitoba front-line worker explained:

> We are locking people up for having a drink, maybe for being alcoholics, for smoking a joint, for not getting up in the morning. Maybe we're locking people up for getting home late, for not having a watch, for not having an alarm clock — for having the audacity to live with people that don't have an alarm clock. (Cited in Comack, Fabre, and Burgher 2015: 11)

GOING TO COURT — AND PLEADING OUT

In 2014/15, 328,026 cases were completed in adult criminal court in Canada. Of those cases, most (77 percent) involved non-violent crime. Theft (10 percent), impaired driving (10 percent), and failure to comply with a court order (10 percent) were the three most common offences of the cases completed. The median amount of time from an individual's first court appearance to the completion of her or his case that year was around four months (121 days); Manitoba averaged over five months (151 days). It took an average of five court appearances to complete a case; Manitoba had the longest averages at seven appearances (Maxwell 2017: 5, 11).

During a criminal trial, the onus is on the prosecution to prove that the accused person committed the crime. In every criminal trial, the Crown must prove two elements of any offence: that the accused person committed one of the activities prohibited by the Criminal Code or other federal statute (*actus reus*); and that the accused person demonstrated the required intent to commit the activity (*mens rea*). Most criminal trials focus on whether the Crown has proved those elements beyond a reasonable doubt, although the law also recognizes certain justifications or excuses for an accused person's actions (such as duress and self-defence). The defence of self-induced intoxication, however, is very limited in law. It can be used as a partial defence to specific intent (such as the intent to kill for a murder charge), but it is not a defence to the general intent of other crimes such as assault or arson (see *R v. Tatton* 2015).

Some 63 percent of all completed criminal cases in 2014/15 resulted in a finding of guilt by the court (Maxwell 2017: 6). This figure, however, includes both guilty pleas and findings of guilt after a contested trial. Very few criminal cases actually go to trial. In Ontario, for instance, only 4.8 percent of all criminal cases in 2015 went to trial (Kari 2016). Debra Parkes and Emma Cunliffe (2015: 231) note the gendered and racialized nature of guilty pleas, citing research findings that women plead guilty at higher rates than men do, and that Indigenous people are more likely to plead guilty than are non-Indigenous people.

Many of the women at the WCC pleaded guilty to their charges when they went to court. Still coming down off of drugs, Jody said that she "wasn't of sound mind" when she was taken from custody to her court appearance.

> They took me out of the hole from hallucinating. I couldn't even walk in these shackles. I was so skinny. I wasn't even of sound mind. I had no idea. I've never been through it before. I didn't know who to talk to. I didn't know, you know. So I just went there and pled guilty. And I was shaking. I was so skinny and sick. It was so bad.

Brenda, who was in custody on remand while awaiting her trial date, was also planning to plead guilty to her charges. Now in her forties, Brenda had an early history of abusive relationships, drugging and drinking, and getting into trouble with the law. But when she met her third husband in her mid-twenties all that changed. She started on a different path and eventually ended up taking university courses. In the space of a year, Brenda lost her husband, her brother, and her father to cancer. When her husband died, Brenda said she "lost everything." She added, "I just gave up. I didn't care anymore." She started using drugs and drinking again, and was charged with robbery with a weapon. "My daughter-in-law picked up this guy on the track [where the sex trade operates]. I was standing with her and she picked him up and we went back to his place. I guess she planned to rob him and he ended up getting stabbed. He got stabbed seventeen times."

While she was out on bail, Brenda was charged with an aggravated assault.

> I was drinking in the bar and this guy that I knew, I started drinking with him and we drove to a bar and he actually raped me.... He picked me up in the Northern [Hotel] and we went to the LaSalle [Hotel] and he raped me in between, on our way back to the Northern. And we got into a confrontation outside and I ended up stabbing him.

The police arrested Brenda. "When they were interviewing me I was telling them about the rape. They told me, 'Don't try to use the rape because nobody's going to believe you.' So I didn't say anything about it." Brenda had since decided to plead guilty to the charges:

> I'm not gonna fight it. I don't want to go to court and tell what happened. I'm just gonna take it again like I always do. Take it in silence.... I don't want to go up there and tell what happened. And just, I've been sitting here for fifteen months. I've almost got time served. So I'll just take it like I've always done, by not saying anything.... 'Cause I just don't want anyone to know that that stuff's happened to me.

For some of the women, with little knowledge of the law and the legal process, pleading guilty seemed to be the most expedient thing to do. In Susan's case, criminal justice intervention was the result of her disreputable status as a "drug addict." Susan and a friend were at a "party house." They left the house to go to a nearby store to buy a lighter. Susan was carrying a loaded crack pipe, and she put her sweater over her shoulder to conceal the pipe. Seeing the lump, the store clerk thought that Susan had a gun under her sweater.

> I had a twenty-dollar bill. I was trying, I put it on the counter and she was serving up other customers and I was last. And I said, "Can I get a lighter?" 'Cause I was trying to do my hit. And she put change on the counter. She said I only gave her a five. I said, "I want my money." And I argued with her. And she said she was going to call the cops. And I said, "Give me my fuckin' lighter." And she thought I had a gun. And she put up her hands and she started yelling. And she ran out of that store.

The police arrested Susan two weeks later on a robbery charge. "And I didn't even do that. I didn't even rob that store." Because there were no cameras in the store, Susan said, "It was my word against hers. And they believed her." She was convicted on the robbery charge and sentenced to eighteen months' incarceration. Susan was well aware of her marginalized status: "I was an addict on the street that had no fixed address and they took it seriously. So I got that and I didn't know anything about appealing it. I didn't know anything about taking this to trial. All I just knew is, like, 'Okay, I'll get this over and done with. I want to go home.' And I didn't know."

Heather, who had grown up very "ghetto," had been involved in the sex trade, but when I spoke to her she was facing criminal charges for the first time, and there were several: attempted murder times three, arson (disregard for human life), destruction of property, and possession of an incendiary device. The charges were all in relation to an attempt to burn down the house where the father of one of her children was living. But Heather doesn't remember much of what happened, just "bits and pieces." She was high on pills at the time. Her intention in getting high, she said, was "to forget about all the problems that I was having with my previous baby's dad. And I would just get away from everything and everything would just go away for a while."

Trying to reconstruct the events, Heather remembered seeing her ex-partner earlier that evening and talking to him on the phone.

> I'm not the type of person to lash out unless something bad is happening. So I really believe that there was an altercation between me and him that night because I wouldn't have just walked up to the house and — you know what I mean? That's not in my nature. That's not the type of person I am. I couldn't care less what you've done. I don't believe in taking the life of someone else for no reason, you know.... And there has to be more to my night.

While Heather said she initially told her lawyer she "wasn't pleading out to anything I didn't remember," she ended up pleading guilty to the arson charge. "My judge even almost didn't let me plead out because he said if I didn't remember anything, 'How is she going to take responsibility to plead out?'" Heather received a sentence of thirty months' incarceration and eighteen months' probation. The other charges were stayed.

Pleading out, however, sets the stage for further criminalization down the road. As Heather put it, she "lost everything" that night — including a previously clean record. She believed that the cops were not so likely to "bother you" if you didn't have a criminal record — and that even "not being on welfare helps you stay under the radar." But after pleading out, things were different. If she went back home to the North End and something bad occurred and the police turned up: "I'm getting arrested because I have a criminal record. I'm getting detained and I'm getting asked twenty-one questions and I'm probably going to get threatened with jail time if I don't talk. That's what will happen."

TAKING THE RAP

Other women pleaded guilty or "took the rap" for offences that they didn't commit. In some cases, they made that decision due to loyalties to family or friends. In other cases, taking the rap seemed to be the only option when the alternative was to "rat" on the person who was really responsible for the offence, which might have generated even more serious consequences. In their investigation of the notion of "wrongful conviction" as it applies to women Parkes and Cunliffe (2015: 231) make the point that confession to a crime can spring from "social or ideological pressures to take responsibility for harms for which one may not be legally responsible, but for which one may feel morally responsible." That would seem to be the case for Jackie.

Jackie's Story

In her early thirties when I spoke to her, Jackie didn't have a previous criminal record. Still, she had ended up in custody with a raft of charges — home invasion, aggravated assault, assault with a weapon, break and enter, theft, and domestic assault — all of which happened on one night. Jackie said, "I can't really remember what happened. I was drunk .... But I know some bad shit happened to some people. And it wasn't meant to go down that way. And my brother was involved. That's all I'm going to say. But I did take the rap." Jackie explained that her decision was tied to her relationship with her brother:

> 'Cause I think I owe it to my brother because this one time we were drinking, me and my brother, and we were having a good conversation and he goes, "Can I ask you something?" I was like, "What?" He goes, "When we were small why did you leave me?" And I couldn't answer him. And he's like, "I got molested too by my older two cousins." That — my uncle? His daughters did that to my brother. And I felt really bad. I was like, "Well, I don't know." I was

like, "I can't answer that right now." He goes, "Yeah, you can." He goes, "We're both grown up now," he said. And he was mad and I got scared and I just, I caved in, I couldn't talk. And then I felt like I owed it to him to take this rap 'cause he has a little girl and I want him to be there for his little girl.

The incident that led to her charges was apparently connected to an encounter that Jackie had with her ex-boyfriend. She had been at a bar with another man. When she went outside to smoke a cigarette her ex-boyfriend and his friends followed her. Jackie ended up being badly beaten and woke up in the hospital, surrounded by her family members. And "shit happened" right after that. It seems her brother went and "home-invaded," as she put it, the house of her ex-boyfriend and his friends and "kicked the shit out of them. They didn't know who my brother was or his name. But they made it sound really bad, like we attacked them with knives and bats and sticks and shit. No. It was only one person and one thing, whatever."

Jackie reasoned that it was a case of retribution.

If he didn't jump me, if he didn't beat me up for leaving him that wouldn't have happened to him, you know. 'Cause my family doesn't like seeing me in the hospital half dead. Whose family likes that? It's like an eye for an eye sort of thing, you know. My family, and my brother especially, I'm close to my brother. I grew up with my brother. Of course he's going to back his big sister up, you know. And I took the rap. I was the bigger person. I took the rap for him 'cause that's my little brother. I protect my little brother.

Jackie pleaded guilty to aggravated assault, assault with a weapon, break and enter, and two breaches. "Everything else got dropped." She was sentenced to twenty-three months' incarceration and three years' probation.

Natalie's Story

Also in her early thirties, Natalie had no criminal justice involvement until her current charges. Her best friend was involved in the drug trade and part of a gang, but she "didn't see him that way. He was just somebody I grew up with. He was my friend." When she was about eighteen she and her friends went to a rave. "Somebody there had a gun and shot into the crowd." Her friend pushed her out of the way, and, she said, "ended up taking a bullet in the shoulder that would have hit me.... So there isn't anything I wouldn't have done for him." Natalie's friend died four years later.

> He overdosed on drugs after a party that we were all at, which I kind of have some guilt for because I had taken all of his cocaine away from him. And because he didn't have any of that he did some pills that some other girl had given him. And just the reaction of all those different drugs together, he had a heart attack. And he was only twenty-four.

Her friend had been involved in drug-dealing, and Natalie would help him out on occasion. "He had asked me to help him at parties and at the bar and stuff like that, and selling drugs. And 'Sure, Absolutely, man. You know, whatever you need.'" When her friend died, Natalie took over his drug business. "Instead of dealing with my grief, which I still haven't dealt with over him, I kind of just took over his life." In addition to paying for his funeral, she was also working to support his partner and son, "'Cause he would have done all that for me, you know."

Natalie was attending school and selling drugs in a bar on the weekends. She made up to $300 a night. Her plan was to stop selling once she had her degree and could support herself and her son legitimately. But she was also living in one of Winnipeg's inner-city communities, next door to a gang house.

> I guess they had a fight one day that ended up with my doors and all my windows smashed out. 'Cause it had broken out onto the lawn and it just got out of hand. And I had to call the police. And nobody was charged because there was so many people at this party that I couldn't identify who smashed my windows. The police couldn't arrest anybody. So, yeah, I spent two months living there with plywood on my windows. Housing didn't even care. There was prostitutes on the corner, glass in my yard all the time. My son was getting older. I didn't want to live there anymore. So I moved in with my cousin and her boyfriend. That's one of the worse things I ever did.

Natalie and her son were alone in her cousin's house one night when the police showed up. "The house got raided at three in the morning and they found four ounces of cocaine in his bedroom, her boyfriend's bedroom, and prescription pills and all kinds of stuff." Natalie was the only adult present in the house, and the police charged her with drug possession and trafficking.

I could have taken it to trial because none of my fingerprints was on anything. It was all theirs…. There was really no evidence against me. But her boyfriend happened to be a full-patched Hell's Angel. So I'm obviously not going to say who he is. And they wanted me very badly to [name him]. They brought me pictures. Even when I came here, for the first two weeks I was here detectives were saying, "Come on. We can make this go away. It's not even you we want. Just tell us who this is." And I wasn't prepared to do that. I grew up around those people. I know what happens. And maybe if I had known how much time you get for trafficking I might have thought a little differently [chuckles]. But, yeah, I didn't even go to trial. I waved my right to bail. I decided I was just going to plead guilty. And in my mind I could get out on parole faster and back to my son than sitting here and waiting for a trial. So that's what I did.

While she was waiting for her court date, Natalie was offered bail to a drug treatment centre. "But one of the conditions is you have to have a drug addiction or be involved, do drugs all the time." Initially, she was going to take that option, "'cause I really didn't want to be in here. I was told I could have weekend passes to see my son and stuff like that. I signed the papers. I was going to go. And then it's just the guilt, I guess. Every single girl that's in this jail is here for one way or another 'cause of drugs — because she was high, broke the law, or broke the law to get money to get high." Natalie called the director of the treatment centre and told him, "I don't have a drug problem. I was just trying to get into your program to get out of jail."

She believed her decision was tied to what happened to her best friend. "I didn't want to take a bed away from somebody who needed to be there instead of putting a needle in their arm or something, you know what I mean?" The Crown asked for a five-year sentence, but the judge — impressed by her decision to forgo the treatment centre — sentenced Natalie to thirty months' incarceration.

IT'S NOT OVER YET

For some of the women, the restrictive conditions encountered on bail prior to their court appearances were imposed again after they had served their time in custody and were let back into the community on a conditional release. Under the law, both federal prisoners (except those serving a life sentence for murder) and provincial prisoners are eligible for conditional release (or parole) after serving one-third of their sentences or seven years in custody, whichever is less. Conditional release means that a parole officer supervises the person, often with special conditions attached (such as abstaining from the use of drugs or alcohol, not associating with certain people, not frequenting certain places, or participating in counselling, treatment, or random urine analysis). If not otherwise released on parole, federal prisoners (excluding those serving life or indeterminate sentences) can be granted statutory release at two-thirds of their sentences. Individuals on statutory release are required to follow standard conditions that include reporting to a parole officer, remaining in a geographical area, and obeying the law and keeping the peace for the remainder of their sentence. As in parole, statutory release can also come with special conditions attached. In exceptional circumstances, individuals who are considered to pose a threat of serious harm or violence may be denied statutory release and held in custody until their sentence ends at the warrant expiry date. The conditional release of prisoners is governed by the Corrections and Conditional Release Act and administered by the National Parole Board for both federal and provincial prisoners, except in those provinces that have their own parole board (British Columbia, Ontario, and Quebec) (Parole Board of Canada n.d.; Office of the Auditor General Canada 2015; Community Legal Education Association 2013).

Prisoners released on parole generally have high rates of success. In 2014/15, for example, of the 948 people on federal full parole, 87 percent of the stints were successfully completed, meaning that the person was not returned to prison for breaching conditions or a new offence. In that same year, of the 5,902 people on statutory release, 63 percent were successfully completed. In both cases, revocations were most likely to occur for breach of conditions and not for committing a new offence. Some 79 percent of both revoked paroles (121) and revoked statutory releases (1,697) in 2014/15 involved breaches. None of the paroles and only 2 percent of the statutory releases were revoked for a violent offence (Public Safety Canada 2016: 96, 98).

Indigenous prisoners are more likely to be denied parole and compelled to serve their sentences until the statutory release or warrant expiry dates (Public Safety Canada 2016: 91). Several of the women talked about their experience in gaining their freedom and in trying to abide by their release conditions once they had been let back into the community.

Helen's Story

Helen was sentenced to a federal term of imprisonment in 2010. The offence involved stabbing a woman in front of a hotel. She had managed to quit drinking for a year, but lapsed one night. Helen remembered heading out to look for a street-gang member who had been harassing her family.

> I was after him because he was beating up on my grandchildren and my son, giving them black eyes. He was trying to make them run, you know, to sell drugs and all that. These are twelve-, eleven-, fourteen-year-old kids he's muscling up. And they were throwing them in vans and beating them up and ripping them, taking their shoes, their new shoes or their gold [chains], whatever they had. He was doing that. And he hit my son, hey. And I'm very protective over my kids, right.

On her way to where she thought she could find this man, Helen was walking past a Main Street hotel when she came upon a fight between two women. One of the women was yelling, "My brothers are MWS [Manitoba Warriors]." Helen's recollection is spotty, as she was "comatose, I was blacked out" from drinking. But she recounted her understanding of what happened next:

> When I heard "MW" ... it must have reacted in me 'cause I was mad at this gangster, right, for torturing my son and my grandchildren. So I said, "Who the fuck cares about Manitoba Warriors," I told her. "They go around hurting kids," I said. And she started swearing at me.

> And they said I went up to her and I stabbed her. And I stabbed her in the heart, not in the heart but I hit her artery? And then I guess they said — but when I left she was still fighting with that woman when I left. 'Cause I just went up to her and I went and I kept walking. That's what they said, I kept walking.

The police apprehended Helen soon afterward. She said they threw her to the ground, "into a snowbank." Then they handcuffed her and threw her into a van. "They said, 'you fuckin'—.' And then they just started swearing at me and everything like that. And then they said, 'You're going down for murder' and all this." Helen ended up pleading guilty to a charge of aggravated assault. She told her lawyer, "I want to get it over with. I just want to do my time and I want to start here and, you know, I almost took somebody's life and it woke me up."

The court sentenced Helen to five and one-half years in prison for the assault. Assessed as having a high risk to reoffend, she was later denied parole:

> I was tagged as high risk because I carried thirteen convictions of aggravated assault. Well, I didn't get convicted for all thirteen of them but … they'll never disappear. They'll always be there, you know what I mean? I didn't know that…. Now that I think about it, I should have never pleaded out. I always pleaded out guilty because I wanted to get out of jail and get it over with, you know what I mean? If I would have fought those cases I wouldn't have carried so much. But I never knew. I didn't know the system. I didn't know the law…. 'Cause some of those things that I carry I didn't do. If I would have fought them I would have probably won some of them. Then I wouldn't have had so many. But … I didn't know the court system. I didn't know. I just wanted to get out of jail.

Helen was eventually granted statutory release to a halfway house. "I was really happy when I got there. I just loved the place, the way it looked." But troubles soon emerged. There were no locks on the bedrooms doors, and Helen's belongings were stolen the first time she went out. Helen also said that several of the women at the halfway house were selling drugs, and "there was men coming in there, going upstairs, you know…. I didn't feel safe there when I seen stuff like that." After staying for five months, Helen "walked out of there," which put her in breach of her release conditions for being unlawfully at large. She turned herself in and was taken into custody.

Some eight months later Helen was again released from custody. One of her conditions was to abstain from alcohol and drugs. She had not been drinking since she was released from the federal penitentiary. She had come to understand that, as she said: "I can't drink alcohol because that's been my painkiller for how many years for all that stuff that I've been through. But I'm violent when I'm in that because that's probably when everything comes out…. I have no control over myself when I have that alcohol." She does use marijuana, "And that's it. And there I don't black out, right." Marijuana is a form of self-medication for Helen. As she explained, "I have arthritis. Instead of taking medication I use marijuana for pain. And plus I'm anemic. I can't eat." Smoking marijuana, she said, "makes me want to eat…. It just makes me feel better. It helps me out in my days, you know."

Nevertheless, Helen was scheduled to submit to a urine analysis as part of her release conditions. Knowing that she would fail the test, she turned herself in and was again taken into custody.

Sarah's Story (cont'd)

Sarah received a five-year federal sentence for the incident that occurred at her house when her daughter and a female acquaintance got into a fight. She was sent to the Edmonton Institution for Women and spent the last year of her sentence at the Okimaw Ohci Healing Lodge in Saskatchewan.

While she was in the Edmonton Institution, Sarah got into fights with the other prisoners and ended up in segregation. "I was so angry, a really angry person. No one could say nothing to me. I was always right, you know. So and, yeah, I went into the segregation, did my time." Sarah also had conflicts with the guards:

> I was so angry with some of these guards, the way they were pushing me around. "You know what? I've had enough of you," I said. "You know, that's enough," I says, "Just, you know, leave me alone." They were pressing buttons on me to see how angry I would get. And I can get pretty angry or I could just shut off the world. I could just stay in my room, blank out in my room and stay there for days. And they'll have to knock, say, "Are you okay? Are you alive?" "Yeah, I'm okay." And I don't know where I've learned that. That was another way of coping. Shutting everybody out. And I find I still kind of do that because I still have those trust issues.

At one point Sarah refused to go to lockup. When the guards took control over the situation and got her back to her room, she was "cut off from everything, you know what I mean? So that was my punishment." When the Elders came and talked to her, she "finally broke down" and asked for help.

Sarah worked closely with one of the prison counsellors and did an eight-month Behavioural Health Therapy course. "I had to take it twice because the first time it just wouldn't click to me. It wouldn't click." After that, she took a program called Spirit of the Warriors. "When I went into Spirit, oh my god, I found, I went for, how many months? I cried every day and I almost wanted to quit. Every day for four months I cried. And just because I was talking. I was finally opening up all my hurt, all my pain, you know?" Looking back on that experience, Sarah recalled:

That was important for me to find out who I was. That took me a long time to understand me. It took me a lot, I guess because I was blocking, blocking shame. Shame does a lot to a person too. Because, you know what I mean, no one could really say, "Okay, you know what, my brother was fucking me," you know what I mean? Or things like that, you know what I mean? It's not right, of course, it's not right but you didn't know any better. You were a kid. You're getting raped and you don't even know that. And then, as you get older, "Oh no." You see that person and you know it's wrong, but you hide it. It's a secret. And that's why we build so much anger.

Sarah had a number of assault charges on her record. "Some assaults I didn't even do, but I pled out to them just to get out." While Sarah made progress in coming to terms with her anger, because of her record for violence the Parole Board was not prepared to release her at the statutory release date (two-thirds of her sentence). She served the full five years, right to her warrant expiry date.

Just four days before she was to be released, the Crown in Winnipeg subpoenaed her, "'Cause they wanted to put a Section 810 on me." Under Section 810 of the Criminal Code, restrictive conditions can be imposed on prisoners' release into the community once they have reached their warrant expiry date if there are reasonable grounds to suspect that they may commit a serious personal injury offence. Sarah told me that everyone at the healing lodge, even her counsellor, was "surprised" about the subpoena. Her counsellor, she said, couldn't believe it and told her, "You worked so hard for this."

Sarah was flown to Winnipeg on a Friday, taken to the Remand Centre, and then driven to a mental health unit. "And they take me all the way to Notre Dame [Avenue] and say, 'This is your home' and then put me in a mental health unit, where it was just twenty-something men and one woman: me. I says, 'Well, I don't have mental health problems like them, you know.'" Sarah described what it was like at the unit: "It was not nice when I walked in there. They put me in a room where they had a guy out of Stony Mountain [Penitentiary] but [he] ran off. And I went to pull up that blanket and it just smelled like urine. I looked and it was mouldy, and I says, 'I'm not fuckin' living here.'"

The parole officer told her to "just hack it out for the weekend. We'll get you out of here." But "they didn't do that. I couldn't even sleep at nights. I had men squirting tons of cologne on them 'cause I'm the only woman.

Coming to my door, giving me smokes, asking me things. I said, 'Okay. Don't bug me no more.' … It was creepy." After two weeks Sarah phoned the parole officer and told her, "'I don't give a shit if you breach me. I'm getting the fuck out of here.' I packed and I was gone." A warrant was issued for her arrest. Sarah was picked up a week later, and got a year for that breach.

Sarah ended up serving the one-year sentence in the Remand Centre. But that did not end her incarceration experience. When she was released, one of her conditions was not to associate with anyone known to have engaged in criminal activity.

> I didn't realize they were talking about my kids. My son was a criminal, but he hasn't been in jail for years. They breached me because of that. Then they breached me because I — what else did they breach me for? I can't even remember. I was … with a group of people that were all criminals but it seemed like I was doing a criminal activity or something like that, I don't know. I was at the [Salvation Army] Booth Centre. Oh, come on! How many criminals are in that building? You know what I mean? They just found everything to put me back in.

THE ROLLERCOASTER RIDE

The women's accounts make it clear that crime is by no means a straightforward matter. More often than not, the circumstances that caught these women in the criminal justice net are messy and complicated affairs — to the point at which it becomes difficult to separate out the categories of "offender" and "victim" because those boundaries are so often blurred.

In these terms, the discrete crime categories applied to these women become severed from the social contexts in which their law violations emerged. The problems, conflicts, and dilemmas generated as the women endeavoured to cope with their lived experience of trauma, including their histories of abuse, their grief over the loss of loved ones, and the violence they encountered not only in their families and intimate relationships but also in the inner-city spaces where they reside — they all arise in this given social context. For so many of the women, coping with trauma meant turning to drugs and alcohol, which only exacerbated their troubles and ensnarled them in the criminal justice net. Christine described this process as something akin to a rollercoaster ride:

Like, I'll be up and down. And when I'm up there and I'm doing good. I'm trying to be in sobriety, do good, get my kids back, in programs. And then something happens with a family member or I lose someone, and I fall down. Then I start using again. And then when I'm using I'm out there stealing. Then I'm out there fighting. Then I come back here. And then I'm doing good. Then something happens again. And it's like a rollercoaster. I'm up and down, up and down, you know? When I hit rock bottom and I just dig myself out of that hole then I'm doing okay and trying to get out of there.

Through its construction of "normal crime," the criminal justice system imposes its own truth onto the women's lives, fashioning an account that focuses on individual autonomy and culpability. In the process, the broader social conditions — the structural barriers and systemic factors — that have contoured and conditioned the women's lives get easily lost from view. This is not to say that the women are merely victims of their social circumstances, with no agency of their own. Ultimately, as they themselves acknowledge, they must accept responsibility for their actions and behaviours, especially when they cause harm to others. Yet, focusing solely on individual responsibility cannot resolve the broader social conditions that engender the women's law violations.

Once caught in the criminal justice net, the women encounter further challenges and further trauma. Restrictive conditions such as abstaining from using drugs or alcohol, being of "good behaviour" (a rather imprecise term), or not associating with other individuals who have criminal involvement (including their family members and friends) essentially require the women to refrain from living the life that they know, what has become their "normal." The imposition of these restrictions sets the women up to fail and drags them deeper into the criminal justice net as they are charged with more criminal offences for breaching their release conditions — a situation that will most likely result in convictions, more time in custody, and a longer criminal record. Those held in remand custody — sometimes for months, sometimes for years — have a strong motivation to plead guilty "just to get it over with." In the meantime, they are all tasked with the challenge of dealing with their experiences of confinement.

CHAPTER SIX

THE PRISONING OF WOMEN

Incarceration — the deprivation of liberty — is the most extreme form of punishment available in our society, the most severe method by which lawbreakers can be made to pay their dues, receive their just desserts, or suffer the consequences of their actions. As punishment, imprisonment ostensibly teaches lawbreakers a lesson so that they will refrain from such actions in future. At the same time, modern penal policies and practices are intended to reform or rehabilitate so that the offender can be successfully reintegrated back into society as a law-abiding member. In these neo-liberal times, prison is where offenders are to be "responsibilized" or made accountable for their choices. For women prisoners in particular, gender-responsive programming has been developed so that they can be empowered to become self-reliant and conforming neo-liberal citizens.

Feminists initially embraced empowerment as a strategy for "transforming the structure of societal power relations that allow women to make choices and regain control of their lives" (Hannah-Moffat 1999: 32). In the neo-liberal carceral context, though, empowerment takes on a different meaning. The lawbreaker becomes responsible for her own rehabilitation: "She is responsible for her own self-governance and for the minimization and management of her needs and of her risk to the public or herself" (p. 32). Nevertheless, the choices that incarcerated women are empowered to make "are limited to those deemed by the administration, and not necessarily the prisoner, as meaningful and responsible" (p. 33). As well, women's crimes are decontextualized; "the social, economic, and political barriers experienced by women, and marginalized women in particular," are not the focus of correctional attention (p. 34). Instead, change-making is to occur *within* the individual woman. By reconfiguring her thought processes and attitudes (including the management of her anger) through strategies such as cognitive or dialectical behavioural therapy, the criminal woman's risk to reoffend is thereby reduced.

In these terms, prison is a contradictory site. On the one hand, the primary purpose of the prison is to exact punishment on its captives. The loss of freedom is fundamental to the carceral project, and prisoners are subject to the authority and control of their keepers within this highly structured environment. Resistance to the prison regime by the prisoner can lead to further punishments in the form of administrative charges, segregation, more time in custody, and other disciplinary actions (Martel 2006, 2000; Parkes 2015). On the other hand, prison is a treatment centre in which women are to receive help in dealing with their trauma by means of therapeutic programming, counselling, and other resources — which leads them to expect that they will not only be given access to those resources, but also be treated by correctional staff in supportive and respectful ways (Pollack 2009). This tension between the prison as a site of punishment and a site of treatment sets the stage for inconsistent and conflicting experiences of imprisonment. For the most part, however, punishment inevitably trumps treatment.

In *Women in Trouble* I raised the issue of whether "prisoning" — the process of imprisonment and the women's experiences of that process — enabled the women to resolve their troubles. By the 1990s, at a hundred or more years of age, the Portage Correctional Institution was long past its prime. As one of the women described it, "This place is a *dump*. This is like the next stop to hell" (Comack 1996: 127). Similarly, Bernice, who had spent a year in the PCI in 2006, described the jail as "something else. It was old, it was ugly." In addition to its physical problems, the PCI was overcrowded with women. While the official capacity of the jail was thirty-five prisoners, eighty-five women were being held in custody there at the time of its closing in 2012.

The opening of the Women's Correctional Centre in February 2012 promised a new era in the management of incarcerated women in Manitoba. Its much larger space and greater capacity reflected a design informed by the broader correctional shift to a gender-responsive approach. As the superintendent of the WCC told the media during a tour of the facility prior to its opening, women need different jails than those designed for men. "We can't just take a male facility and paint it pink and say, 'There you go, girls'" (Kusch 2012). Nevertheless, despite this new and improved facility, questions about the prisoning of women persist.

With trauma figuring prominently in the women's lives, we need, then, to ask: does the WCC constitute a place in which the women can begin to heal from their lived experience of trauma? Or does it merely add another layer to that experience, exacerbating the women's troubles? As with most social issues, the answers to such questions are complicated. For many of the women, prison offers a refuge or escape, a temporary reprieve from the threats on their lives on the outside. Similarly, prisoning constitutes a time out, a chance to recover from the toll on their lives of drugging and drinking, a chance to "get clean" and gain clarity and perspective on where they have come from and how they might move forward. At the same time, prisoning incurs a number of costs. Control and containment, the defining features of the prison experience, generate ongoing stresses that undermine the women's mental and physical health.

Prisoning also involves the disruption of the women's relationships with children and other family members, and of whatever supports and resources they had managed to secure in their life on the outside. This disruption becomes especially acute for women who have been cycled in and out of custody over time — women who keep "coming back to jail." For these women, prisoning has become another part of their "normal." It adds another layer to their lived experience of trauma. Not only do the women become institutionalized; each time they are released they have to "start all over again" to rebuild their lives in the community.

GOING TO JAIL

For many of the women, going to jail was a conscious decision. They knew that their lives were spiralling out of control and they had to do something about it. Getting incarcerated was a way of breaking that downward spiral.

Shannon had spent the previous five years addicted to opiates. "And then it got too much. It got way too much…. It was just too much drugs, too much shit. I mean, when you get into needles that's when you know things start getting ugly." In addition to opiates, Shannon started shooting other drugs, including coke and speed, "anything I could fit into a needle." She had tried to go to treatment, but she said: "There's no way I could do it on my own. Like, fuck that. You'd basically have to put me beside a locked door to get me to stop." Although Shannon had been living in another province, she had outstanding warrants in Winnipeg for "prostitution, drug possession, same old thing." She said she knew she had to return to jail in Winnipeg. "So, yeah, that's what I did. I came back and I came to jail and I threw up for about a month."

Doris had been using crack cocaine and working in the sex trade. Her life had gotten to the point where she was contemplating suicide.

> Something stopped me. I thought of my kids. Something was tell-
> ing me, "You have kids. Don't do it" and stuff like that.... And I
> felt bad and then after I realized it, I was, like, I think I better go to
> jail to clear myself. Otherwise I would have been bony and would
> have went to go do worse for myself, sell myself so much, smoke
> crack.... When I came to jail I looked like shit. I was skinny, bony,
> didn't want to eat. I didn't look normal 'cause I was so cracked out.

Mary said that getting picked up by the police "saved me." She sold drugs
to an undercover officer, and "two minutes later I had police pulling me out
of the cab. Drugs flew everywhere. I had, like, one thousand, one hundred
and sixty dollars on me. So. I had all the drugs and my IDs — all my drugs
and my IDs were in the same pocket. And it was like I just didn't give a shit
anymore. I wanted to come to jail. I knew I was on a downward spiral. I
knew I was self-destructing myself, you know."

For previously incarcerated women who could no longer cope with
their troubles on the outside, going back to jail seemed the only option.
Donna had spent almost five years in the federal women's prisons, serving
a sentence for manslaughter.

> I felt like I was falling through the cracks because when I got out I
> was told that I would have all these resources to help me if I started
> struggling. And when I needed those resources they weren't there.
> And I started getting stressed out. My older children are in that
> phase of their life where they're experimenting with this and that,
> and my seventeen-year-old daughter got pregnant. When I needed
> someone to talk to about my issues and that, there was nobody.

Alone and without supports, Donna ended up being reincarcerated when
she breached her release condition of abstaining from alcohol. "When I
relapsed I was basically just giving up. 'Cause it seemed like the only one that
was trying to improve their life was me and everyone else was just — they
weren't trying.... And I just gave up and went and sat in a bar, got drunk,
ended up in the drunk tank, and came back to jail." Donna said, "It was just
easy to give up. 'Cause I knew what would happen. I'd just come back to jail."

While going to jail may seem a viable option given the women's troubles
on the outside, their experience of imprisonment is very much conditioned
by the particular space inside the facility where they are housed.

CARCERAL SPACE AND THE EXPERIENCE OF CONFINEMENT

Criminologists and geographers have attended to ways in which prison as a social space governs the experience of incarceration (Moran 2012, 2015; Hancock and Jewkes 2011; Moran and Jewkes 2015). Much of this work draws on the writing of Michel Foucault (1978), who wrote: "Space is fundamental in any form of communal life; space is fundamental in any exercise of power" (2010: 252). In this respect, the prison represents "a particular organization of space and human beings" in which "the mechanisms of power are being deployed" (Rabinow 2010: 18). An understanding of the women's experiences at the WCC, therefore, necessitates an awareness of its spaces — and of how power plays out within those spaces.

Like many of the jails and prisons in the province, the WCC is located outside of the city limits. While not as distant as the Portage Correctional Institution, which was some 100 kilometres from Winnipeg, the WCC is nonetheless not easily accessible. The jail is situated on an off-road of the main highway leading out from the western edge of the city. Family members intent on visiting a prisoner require access to a motor vehicle to make the trip, and in making the trip they would have to look closely to be able to detect the WCC on the flat prairie landscape.

The old PCI was an imposing structure with limestone walls and barred windows built according to nineteenth-century prison architecture. The designers had the words "Provincial Gaol" carved into the stone above the main entrance. Inside the front door was a small foyer that served as a visiting area. Adjacent to the foyer was the main security office, with a guard stationed there. Administration offices were located to the right and left of the foyer. A series of key-operated gates and doors inside the main entrance led to the main part of the jail. While most of the women were held in dormitory rooms (complete with heavy doors) on the two floors of the building, a large room at the rear of the second floor of the building contained traditional cells with floor to ceiling bars. The kitchen and dining facilities were in the basement, along with a segregation area or "the hole," a windowless room with three cells. At the front of the second floor, three rooms served as classrooms, meeting rooms, library, and recreation area. The only outdoor space consisted of a small yard surrounded by a high chain-link fence.

From the outside the more spacious WCC has the look of any number of modern institutional buildings (save for the barbed wire along the top of the high chain-link fences.) Inside the main entrance is a large waiting

Portage Correctional Institution. Photo by author.

room. A guard is stationed behind a glass partition next to a metal detector that visitors have to pass through before entering the separate visiting area on the other side. Beyond the visiting area is a large rotunda, which leads in both directions to the various units on the main floor where the women are housed, as well as to the large kitchen facility where meals are prepared. A wide staircase leading up from the rotunda provides access to the administration offices and medical unit, located on the second floor.

Despite its official capacity of 196 prisoners, the jail has consistently exceeded that number since its 2012 opening. In June 2014, when I was

Women's Correctional Centre, Headingley, MB. Photo courtesy of Manitoba Corrections.

visiting the WCC to conduct the interviews with the women, the count was at 199. One year later, in June 2015, the count was up to 257. As of June 2017 the count was 277. It had reportedly gone as high as 300 women at one point.

On admission to the WCC the women are assessed according to their risk level and assigned to one of the units based on their security classifications. The "General Population" (GP) is housed in three separate units: Alpha, Bravo, and Charlie. A command post is situated in the centre of the area that houses the three units, with correctional officers stationed to maintain visual and camera surveillance of the units and operate the doors. Each of the three units has a common area lined on two sides with cells that feature heavy metal doors with small windows. A shower room is located at one end of each of the units. While meals are delivered to the units on trays, Charlie and Bravo also include a small kitchen area where the women can prepare coffee and small snacks. A classroom adjacent to each unit at the other end offers a space for programs and meetings with outside groups or organizations. Adjacent to each unit is a small exercise room that hosts a treadmill and elliptical trainer. The area also has a smaller room where one-on-one meetings can occur.

Overcrowding has had an impact on the living conditions of the women housed in General Population. Charlie Unit, for instance, consists of sixteen

Women's Correctional Centre, Charlie Unit. Photo courtesy of Manitoba Corrections.

cells (each with two beds). By adding mattresses to the floors of each cell, the unit's capacity can be expanded from thirty-two to forty-eight women. To manage the larger number of women, the unit is then divided into four tiers of twelve women each. The women are locked in their cells for twenty-one hours a day, and each tier is allowed into the common area on a rotating basis for one hour at a time, three times a day. During that time the women can shower, use the phones, watch TV, or go (four at a time) to the small exercise room. Occasionally, they are allowed to go outside to a small yard adjoining the unit.

Maureen talked about what it was like to be locked down for twenty-one hours a day in Charlie:

> It's hard, it's most certainly hard. I'm barely moving around.... Like, there's three girls in a small-ass cell that's designed for two people, you know. They cram three of us in there and it's just, it's hard. It's hard to live with people that you don't know. You can't co-operate because one wants the radio blasting, the other one doesn't. I want to read and I want to take a nap but they want to scream out the door. It's hard, most certainly it is. But what do you do?

Alpha and Bravo are more open units; the women are allowed into the common area of the units for the better part of the day. Alpha holds the women who work in the kitchen and stores, so they have more mobility as they leave the unit each day to complete their shifts. As Jody commented, "Alpha's probably one of the best places to be in here just 'cause you can work, your time passes. But other than that, it's the same."

Delta is in another part of the WCC. Initially referred to as the Special Needs Unit, the unit holds women who have mental health issues (such as depression and anxiety) and so have difficulties managing in General Population. Its configuration is similar to the units in General Population; it also features a common area lined with cells, an exercise room, and an outdoor space. Correctional officers are stationed at a desk at the entrance to the unit. In addition, the area leading into the unit has two small rooms used for one-on-one meetings with the women.

Lori had spent her first two weeks of incarceration in General Population. "Alpha was *way* too much for me. It was a lot of girls, a lot of yelling, a lot of conflict. And it triggered too many of my mental illnesses to the point where they moved me to Delta." The unit has a calmer feel to it, although Lori commented, "It depends on who's here, how many girls are here. 'Cause a lot of us, if you get a bunch of us that are on, like, a higher level that day, the volume and the noise goes way up." The advantage of being in Delta is that "Everybody here has their own problems, so it's easier for them to understand everyone else. Nobody judges anybody for your problems in this unit."

Dianne asked to be moved from General Population to Delta.

> The minute that I got there I was just, I took the first week, like, my body was so in high gear from being in GP that the first week I was just like "Whoa." I was just knocked out. My body was just so out of whack I just had to take that time to rest and let my body come down.

Dianne had hesitated in making the request to be transferred to Delta. She was aware that the social stigma surrounding those with mental health issues follows the women into jail:

> At first I thought, "Wait a minute, I don't want to get labelled [laughs]. I don't know if I'm good with that." But, yeah. Like, in GP a lot of the girls are very ignorant about stuff like that and that was why I was a little bit concerned about it. But then now that I'm back [in GP] and everybody kind of sees like, "Oh yeah, she still has her marbles," you know what I mean?

Kilo, a unit designed to house federally sentenced women, is a separate structure located at the rear of the complex. The women in Kilo are responsible for making their own meals but are required to report several times a day to an area adjacent to the rotunda in the main building, where correctional officers are stationed. The area also has tables where the women can congregate and a large spiritual room. Sarah talked about what she saw as the difference between Kilo and the federal women's prisons:

> It's very boring. Sure, sure the house is gorgeous and everything, but it's like this, you get only eight people on your PIN, whereas in federal you can phone anywhere you want. But here it's very limited. There's no programming, no jobs [chuckles]. There's nothing. Whereas when we go to Edmonton there's a community, there's all kinds of stuff. Go to Okimaw Ohci, there's a community, there's all kinds of stuff happening. You can go there, there, there, whatever. But here, there's nowhere.

When I visited in June 2014 the Kilo unit had only six women in it. The following summer the decision was made to no longer hold federally sentenced women at the WCC. Instead, they were to be transferred to either the Edmonton Institution for Women or the Okimaw Ohci Healing Lodge in Maple Creek to serve their sentences.

The WCC also features what is referred to as the Secure Step Down Unit, which includes the Echo and Foxtrot units as well as four smaller units (Golf, Hotel, Indigo, and Juliet) comprising segregation cells in which the women are kept in lockup for twenty-three hours a day. The women start their time in Secure in segregation or "the hole," and after two weeks of good behaviour are moved up a level. As Alicia explained:

> [In the hole] you get two half-hour breaks there a day and then if you're good over there and no, like, freaking out or anything like that they'll move you to Echo or Foxtrot, which is one hour out a day. And you have to make levels. When you go into Echo and Foxtrot you go in as a level two and it takes two weeks to make a level and then you're level three and then two more weeks to make a level four. And then you stay at level four for two weeks on good behaviour and they'll move you to GP.

Women can end up in Secure for a variety of reasons, including being assessed as "high risk" on their admission to the WCC, for fighting with other inmates, for talking back to the guards, or for consuming illicit drugs or alcohol.

Avery had been "red-flagged" when she arrived at the WCC because of troubles she encountered in the Remand Centre. Avery said that the Remand guards handled her roughly and she started "freaking out." So when she arrived at the WCC she was assessed as a high risk: "I had to wear handcuffs in the shower for a month and everywhere I went I had to be shackled up, like, my feet to my waist to my wrists." Trying to make it to the next level in the Step Down Unit can be akin to the game of Snakes and Ladders. Avery never made it up the levels. She would get to the end of the two-week period and then, "A day before the review I would, something would happen and I would just freak out." She eventually ended up being transferred to the Delta Unit.

> I wasn't going to make it through the levels just 'cause I'm pretty sure 'cause of my mental health, it wasn't doing good. Like, especially if I have depression and ADHD. I've been in here for seven months, first time in jail and locked up twenty-three hours of the

day, every day. I'm not going to get better. If anything I'm going to get worse, you know.

Avery found that being in Delta was "way better" — but "it's still jail."

Alicia ended up being put in the hole after getting into a fight with another woman in GP. The woman had told her to "shut up. And I was like, 'I'm not going to be quiet and put my tail between my legs just 'cause you tell me to.' And then she came at me and I wasn't going to just let her fight me. So I fought her back."

Annette said that she was being held in Secure "because I'm a very lippy girl. And I was in Bravo Unit and I got in a little bit of trouble for being lippy and they brought me here [to Secure]. And here you're locked up twenty-one hours a day.... So it's like, you know, there's nothing to do but sleep and read and eat. And it's just, it's awful, I hate it."

Consuming illicit drugs also merits time in Secure, as well as being dry-celled (placed in a cell without plumbing facilities). Jody was dry-celled on her admission to the WCC. Prior to being taken into custody she had been doing "hydromorph's, oxy's, all the crazy opiates, like, really strong for eight months straight every day." This was her first time in jail.

> They brought me in and they dry-celled me for nine days and it's like crazy withdrawals you go through. And they just really didn't even take it serious.... And then they put me in the hole and I started hallucinating really bad. And they weren't giving me nothing. Like, they wouldn't even give me a Tylenol, not Advil, nothing. And people die from withdrawal from that kind of stuff.... And I was hallucinating. It was really bad. It was like I wasn't seeing with my eyes, it was like in my head. It was really bizarre. I thought my mom was outside. I thought they were holding me against my will and the news was outside and they wanted to interview me and all this crazy stuff. I don't know, man, it was so bizarre and, like, I don't know, it was really bizarre.

Jody ended up spending six weeks in Secure.

> It was really hard. You don't get a radio and you don't get nothing. I was going crazy, 'cause I just stopped hallucinating and all that stuff too and I'd never been jail so I just, I didn't know what the hell, you know. I just knew I had to stay strong and keep it together 'cause I knew it wouldn't last forever being down there.

Tannis and Molly were dry-celled after they had consumed crystal meth. The drug had been smuggled into the WCC by another woman. They described being dry celled:

> It's really shitty in there 'cause all you have is that little mattress and … the guards have to watch you 24/7. They always have to watch you in case you're trying to grab the drugs. They watch your hands and your feet and your face, they say. When you're trying to sleep too they say, "Well, we need to see your hands. So you have to have your hands and your face showing all the time." And when you need to pee or poop you've got to tell them so they watch you pee and poop. And even when you shower they watch you shower, two guards, two female guards watch you shower. And I was in dry cell for six days 'cause it took, and I had to take three poops. I had to take three poops. (Tannis)

> It was pretty rough in there. They, I don't know, it's really degrading. They watch you shower when you're naked and they give you nothing in your cell. It's cold in there, a little mattress with no sheet and one blanket. You don't get any brushes or sometimes they wouldn't even let us have a toothbrush or whatever. For a couple of days we wouldn't be able to shower and then the shitty meals and, yeah, I don't want to ever go through that again. (Molly)

After their time in dry cell both women were placed in the hole. Tannis spent fifteen days there:

> It's quiet. You're in your cell all day by yourself. Can't have nothing. Not allowed to have anything, just a paper, pen, and a book. And you're only allowed to have one break in the morning for half an hour and one break in the afternoon after lunch for half an hour. So, yeah, two half-hour breaks. And they, the hole, I don't know, you get your meals, you get your, it's just, you're not allowed to have anything, that's all. It was just lonely, though, 'cause you don't have a roommate or anything like that.

Melody was placed in the hole for being drunk. One of her cellmates had made homebrew. "I was supposed to be the tester and I tested it and I got drunk from it. I got thrown in the hole for fifteen days." Melody said that the hole had its advantages over being in General Population:

I kind of liked it in there 'cause it was so nice and quiet and — but I hate the slamming doors, guards slamming doors. I hated it, but other than that I liked it…. But sometimes I just felt lonely. I wanted to get out of there, but I liked it in there. It was nice and quiet, better than being in Alpha and Bravo. It's so noisy. I think that's where, like, when all the noise, it just makes me have anxiety in my head. I'm just holding my chest. It's like my heart's going to pop out of my mouth or I can't breathe and I just have really fast breathing. And I guess that's anxiety.

Jennifer spent eight months in Secure. She said: "It was hard at first. But then I got used to it." She said she could have got herself out of Secure earlier but she became "used to doing segregation time, being locked up and only coming out for a little bit at a time a day. I was scared. I was scared to be around too many people." She said she kept telling herself, "What if, what if I get angry, what if I argue with someone and fight? I don't want to do that." When we met, Jennifer had just been moved back to General Population. She told me, "It's a little bit overwhelming but I think I'll get used to it. I just have to adapt to being around people again because I've been locked up so long in a room."

Maureen was in the hole for eleven days. Like the other women, she found it a reprieve from the noise and crowded conditions in General Population:

I didn't mind it. I'd rather be over there than over here. It's quiet. You get your own room, you know. The rooms, the small rooms that they have over here [in GP] with three people in them, the rooms in the hole, like, you get one room to yourself that are bigger than the small rooms over here, you know. So I didn't mind at all…. I was totally okay over there. You learn to function just fine. But coming back to GP to the noise, to everybody having to live together, it's not an easy thing to do, that's for sure.

Clearly, the particular spaces in which the women are confined inside the prison — and the mechanisms of power deployed in those spaces — very much condition or contour their experiences of confinement. Women who are housed in the Charlie Unit are locked in their cells, along with two other women, for all but three hours of the day. Ironically, despite more restrictive conditions — including being locked down for twenty-three hours a day and having to wear handcuffs and shackles when being moved — the women who end up in Secure for breaching the rules of the institution find it an improvement over being held in General Population, given its noise volume and cramped spaces. Regardless of which unit of the WCC the women are located in, they are confronted with the challenge of doing their time.

"DOING TIME"

Time is measured in a number of ways in prison. The sentence a prisoner receives — the days, weeks, months, or years that they can expect to be incarcerated — is one measure. Time is also "the basic structuring mechanism of prison life" (Sparks et al. cited in Moran 2012: 309). When to get up in the morning and go to sleep at night, when meals are delivered, when the medicine cart comes around, and when visits are allowed are all determined for the prisoners. In addition to "clock time," which measures off the hours, minutes, and seconds of the day, prisoners also encounter "experiential time" (Moran 2012: 309). Due to the repetition of daily routines, time may seem to stand still — like in the movie *Groundhog Day*, where one day repeated itself over and over again. Or time is perceived to be flowing more quickly outside than inside the prison, given that events in the lives of others (children, partners, relatives, friends) may seem to be passing the inmates by. Time, however, is tightly entwined with space in prison (Moran 2012: 307). In the same way that prisoners have limited control over the space, they have limited control over their time, including their daily routines. The women therefore face the challenge of "doing time" in this confined space.

For some of the women, doing time is made easier by the jobs they are assigned, such as working in the kitchen and stores, doing laundry, or cleaning floors. Brenda worked as a laundry trustee, which meant getting up at seven each morning. "It keeps me busy," she said. Working at these various jobs also had the added benefit of earning a meagre wage. Tina was initially assigned to work as a unit cleaner, and was paid $2.20 a day. When she was moved to laundry, her pay increased to $3.20 a day. Tina said that "every two weeks it goes up fifty cents until you reach four-seventy." Jody had a job working in stores.

> I'm in Alpha and I've got one of the best jobs in here, which is stores…. So we fill all the bottles, the flooring bottles, disinfectant bottles, we bring in all the deliveries at the delivery door on a pallet jack, like, kitchen deliveries, whatever deliveries. And then we do inventory, we clean up there in that area that we have and we bring all the unit orders to them, stuff like that. But it took me

a long time to get to that job. I've only been working in this job for like a month, month and a half.

Jody commented, "Other people that don't have work every single day they just sit around and play cards all day. There's really nothing. It's really, you feel like you get really stupid in here and real slow, yeah."

Other women's accounts confirmed Jody's assessment. When asked what their typical day looked like, their responses were similar. For Ellen, a typical day involved "nothing, really. I just get up, try [to] use the phone, play cards, eat, read, go to the gym, maybe try [to] watch TV. That's it. There's not much you can do in here." Maxine said her day involved "Just mostly sit around with a group of friends that I have here. Play cards, watch TV, nothing really much to do." Jessica said, "I just lay there and listen to my music all day and come out for my breaks three times a day and go on the phone." Maureen pointed out that in Charlie, "Right now we've been on lockdown for the last two days. We haven't even got out of our cells." But when she does get her hour-long break she usually watches TV, uses the phone, or does circles in the unit, walking laps. A key component of doing time, then, is dealing with the overwhelming boredom, which comes with its own challenges.

One activity that several of the women said helped them to cope with doing their time was beading. Drawing on their Indigenous culture, the women fashion colourful earrings, key chains, and other items using small beads. According to Wanda:

> Beading's a really, really, is a stress reliever, I guess. It keeps you calm and just focused on that one topic right there…. That's the only way to get by your time in here is to focus on what you're doing right there in that moment in that day, not to worry about tomorrow, not to worry about yesterday. It's to focus on today. It's the only way to get through with it in here. Otherwise you're just going to be stressed out, crying in your room, you know. You're not going to be able to handle it. And that's how I really feel right now. I really feel, like, I just want to, I don't know, I just want to go in my room and cry all day. But that's not going to help anything.

Annette also found beading to be an effective coping strategy. "While I'm beading, right, I just put my music on and I listen to it and I just forget … and then you see the blue guys [the guards] again, and it's like, 'Oh shit. Oh yeah, I'm in jail.'"

Beading is a temporary reprieve. The women in General Population were only allowed to do their beading in one of the small rooms adjacent to their unit. The room holds seven women, and their time is limited. As Harmony remarked, "It frustrated me because you got that hour or however long you can go to do it but you're trying your hardest to get it finished."

NEGOTIATING RELATIONSHIPS WITH THE OTHER WOMEN

Doing time also involves the challenge of negotiating relationships with the other prisoners — especially living in such close quarters, where, as Cheryl said, "everybody knows everybody's business."

Some of the women were sharing cells with relatives and friends. Alyson, who was rooming with her sister, said: "It's a bit easier to do time with your family. Yeah, 'cause I have another, one of my kids' dad's cousin is with me, too. Yeah, it's good to be with people that are from your reserve, too." Other women formed intimate relationships while they were incarcerated — what the women referred to as being "gay for the stay." Doris, who had a relationship with her baby daddy on the outside, said, "We're faithful to each other and, well, in here I'm not [chuckles]. But you got to do what you got to do, right, to cope with your feelings." Mary talked about the difficulties of maintaining an intimate relationship in such confined quarters: "We have good days but then, like, everybody just, I don't know, it's hard to deal with 'cause if you were having an argument with your partner out there you could walk away from them, get away from them, as opposed to in here when you argue you're stuck in the same room. It's very annoying [chuckles]."

The potential for drama is heightened in such close quarters. As Jody explained:

> Right now the people in our unit get along pretty good, except for the little fights roommates have just 'cause they're always together, right. But sometimes there's lots of drama. It just depends who comes around. 'Cause girls date girls and then there's drama, or they get jealous or this or that, or girls just have their own issues going on in their lives and they take it out on other girls and get angry and stuff.

Lynne agreed: "There's so much drama in jail. There's lesbian drama, there's, you know, this person is saying this person [did this or that]. It's just a lot of drama, honestly. And I don't like being dragged into other people's drama and that's kind of what's happening. So I just ignore everybody."

Lynne had been working as a laundry trustee but she quit the job. "'Cause I kind of have to talk to everybody and everybody has to kind of come up to me for certain things. So I figure if I just quit and just do my time it will be easier."

Gossip is another feature of life in the close quarters with other prisoners, and an outgrowth of the boredom that accompanies doing time. As Christine noted, there's "so much gossip.... The gossip gets to you and everything. It's just, oh my god." The women do their best to avoid getting caught up in the gossip that is being spread around. Margaret said, "I can't stand the gossip, you know what I mean. It drives me insane. Like, why? Why gossip [chuckles]? Can't we just let each other be free and not gossip about each other? So I try to stay away from that as much as I can." Doris also tried her best to avoid the gossip: "There's a lot of drama going on, and so a lot of people say, 'Hey, this girl's talking about you,' 'Hey, that girl's talking about you.' But I don't pay attention to that. I just keep to myself and do my time because I want to get out of here. I've been here too long. I want to go home and see my family and my kids."

Brenda acknowledged the difficulties encountered with some of the women in her unit:

> Some of these women drive you crazy ... 'cause they're mouthy and they know that you can't touch them — or they think you won't touch them 'cause of the guards. But usually they stay out of my way.... It takes a lot of control to walk away.... Takes everything in me to walk away sometimes. It gets to the point where I'm just shaking inside, where I just wanna go beat the crap right out of them.

Brenda resists that temptation for the sake of her daughter.

> It's my daughter that keeps me out of the hole, I guess, might as well say. Because she has to talk to me every day.... She's all alone out there now her dad's gone. So she's got nobody. And she tells me, she says, "Mom, I feel so alone.... I have nobody." So she gets suicidal. She ended up in the Emergency one night, she told me. So that's what keeps me under control in here is my daughter. If it wasn't for her I'd probably be living down in Secure [laughs].

Some of the older women had gained perspective on doing time from their previous experiences of incarceration. Janice, for instance, saw the younger women as "playing a role" when it came to spreading gossip:

I don't gossip. So if I have something to say I usually say it to the person that's involved. And when I'm told something about some-body else I keep it to myself. I don't want to spread stuff around. I just, it's not me. I've never done my time like that. I'm not about to start. 'Cause a lot of it's just like, it's child's play in there sometimes with the girls. But I try to remember, "You know what Janice? You were that age once and you busted your ass trying to prove yourself to the older ones." So I guess that's what they're doing too. I don't know. Some of them play their role, I guess. But I just say, you know, "When I was that age —" I give them some leeway because I know how it is at that age. I know how it can be.

Given that one of the primary strategies the women use to navigate their relationships with the other prisoners is to keep to themselves, some of the women found that the four tiers in Charlie worked to their benefit. Molly commented:

A lot of people don't like that you have to be in your room all the time.... I like the time to myself in the cell 'cause I feel like I really don't want to be around a lot of people and, like, yeah ... I just appreciate things more and I'm happy being alone and it's just the way I feel inside, that I'm happier. Yeah, so it doesn't really matter to me [being in Charlie]. I'm dealing with my time better now.

Doris also said she preferred the four tiers in Charlie: "There's only three rooms at a time [that are released into the common area], and I like that [because you] don't have to communicate with all the other girls. Oh, some of the girls I don't even like in my range. Some girls don't even like me. I'm getting along good right now."

Christine spent most of her time in her cell listening to music and writ-ing a journal. "I just keep to myself. If I have good roommates I'll talk to them [but] I don't share too much. 'Cause I don't want to put [too much on them] 'cause they have their own stuff, you know, every woman has their own stuff. I don't know what's in their past unless they want to share, right." But Christine also said that when she was let out into the common area of the unit on the hour-long break she became a different person: "In my room I keep to myself, I'm more calm and quiet. And then when I come out I put on this mask where I'm loud and I'm hyper and I'm just, like, out of there. I'm just glad to be out of my room 'cause all that, I leave all that negativity in that room and I come out feeling different."

One of the reasons that Christine "puts on a mask" is that "I don't want women to know my weaknesses and to use those weaknesses on you in here. 'Cause once they know that they can use that on you. I know that, I've seen it, you know what I mean?" Christine elaborated on why the women use this strategy:

> To make themselves feel better, I think. You know what I mean? Like, just throughout the day you need something to make you feel good through the day, get you through the day or you feel powerful or —

> [It's a power move?]

> Yeah, exactly. That's what it is, you know, these bigger women. And I'm small, you know what I mean. So my smallness, I have a loud voice for it. And that's my advantage where I can defend myself with my words.

Christine's strategy seemed to work. She had "only fought once [since] being locked in here," and, she said, she didn't like doing that. She "made amends" with the woman.

> We talked it out when we were in the hole. I said, "Holy, man. You came behind me and tried to fight me. We're women. We should have talked about it. Like, be friends. We're supposed to be friends." "I'm sorry. Ooh, my god. I let everything get to me. I just wanted to fight." I was like, "Well that wasn't the way. You should have just talked to me, you know what I mean." But, whatever. We both got to let out some anger.

Despite the drama, the gossip, and the conflicts that can break out, the women do draw upon each other for support. As Carol commented: "These women in here are teaching me." A lot of them, she said, had been in something of the same situations as she had. "And it made me feel that I wasn't alone, like, really, really alone anymore. I just didn't know or wasn't allowed to know how to get help. Yeah. And then these women are, I learned a lot from these women."

The older women especially are able to gain the respect and trust of the younger women. Janice explained:

> I think for me it's because they see I'm older. And a lot of them

— and some of the women know where I've been or they know me. So it's a respect, I guess. I'm their voice in there, in Bravo I'm their voice. The girls come to me. I remember a girl was calling me her case manager. She says, "You do more for me than my own does.... You're the one that shows me how to fill stuff out, how to word it and stuff like that." And I'm like, "Yeah."... You know, these girls come to me because they want to know what they might get. "Well, I'm not a lawyer but I'll tell you what I think from what I know, from what I've seen and heard over the years. This is what I think might happen." So they trust me on that part.

Tina saw herself as taking on a particular role with the younger women:

I get along pretty good with all of them, most of them. There is a couple that I don't really like. But, I mean, I think I'm the oldest one in here in our unit. So a lot of them respect me.... There's a few that are kind of rude and stuff. But I think because I'm the oldest they — and I want them to respect me so I have to respect them.... I'm like a role model, a mother that, you know, my room-mates — it's like, "Agh, I can't stand it when it's dirty in here." And even if something's on the floor, if somebody spills something, a lot of them just leave it there. I'll go and wipe it up. And I'm trying not to do that as much because I shouldn't have to pick up after them. But as a mother —

As a way of resisting the conditions of their confinement — especially in Charlie, where they are locked in their cells for the better part of the day — the women sent "kites" to each other across the unit to the cells on the other side. Jessica explained how the kites work: "Floss and a soap and a note inside of it and you throw it across the range and get it in a room.... You just throw them, throw them on the floor and they slide."

As Christine noted, sending kites was a way of being sociable, of connecting with other women in the unit. But getting caught ran the risk of being labelled a troublemaker and could result in administrative charges, leading to a longer sentence and time in the hole.

I'm trying to make my way to a unit where I could be out and socially connect with everybody, instead of sneaking and trying to pass a kite here and there. That's what gets me in trouble. You're trying to talk to another inmate, another person — 'cause I don't

like calling women inmates — another person and then sliding
them a kite. And then I'm getting busted, you know what I mean?
Or talking to another tier. That's why I have a hard time making my
way on this side. Because I want to — I'm a people person, I'm very
sociable, you know what I mean? I'm an outgoing person. That's
my personality. And I like to talk and socialize. And it's so hard to
socialize with a little small group. Or when I have other friends,
other girls I'm friends with in the unit, and I can't talk to them
'cause I'm getting in trouble for talking to them.

While many of the women adopted the strategy of keeping to themselves
and doing their own time, this strategy was not always possible. Natalie was
aware that "what anybody does in this unit affects everyone."

I haven't done anything wrong here. But other girls do. They pass
kites.... They sneak into each other's rooms. They yell around at
night, all night. I don't even talk to anybody. I barely come out
of my cell when we are allowed out. So I don't want to associate
with anybody. I don't want to be labelled as a troublemaker. And,
unfortunately, I have two other girls that live in my cell. And they
pass kites and they get caught. Because I'm not ratting them out,
then I'm involved.

Natalie recounted one incident where she was being held to account for
the actions of her cellmates:

A couple of weeks ago one of the girls snuck her girlfriend into our
room. And I didn't know that. I was bringing back my tray. She was
already hiding under the desk. And as soon as I walked in and they
closed the door behind me, I seen her. And I said, "Oh, guys, I'm
trying to get to Kilo. You're going to get us all in trouble." But you
don't rat people out in jail. So I laid down on my bunk. I faced the
wall. I did what I was supposed to do. I was where I was supposed
to be. But again, because I didn't buzz the guards and tell them that
she was in there, then I'm just as guilty. So that gave me another
month in here.

Natalie was also aware of the contradictory ways in which "risk" plays
out in the prison. She talked about her parole officer explaining to her how
they assessed risk levels, "a risk to reoffend."

And I'm somewhere between medium and high risk because of my unhealthy relationships and the fact that I — the way they see it is I'm in jail because I did illegal things to help my partners or my friends or, in essence, been taken advantage of, is how they're putting it. And, yeah, to some degree, yeah. I mean, I wouldn't have been selling drugs if it wasn't to help [her friend who had died] [blows her nose]. I never would have started. My mom was addicted to cocaine. I never would have got involved with that. And if I didn't need more money to take care of [her friend] and his kids and his family — there's a lot of money in that, you know.

In risk-management terms, Natalie is responsible for addressing her own risk to reoffend. Yet she is also held responsible for the actions of other prisoners. As she put it: "Apparently it's my responsibility to contribute to a healthy institutional community and to let the guards know when other people are doing wrong, when I thought I was just supposed to for once worry about myself and govern myself accordingly."

RELATIONSHIPS WITH CORRECTIONAL OFFICERS

The women must negotiate relationships not only between themselves but also with the correctional officers. The differing power positions in the relationship with the officers are visibly demarcated by each group's attire. While the women wear loosely fitting grey pants and tops, white socks, and plastic slip-on sandals, the correctional officers are neatly dressed in fitted navy blue uniforms and black leather shoes. Much like in the military, rank is visible on the officers' uniforms. The women are aware of the hierarchy that exists among the correctional officers. For instance, the women call the Senior Unit Officers the "three stripers" based on the stripes on the shoulder of their uniforms. As Jessica noted, "They get to say what will happen."

The contradictions between prison as a site of punishment and a site of rehabilitation come to the foreground in the women's relations with correctional officers. As guards, they determine the regular routines of the unit (such as whether the women are allowed outside on a particular day). They also enforce the rules of the institution, which sometimes means using force to do so. Those correctional officers acting in the role of case managers, however, are also charged with providing counsel, support, and encouragement for the women. The women's accounts reflected these contradictory roles of correctional officers — as keepers and as helpers.

Several of the women found correctional officers who were supportive and helpful. Doreen said of her case manager: "He's a really good case manager and he's kind of like a father figure that I don't have. Yeah, he's really good that way." Carol talked about how one of the guards had offered helpful advice: "This one guard, [her name], she's very nice." When Carol "told her a little bit what was going on," the guard said, "You know, you've got to think about you, too." As Carol said, "I've never thought about myself. I never took time for myself. And she said, 'Maybe this is' — how did she say it again? — 'I'm forced to take care of myself in a way in here, even if it is in here.'"

Similarly, Jennifer spoke about the insights she gained from her case manager in terms of making connections between her use of drugs and violence and her trauma experiences:

> She said me being high and doing all those violent things, I was letting all that buried stuff come out. And she said the only way I could let it come out was because I was high and I had no control over myself. And I never grieved, either. After something bad happened to me, I let it happen and then it was done. And I'd just go on with the next day, you know, until something bad happened again. And I never talked about it or tried to heal.... I didn't want to blame what happened to me on the things I did. But she made me realize, like, "That is part of the reason why you did what you did because you were hurt and you hurt somebody else. Yeah, you were high. But that's when you had the courage to do it was when you had that" — what did she say? [pause] — like, the drugs made me have no awareness, just do it, who cares, you know. No conscience, I guess.

> But she said, "No matter what you do in life, after you forgive yourself and forgive people what they've done to you, then you can go on." And I have been able to go on. But I've talked with her so many times and after she gave me so many scenarios of how someone will just hurt somebody for nothing, she's like, "That's what happened to you. You didn't do anything to get hurt." And she made me realize the things that affected me in life is what I did to those people. But I'm not forgetting that I hurt them. I'm recognizing that I was wrong, that I shouldn't have did it. And it's not only my fault. It's the things that have happened to me.

Other women expressed a keen awareness of the power dynamic that plays out between the prisoners and their keepers. Heather commented:

> It's very military here. I've heard that term quite a bit since I've been here. And it's when they want to do what they feel like doing. It's not when you think you should get whatever. And the new guards, too, they're very — ignorant. It's like they've only been working here a month and as soon as they walk on the range they're already sick of you. It's like, "You haven't even been working here long enough to not like me."

The women also believed that the treatment received from the guards differed according to the unit they were housed in. Molly thought the guards were "kind of stricter" in Charlie than in Alpha or Bravo, where "they're more lenient and nicer. I don't know why they're like that in Charlie." Molly's strategy for dealing with the guards was to "just ignore them. 'Cause, I don't know, it's something to do with them, not me. I think they were bullied when they were younger [chuckles]."

Janice's main challenge in doing time was interacting with the guards:

> It's always with the guards. That's where I get stuck here. I know to mind my Ps and Qs but with the guards sometimes it's hard. And I think it's because they're younger than me … and I try to do it the respectable manner but sometimes it gets taken out of context. And so they punish me for it. And I try to tell them, too, like, "I'm not trying to undermine you and I'm not trying to put you in your place or centre you out. I'm just stating my opinion." But sometimes I'm too opinionated. And I know that.

How the guards specifically chose to interact with the women was also a matter of concern. Helen commented on the language used:

> They swear at us here, you know what I mean. The guards actually swear at, just look down at us.
>
> [What do they say?]
>
> I don't know. They say, "Fuck this, fuck that." They talk like that. And not all of them are like that but some of them, the men are like that, hey. They have no respect for women. They just, I don't know. I don't like half of the guards here. They're kind of disrespectful.

It seems like no matter where we stand, us women, we're always being — we shouldn't be treated like that. We're already doing time, you know what I mean. We're missing our family, you know. And they still treat us, like, you know.

Alicia maintained that the guards "do some stuff that is uncalled for."

For instance, yesterday I asked for Tylenol 'cause I had a deadly headache. And they come to the door and they gave me Tylenol and they slam that thing shut, really hard. And in a little cell that's really loud. And isn't it common sense? "Hey, this person's asking for Advil. Hey, this person has a headache. Maybe I should shut the thing quietly." They don't think like that. And I think it's wrong to treat people like that, just because we're wearing grey. I think it's wrong to mistreat people.... I find it's very wrong and they do that a lot of times.

Margaret put the guards' treatment of the women in a broader context: "You know, you have women who grew up in abuse, getting yelled at their whole lives. And then you have guards come in here yelling at them. You know what I mean? It belittles them. They don't feel safe."

In the same way that difference and diversity are prominent among the women held at the WCC, the women see marked differences between the guards. As Maureen commented: "Some of them are just ignorant and they shouldn't have the job that they have. And then you get other ones that are great, you know. Some of them are great guards. They treat us like we're not children, we're women, you know. Some of them [the prisoners], yeah, you bet they act like children, but not all of us do." Alicia made a similar distinction:

Some guards are super, super nice and some guards are respectful, you know. They look at us like, "Hey, I'll treat you as a human being, just treat me the same way." You know what I mean? And that's understandable. You should treat people the way you want to be treated. But there's some guards, they walk around here like their shit don't stink. They're on the good side of the line so they treat us like shit. They'll sit there and they won't talk to us and they'll just mean mug us and just treat us like a piece of shit. And it's not good. And when we do try to string up a conversation with them, they'll totally just shut us down. It's just like a slap in the face. When you're trying to say, "Oh, good morning" to them or something they'll look at you like you're disgusting and just walk away. There's guards like that.

Natalie said some of the guards were "really nice," but that they were not generally allowed to practise good relations with the prisoners:

> They get in trouble for being kind to us. And they've told us that, you know. So most of the time we're really disrespected and treated really badly. And I was told if I want to be respected I shouldn't have come to jail, which I don't understand because I'm still a human being. And I figure as long as you show respect, you should get respect. But all we ever hear is, "You're wearing grey and I'm wearing blue. So you do what I say."

Not surprisingly, then, the existing power dynamic was difficult to overcome.

MAINTAINING RELATIONSHIPS ON THE OUTSIDE

Overriding the women's relationships with each other and with the guards was their concern for relationships on the outside, especially with their children. Christine had not seen her children for some time, and that, she said, was "painful." "Are they going to forget about me? Are they going to stop loving me? You know, they're going to be mad at me and disappointed. They're going to have those feelings to me, the feelings I had towards my mom, you know. I never ever wanted that." Brenda also worried for her children: "As long as I know my kids are okay then I can sit here and do my time. I think the only thing that makes my time hard is when my kids are having hard times. And that's what makes it hard for me. But if I know they're okay then I'm okay. I can do my time just as long as they're okay."

The main form of contact that the women have with the outside is the phone, but the institution's rules of engagement limit that contact. At the time I visited, the restrictions included limits on long-distance calls and a PIN system of only eight numbers, which were later changed. The prisoners were also only allowed ten minutes per phone call. As Margaret told me, "It's hard for some people, right. A lot of the women out there [in the unit] have family that have criminal records. They can't put them on their PIN because of that. So they don't really have anyone to talk to. You have a lot of women come in from out of town. They can't have out of town numbers on the phone so that really sucks. I feel sorry for those girls."

Another source of contact with the outside is through arranged visits. The WCC features a visiting area. While some of the visits have to take place in a room with a glass partition between the prisoner and the visitor, others can occur in a larger room where prisoners can sit with their visitors. A play area with toys is also provided when children come to visit. Some of the women, however, found visits with their families too difficult in prison. Alicia said, "I would never let my kids see me here." Brenda talked about how hard the visits were for her daughter, especially since no contact is permitted:

> 'Cause when she used to come and visit me, I don't know, she used to cry when she used to see me come in. 'Cause there's a guard there watching us and — some of the guards wouldn't even let me hold her hand. Whereas she's used to us hugging and everything all the time. And here I couldn't hold her or hold her hand or nothing. So she was crying when I'd come in and crying when I'd leave. It was hard on her.

Annette was more resigned about the visits with her kids, deciding that the time she got — an hour every two months — was "better than nothing."

> I like it but then I don't like it because I can't take them outside, they can't eat lunch with me and stuff, right. And my daughter one day she's like, "I'm hungry mom." I was like, "Yeah, you guys will be leaving soon." And she's like, "But I want to eat lunch with you." And it's like, "Well, you can't." And then they asked me for money for the vending machines. I don't even got money. I was like, "I'm not allowed to have money." I don't know if they know where I am. They've never brought it up with me or nothing. Like, they're old enough to know what jail is, right. They're five and seven so they know what jail is and whatever and they've never brought it up to me, so. I'm pretty sure they know where I am, though, 'cause on one of the first visits too — a guard won't sit in the exact same room but they'll sit in a room and observe and watch or whatever ... — the guard walks them out and my daughter asked him, "Are you a policeman?" and I think he said, "Yeah." She's, "Well, where's your gun?' I was like, "Holy crap. Little snotty kid with her attitude" [laughs].

The trauma the women encountered on the outside, including the trauma of loss and grief, continued during incarceration. While she was at the WCC Brenda's brother died. She was allowed to attend his funeral, and her children and other family members were there too, including her eighteen-year-old son, whom she hadn't seen for almost a year.

> They only kept me there maybe ten, fifteen minutes. Just enough time to pay my respects. And then I was out of there. And I was shackled and everything. So I just had enough time to hug him [her son] and then I was back into the van and back here. So I didn't even spend much time with my family, to grieve with them a little bit. And my daughter was crying and I had to tell my son to hold her 'cause she was trying to chase after me. And I think they, the guards must have panicked because my nephews and all them were starting to arrive and they're gang members. And they're big. They're huge [laughs]. So they must have panicked 'cause I was only in there, the longest I'd say fifteen minutes, not even that. I went up to the coffin and paid my respects and then I was out of there.
>
> That church was packed. So I didn't have much time with my family. To grieve with them. I barely even had a chance to talk to them. They all hugged me and then I went up to the casket and I sat down and they're already telling me we had to go. And my kids just got there when they were taking me out.

Thinking back on that experience, Brenda recalled, "It was hard. It's hard to lose somebody when you're locked up in here. You can't grieve with your family [pause]. It's really hard [pause]."

MEETING THE WOMEN'S NEEDS

While the women's prisoning includes the challenges of doing time in spaces of confinement, negotiating relationships with the other women and with correctional officers, and maintaining relationships with those on the outside, it also presents the challenge of engaging in self-governance. As Alan Petersen (1996: 48–49) notes, neo-liberalism "calls upon the individual to enter into the process of their own self-governance through processes of endless self-examination, self-care, and self-improvement." Under the rubric of neo-liberal risk management, the women prisoners are expected to undertake their own self-transformation and to heal from their lived experiences of trauma so that, on their release, they will no longer be the risky subjects who pose the same threat to social order that they were on their entry to the institution. What are the prospects of successfully undertaking such a project in prison?

A basic feature of undertaking self-governance is maintaining physical health and well-being. Prisoners have been found to have a higher likelihood of experiencing chronic health problems than are people in the general population (Nolan and Stewart 2017; Zendo 2015; Chesnay 2015). From a social determinants of health perspective (McGibbon 2017; Raphael 2010; Vigianni 2007), such findings are not surprising given that individuals who end up incarcerated are also more likely to come from circumstances of complex poverty and social exclusion. When added to the mix, the lived experience of trauma heightens the potential for health problems. Nevertheless, while the women may bring chronic health issues with them into prison, prisoning itself is also a health issue.

Much has been written about the health of women prisoners and the move to develop "health promotion" initiatives in prison (see, for example, Smith 2000; Sim 2005). Less attention has been paid to the ways in which incarceration promotes ill health. While the conditions of confinement and the challenges of doing time generate stress and "dis-ease," the access to basic needs, including food, exercise, and fresh air, also has an impact on health. The women at the WCC were not convinced that those needs were being adequately met.

One woman, Natalie, bluntly said the food served was terrible. "I've had French fries and burgers and greasy food nineteen times in May. Like, that's a lot." Heather also commented on the quantity and quality of the food: "They put lots of food on the trays and everything is deep fried." Like many of the women, Susan gained a lot of weight during her incarceration: "I really don't like eating the food here." She said, "All this weight is just from being in here.... A person can gain five pounds a week just eating the food in here." Alyson mentioned that she had gained twenty pounds in jail and was now "the biggest I've ever been." Heather talked about how food was a way of dealing with the boredom — and a source of comfort — in prison: "You're hungry all the time because there's nothing to do. You just sit and play cards and eat. And I do a lot of eating. Sometimes I eat 'cause I'm upset [chuckles]. I try not to."

Coupled with the food was the lack of physical exercise. As Heather said: "I don't do anything. I don't move. I sit and play cards all day." Part of the difficulty is that the women in Charlie Unit are locked in their cells for twenty-one hours of the day. While the women have access to the adjacent exercise room while they are out of their cells, the time is limited. According to Heather:

> We have a Wii [video game console], we have a treadmill, and we have an elliptical [workout machine]. And it's that small room right there [points]. And only four girls are allowed to go at a time. And it's very crowded. And you really don't get to work out much, especially if someone doesn't want to give you the treadmill, you know. If they want to spend their forty-five minutes on that then you're stuck doing whatever's left lying around. And there isn't a lot. They have one mat that they throw on the ground that you can work out on and that's about it.

Adding to the difficulties of access, the machines were often broken.

If they couldn't get food or exercise, what about fresh air? Going outside is often at a premium — it depends of the availability of staff (and under-staffing is an issue) and the "behaviour of different girls." Natalie said that in Charlie, "They take some of the tiers outside [but] my tier hasn't been outside in—I couldn't even tell you how long [chuckles] .... Unfortunately, if one person misbehaves we all get punished. So it doesn't really happen." Jessica indicated, "In the hole you can go outside whenever you want and on your break. Yeah, without anybody with you." But even then there was nothing to do once outside but "just stare at the walls, I guess." Alicia described the outside area in Secure as "a little square box with a cage over top and it's all cement around." Jody described Alpha's outdoor area: "It's a very small yard, there's just one basketball net and they finally just gave us two picnic tables. Before that we just sat on the ground, yeah." Jackie, who was also in Alpha, said that the women were allowed outside for half an hour. While they were there they would "just sit there and look outside [chuckles]. Just sit there."

The paradox, then, is that under a neo-liberal correctional model, the women become responsible for their own self-governance, including their physical health, but have limited choices and little control over the conditions under which they are to undertake that project. In addition to maintaining their physical health and well-being, however, the women are expected to engage in their own self-improvement and rehabilitation.

When it was in operation, the PCI offered a number of resources for the women being held there: drug and alcohol counselling, community work programs, Adult Basic Education courses, a parenting skills course, and courses on anger management and assertiveness training. An Elder conducted a sharing circle and sweetgrass ceremonies and was available for individual counselling. The prison chaplain presided over church services and religious teaching and counselling. Case managers worked with the women to develop their individualized programs and pre-release plans, and a psychiatrist attended the prison one morning a week. One of the case managers also ran a program called "Abuse Hurts," which enabled the women to begin to understand the impact of abuse experiences on their lives.

The WCC offers a wide range of resources. A separate area hosts a medical unit where a nurse is on staff and a doctor and dentist visit regularly. Case managers work with the women to develop their correctional and pre-release plans. A psychologist (for counselling) and psychiatrist (for assessment, diagnosis, and prescription medication) are also available to meet with the women. While the psychologist is a full-time position (five days a week), the psychiatrist visits the facility twice a week for four hours. An Elder meets individually with the women, and a cultural facilitator holds sharing and drumming circles. A teacher and tutors work with women who are upgrading their education. A chaplain offers religious services and guidance. A variety of programs are also available. In addition to a Positive Parenting Program (Triple P), gender-responsive programming is offered, including: Beyond Trauma, a program based on cognitive behavioural therapy and designed for trauma treatment; Helping Women Recover, a program for women who abuse alcohol and other drugs; Domestic Violence Treatment for Abusive Women, which draws on dialectical behavioural therapy concepts to address the ways in which women can manage their aggression; and Emotions Management for Women, which aims to raise cognitive awareness and emotional self-awareness. In addition to group meetings, the women can work their way through workbooks on a variety of topics on their own time. Outside groups and volunteers also come into the prison to offer programs, support, and education. These extras include: the Elizabeth Fry Society, which works with the women to prepare them for their release; Alcoholics Anonymous meetings, for women with alcohol and drug addictions; Open Circle, which connects volunteers with individual women to act as mentors; and Walls to Bridges, which runs a university course that brings students from the outside into the WCC to attend the course with students on the inside (see Pollack 2014). As well, twice a year the WCC hosts a Resource Fair in the rotunda that features some seventy-five agencies and organizations to inform the women of the resources available to them in the community. On the face of it, then, it would seem that the WCC provides the women with everything they need to engage in their own self-improvement and rehabilitation.

Many of the women commented that they had benefited from the resources being offered. Dianne was upgrading her education: "Now that I'm doing my Grade 10 upgrading, I'm actually finding out that I'm pretty smart, you know [chuckles]." Molly had taken the Positive Parenting Program: "It was really good. I learned a lot of stuff. It's made me think of things differently, how I raised my son." Cheryl said, "The only thing that's good about being in here is, yeah, the programs. I went to the abusive ones. I did that booklet, it's called Adult Survivors from Child Abuse. I did that one for myself. I did the ones on addiction. And the beading." Bernice was taking the Helping Women Recover program: "It's helping me, I guess, cope. I'm just letting a lot of things out, just so I can feel a lot better about myself. And it's helping a lot, I find." Mary said she got "a lot of grieving support, I mean, I talk to a nurse about everything, everybody I lost." Jackie talked to the chaplain and the psychiatrist: "I get therapy in here." In addition to meeting with Elizabeth Fry workers to plan their release, several women also spoke about their involvement in the Open Circle mentorship program. As Dianne described it, "It's a healthy relationship that can kind of like help you through this and then help you at the community. It would be like a support, a friend, right."

Many of the women also benefited from the access to their Indigenous culture while incarcerated, especially the chance to sing, drum, smudge, and engage in sharing circles. Maxine talked about the singing: "Actually, it does help. Singing and stuff, those traditional songs is what helps the most. Yeah. Because when you are singing those songs, they're spiritual songs so I feel like my family members who passed on come there. So, yeah, that stuff helps." Mary spoke about the drumming, "It's very refreshing and very invigorating, I guess. It cleanses my mind and everything like that." Natalie commented on the smudging and sharing circles: "So I'm really glad I'm in this program now because it's Aboriginal-based and we smudge and we have a sharing circle. We get to talk and, you know, they all have been really good about listening to my broken heart, I guess [chuckles]." Helen, who was "raised traditional," works closely with the Elder.

> She comes and gets me for one-on-one where I can — I think
> that's where I always vent with her when I have — 'cause I know
> she'll come and see me 'cause she knows, you know, I need to talk,

right. So we'll sew and talk. She brings her blankets and then we hand sew star blankets and then I can vent while I'm sewing, right. 'Cause that's the way I know how to, like, it's one other way that I do it, you know.

Although some of the women spoke positively about their access to resources, other women were more critical. Part of the problem may well stem from overcrowding. With so many women, the resources are thinly spread. As well, the WCC shares similar characteristics with other large organizational structures. The women who had the experience of being incarcerated at the smaller PCI were aware of the difference. As Dianne noted, "I would say being in Portage is like being in Delta…. It was more, a little more one-on-one, it was a little bit more caring, it was a little bit more, less expectation, it was more relationship, you know…. It was more a group-home setting." Janice had also spent time in the PCI, which she said had "more [of] a cozy feeling." In contrast, she found the WCC to be "very institutional. Cameras, guards, so many policies, procedures, and rules in this place. It makes your head spin."

In keeping with the bureaucratic nature of a large organization, to get access to resources the women have to submit request forms, which tend to require long waits to get results. As Jackie noted:

It's so hard to get stuff in here 'cause you have to go through all this shit … you have to fill out requests. And they do it on their time, everything's slow here. And look, I've been trying to get glasses. I get migraines and headaches 'cause I can't see, everything just looks really fuzzy. And I've been putting in request after request. I even tried to, I think of going to [the] Ombudsman. This is ridiculous already. I get migraines because I can't see and I've been here almost a year already, well a year, thirteen months I've been here, and nobody's even come to see me. Not even a denied. At least deny me, you know.

Jackie was also frustrated by the lack of access to the doctor because "you have to put in a request for that too…. So it's always through request forms. So, yeah, when you want to talk to someone [it's] through request forms, request forms, request forms. Sometimes they never get answered."

Access to counselling also appears to be at a premium. Tina indicated, "I'm trying to get in to see the psychiatrist and the psychologist. And I put in a request over two months ago and I still haven't seen them." Donna had a similar experience: "I've asked *repeatedly* to see the psychologist or the psychiatrist and I've been waiting since March [four months]. And I haven't been able to see them…. They tell me that it's a long lineup and there's one, I don't know, I call her the 'gatekeeper,' mental health nurse that you have to see before you can see them. And she decides if you need to see them or not." Margaret did manage to get access to counselling. "When I was seeing the counsellor, I was only seeing him for ten minutes at a time. I saw him three times. I just stopped seeing him because it was just no good." Jody also commented: "I saw the psychologist here for the first time two months ago. I've only seen him twice, and he's kind of a general[ist] 'cause he sees so many people, right."

While the women's access to therapeutic counselling may be limited, some found that the situation was an improvement over what was available on the outside. Lori was able to see the psychiatrist at the WCC once a week. By comparison, "I could go two to three weeks without seeing my psych on the outside and the most you can see them is once a week. So I'm getting more care in here than I ever was out there 'cause there's so many more people out there and they can shuffle through people in here." Lori also commented on the medications she was receiving for her mental health issues while incarcerated:

> I've been trying to get help for years but I've never been in one place long enough to get a proper diagnosis, for anyone to get a real diagnosis to be able to medicate me properly. Since I've been here is been the first time I've been able to sit still long enough to have enough people —
>
> [To give you that support.]
>
> Yeah, yeah. This is the most, the farthest I've gone in my medications and stuff in here.

Nevertheless, the dispensing of psychotropic medications in women's prisons is a contentious issue. Women receive more prescriptions for all types of medications than men do, and specifically for psychotropic medication. Women prisoners are prescribed medications at a higher rate than are women in the general population (Langner, Barton, and McDonagh 2002; Sim 2005; Kilty 2012). As Jennifer Kilty (2012: 163) notes, "The broader societal trend of over-prescribing psychiatric medication … to generate a biological fix to the social ills affecting our lives is even more widespread in prison."

One Canadian study on the dispensing of prescribed medications to federally incarcerated women found that — excluding over-the-counter medications (such as acetylsalicylic acid (ASA), acetaminophen, or antacids) — 80 percent of the 306 women had medication orders, with an average of 3.1 orders per woman; 42 percent of those orders were for psychotropic drugs and half (51 percent) of those women were prescribed two or more psychotropic medications. Regional differences were also found, with the Prairies — where a large percentage of the incarcerated population is Indigenous — showing the highest rate of medication orders (Langner, Barton, and McDonagh 2002). An August 2013 snapshot of federally sentenced women found that 63 percent were prescribed some sort of psychotropic medication (OCI 2014: 21). Another study indicated that Correctional Service Canada spent $20 million on prescription drugs in 2012/13 (OCI 2014: 19). Although similar data are not available at the provincial level, if the long lineups for the meds cart that I witnessed during my visits are any indication, similar practices are occurring at the WCC.

Sarah talked about her experience with prescription medications at the Edmonton Institution for Women:

> They had me on all kinds of pills when I was in Edmonton too, right. There's another story. They had drugged me up so bad that I said, something clicked in me and said, "They're trying to do something to you" [chuckles]. But honestly, there's some people that come out of Edmonton and they're not the same anymore. They're schizos because of all the pills. And they had me on fifteen pills, man, different kind of depression and this and that, all downers. And I hated pills. I just threw out my pills.

Sarah said: "I don't want to be on pills. I think there's better ways of dealing with things than being dependent on pills. Pills I just hate. I always try to talk the girls out of it. I says, 'Why do you want to take [pills] just because you can't sleep?'" Natalie held the same view: "There's one psychiatrist that works here. Everybody that goes to see them comes back on medication. I don't want to be on pills. I don't think I need to be. I just need somebody to listen to me."

For some of the women, the medications prescribed only worsened their mental health. Wanda found, "The meds that they were putting me on were making me even more depressed and angry and I wasn't feeling like myself." Doreen had been prescribed two different kinds of antidepressants,

Fluoxetine and Amitriptyline. She found that the drugs made her more aggressive.

> It put a seal on my feelings and there was cracks in that seal. And every time, yeah, like my sadness would slip out of that crack, it would come out hard. Whenever anger would slip out, BOOM! I was in Charlie, the Charlie Unit, and I was sent to Secure.... I was charged with threatening and intimidation on another inmate. And I spent eighteen days in the unit of Indigo [the hole] and had to work my way back to GP.

The irony here is that on the outside many of the women had turned to drugging and drinking as a way to self-medicate and cope with their trauma, which brought them into the criminal justice net. Yet, once incarcerated they are prescribed drugs in order to manage their thought processes and behaviours, which sometimes gets them into more trouble.

If finding "someone to listen" to them was difficult, the same held true in getting access to the programs. Maureen, who was held in Charlie, commented: "The tier that I was in, not a lot of programs are offered to that tier.... And we don't get very many programs offered to us at all, and if they do it's only one tier at a time, you know." Jody said that in Alpha, "There's not really anything. There's nothing here, really. They have little information sessions that one of the guards will put on for [a] half-hour. It's like a little booklet they'll read to you about stuff, like anger or bad relationships, you know. And they have AA every once in a while." Lynne noted that in Delta, "They don't have that much stuff here." Margaret also talked about the availability of programs:

> We'll have a program every three months or something, you'll go to school every three months or whatever. And you're not even guaranteed to get into a program because it's limited, right.... I think that there's not enough. I'd say if they had more people doing programs, say if they had a program every week, every other week, and people were getting into programs, people would learn more, you know what I mean. Instead of just sitting in the range playing cards and gossiping about each other and not really looking at ourselves.

Even then, some of the women who had managed to get into programs did not find them useful. Harmony had taken the Twelve Step program for alcohol addiction but commented, "It didn't help me though [chuckles]." Cyndi, who was serving a federal sentence, said she had "done everything" in terms of the programs. "I find them all the same [chuckles]. Once you did a couple you find that most of them are the same, but worded differently."

THE MEANING OF PRISONING

Given the contradiction between prison as a site of punishment and a site of treatment — as both punishing and empowering — it is not surprising that the women attached differing meanings to their experiences there. Primarily, though, those meanings are informed by the traumatic circumstances that the women were confronting in their lives on the outside.

For some of the women, prison represented an escape or break from the stresses they were encountering on the outside. Jessica said that being in prison, "I find that it makes me not worry about things. 'Cause out there I worry lots.... There's way more stress out there than in here. And I'd rather be in here." For other women, prison represented a refuge, a temporary reprieve from the threats encountered on the outside. That was the case for Carol:

> I feel safe from the outside. 'Cause nobody can hurt me again, you know, the way they hurt me. [Crying] There's always somebody watching you, watching out for you, like, the guards. I know that sounds crazy but — I actually sleep. I can actually eat. I said, "This is like the most healthy I've ever been." I'm not so worried about anything.

Still, she couldn't help adding, "I don't like it in here, either [chuckles]."

Like Carol, other women saw being in jail as a salvation from their trauma-filled lives, albeit one that was still troublesome. Annette was of the view that, "All in all I think jail kind of saved me. 'Cause the way my life was going, it was going pretty awful ... but I don't like jail." Wanda said being in prison was "keeping me away from all of the drugs and alcohol in that old lifestyle." But at the same time, "it's very stressful and it's very depressing."

At bottom, what brought the women to jail was their lived experiences of trauma. For so many of them, drugging and drinking had become their way of coping with that trauma and all of the accompanying feelings. Being incarcerated, the women found themselves in a state of sobriety (save for the psychotropic medications prescribed). Several of the women commented on what that sobriety had meant for them:

In here I see things clearer. I feel better now that I'm sober. (Cheryl)

I see things a lot more clearer. 'Cause I don't think you go through much of a withdrawal from smoking crack, you know, but it's just to get away from all that and to have my options open. (Maureen)

Being incarcerated, I've been sober for a year and it feels good. I can actually taste food. I wasn't able to, I don't know, it was no good the way I was living and my alcoholism was really bad. (Jackie)

With the clarity that comes with sobriety, some of the women were able to use their incarceration as a time to engage in self-improvement. Jackie and Tina spent time working on their anger. Jackie said that the first time she came to jail:

I used to be really intimidating, I would never be able to sit here and talk to you like this if it was my first time in here again. I was really frickin' mean. Girls were scared to approach me. And 'cause I've stuffed down all my anger and stuff and once I explode I get really mad. I've only exploded twice and twice I got charged and I got taken to the hole.

This time, over the year she had been incarcerated, Jackie had seen a change in herself: "I've changed, I've matured, I know how to handle my anger more and I'm more open to — inmates come talk to me 'cause I just listen. I don't give them advice. I just listen. And after that they're okay. People can approach me now. I was never approachable before. I was really angry at the world."

Tina had also been working on her anger issues, especially towards her mother:

I had a lot of anger … and even just now it's like I'm sitting here, I've taken an Anger Management course and I really feel like — I don't like being here but I really think this place has made me a better person. Just dealing with stuff, dealing with, like, I've been sexually abused by two of my brothers. And I forgave them a long time ago. I've been raped, abused, sexually abused by a lot of guys and I forgave them. But the one person I could not forgive was my mom. 'Cause she's the one, I felt like she's the one that was supposed to love me no matter what and she didn't. I thought she didn't.

Despite all of the challenges that come with doing time — the lack of control, the loneliness, the boredom, and the problematic access to resources — some of the women were able to take advantage of their prisoning as an opportunity to engage in self-examination or self-reflection. As Christine commented, being in jail "gives me a lot of time to think about … all the should of's, could of's, would of's, you know. All the what if's."

One way that some of the women have come to understand their imprisonment is by drawing on religion. Jackie said, "God put me here for a reason. He took me out of that life I was living and said, 'You've got to stop drinking,' you know. He put that in front of me, like, 'You *have* to stop drinking.'" Jennifer also credited God for bringing her to jail: "And from being here I can honestly say I'm happy that God brang me here because what if I would have ended up killing someone or what if I would have killed myself because [of] the path I was on? Because it was only a year that I was getting so badly into drugs. But I couldn't stop myself. Jail had to stop me from doing it." For Jennifer, being extracted from her life on the outside enabled her to begin the healing process: "And now that I'm here fully clean, no drugs in me at all, I'm healing. I'm actually healing from the things that have happened to me."

Ashley found God while she was at the WCC: "I had a spiritual awakening. And it was really, I think he brought me here for a reason because he's tired of me suffering out there." At one point, Ashley had been released on bail to a drug treatment centre, where she resided for eight months. "When I went to treatment I took that as an opportunity for me to try and figure out why I am the way I am and to take time to reflect." Ashley said the program "was really good. I did whatever I can to get the most of it. I didn't waste my time. We had addictions counsellors there so that helped a lot. And we had a therapist there. So I started talking about really deep things that happened to me. And, yeah, just kind of scratching the surface of the abuse that happened." But the healing process is an uneven one, filled with advances as well as setbacks. Ashley ended up breaching her bail conditions when she returned drunk to the treatment centre after being out on a pass. She eventually ended up at the WCC. "And it wasn't until I came here that I realized that God brought me here to try and make me better."

To "make herself better," Ashley used her experience of incarceration to engage in self-examination:

> I've gone through a lot of stuff in my life and I've come to know that what people have gone through really affects how they are today.

So being treated like that growing up I noticed I have a really [big] fear of rejection and my self-esteem isn't very good, so. And I've come to realize all this, you know, just by self-reflecting and start asking my questions, "Why am I like this?" or "Why do I think like this?" And try to figure a connection with some of the reasons why I could be like this.

Nonetheless, while self-examination produced insights into her troubles and how she came to be in her current position, it was not enough. As Ashley said, "Even knowing everything about where everything stems from, it's like, what do you do with that? … 'Cause otherwise naming the problems with yourself and seeing those things, it's one thing. But actually dealing with them and to change that pattern of how you've lived for so long, it's really hard. So it's a really hard cycle to try and break." Ashley's way of resolving that dilemma was to turn to God: "Nothing else was working for me. Trying to get better by myself, it's not working. So I just want to just give myself to my higher power now and let him take care of everything. So wherever God wants me to go, really [chuckles]. Yeah, just surrender, yeah. I've ran out of answers of how to try and help myself."

Surrendering to God was Ashley's answer to the impasse she found herself in, but her narrative also points to a fundamental problem encountered in framing the lives of criminalized women in individualized, neo-liberal risk-management terms. While the women are encouraged to engage in self-examination and self-improvement during their time in confinement, the sources of their trauma are *not* strictly individual or psychological, something that can be rectified by making change *within* the individual woman, in her thinking patterns. Such an approach uncouples the women's lived experience of trauma from its *sociological* basis, from the social conditions and larger systemic processes that generated and exacerbated their trauma. Mary was alive to this issue when she commented: "People come back to jail because they don't have a life out there, you know." Margaret described the women as being "stuck": "They get out, they don't have any family. They don't have that support. They don't know how to ask for help. So then they feel discouraged and they go back to doing drugs or committing crime." Whatever insights or resolve the women may gain during their time in custody, after they get out they still have to contend with the social sources of their trauma.

The women were well aware of the troubles that awaited them on their release. As Mary said, "I'm scared I'm going to go out there and fall right back in the same ruts." Jackie was also fearful: "I'm scared to get out. I want to get out but I'm scared. I have nowhere to go. And I'm scared to start drinking and spiral down, you know?"

On the outside, the women relied on drugging and drinking as a coping strategy to deal with their trauma experiences. While prisoning enforces sobriety, once released they have to contend with the ready presence and availability of drugs and alcohol. Maxine was worried about her ability to avoid drinking, given that alcohol will be all around her when she is released:

> I don't want to drink no more. But I'm an alcoholic so it's really hard to say. I can say "No" to a certain point where I'm sitting and everyone's getting drunk, and I'm like, "Okay, whatever." So that's going to be a hard thing for me, especially being around everyone, you know, [who] drinks. There's only the older people, like my grandpa and them, that don't drink. And all the other people, my family, drink. They drink a lot. And it's just, it's hard. So I'm going to try and work on that hard to stop drinking. Because I do recognize now that it's just trouble for me and it's always going to be trouble for me.

Even though Shannon had made the conscious decision of going to jail to break the downward spiral she was in because of her drug addiction, she was forthright about what would most likely happen on her release: "I'm probably going to get out and go get high." Janice, though, was more cautious: "Drugs? Hmm, the only thing I know is I don't want anything today.... I'm not craving today. I don't want anything today. But tomorrow, well, a whole different story." Jody wanted to quit doing drugs but was "scared" about what might happen when she got out: "If there's past friends that still do them, if I run into them, what if I get tempted, you know what I mean?" Sandra was also intent on not using drugs: "I don't like the dark places I've been when I was doing it." But staying away from drugs will be hard given her life on the outside: "'Cause I know a lot of people that do drugs. I know a lot of people that are in gangs. I know a lot of people that are in and out of jail all the time."

Maureen put this issue in a larger context, commenting on how the lifestyle associated with a drug habit becomes all-encompassing:

> It's not just the drugs that people get addicted to. It's the ritual of it all, you know. It's going on a date, getting the money, calling your dealer, opening the foils, getting your pipe ready. Like, it's all

of it. It's not just the drug itself, you know. So when you break the habit, yeah, okay, people can break the habit of the drug. But it's you [need] to break the habit of the lifestyle. So that's what the hard part is. It was everything. It was my whole life.

Adding to their troubles, the women's time in custody disrupted whatever supports and resources they had managed to secure on the outside. For many of the women, this disruption meant having to start all over after their release. Jessica was not sure where she would live. Before her arrest she had been living in a crack shack. "When I get out I don't even have, I don't know where I'm going to go stay. I don't want to go stay where I was staying or I'll just start doing drugs again." Susan said she was "going to have to start from scratch again."

> Every time I come in here all my stuff, my belongings, they go somewhere. People don't have respect for my fuckin' belongings or something. I come here and when I get out I spend all my money building up my stuff, my clothes, my makeup, my belongings, a lot of shit that I like to have and that. Yeah, I always have a lot of nice stuff. But then usually when I come here, when I get out, the people who I leave my stuff with, they have lost their place or my stuff goes missing or they don't know what happened to it. So every time I come here I start over.

Brenda also "lost everything" when she went to jail: "My house, everything. All my belongings, all my pictures. Everything I owned. I have nothing. The landlord threw everything out." Christine too "lost everything again. My mom came there. She rescued my pictures and my clothes and my shoes, sentimental things. But I lost my furniture and my bed and all that. So again I have to start from rock bottom."

Getting out also means overcoming the variable ways in which the experience of incarceration becomes imprinted on the women's minds and bodies (Shantz, Kilty, and Frigon 2009). Jackie resolved never to lock her doors: "I hate locked doors. When I get out of here I'm never locking my door [laughs]." She is also resolved to never wear grey clothing: "If you see grey every day you get sick of it. I swear to God, I'm throwing out all my grey clothes as soon as I get out."

Leaving behind the imprint of their incarceration experience is especially troublesome for the women for whom prisoning has become part of their "normal." Having spent the better part of their lives in the custody of different systems — the child welfare system, the youth justice system, and now the adult correctional system — they have become accustomed to being in institutional settings. Ellen said her life had "been pretty shaky the whole time growing up.... I was bouncing back and forth from foster homes, group homes, shelters, and whatever." She was also in conflict with the law from an early age. "I've been in the Youth Centre more [times] than I can count." Given that experience, Ellen found that she did not mind being locked up:

> When I first got here, it's funny 'cause I was up at admissions and that lady that was doing my intake, she asked me, she's like, "How come you seem so comfortable here?" And I was like, "I don't know." And then she's like, "How old are you?" And I told her I was eighteen. And she's like, "Oh, that explains it. You've been to the Youth Centre." And I was like "Yeah." And she's like, "Oh, I see." And then whatever. But when I first got here I didn't, I don't know, I'm so used to it. I don't really mind it. There's days where I find it tough and I have to be alone. But I'm so used to being in an institution or group-home settings where people come and go. It's easier for me to be locked up or in a group home or something like that.

Similarly, Shannon said, "By the time I was eighteen I'd been to every lockup in Winnipeg." She discovered, "It should really bug me more to be locked up than it does. It really should but it doesn't."

Ellen's and Shannon's comments reflect the experience of far too many Indigenous people. After all, colonialism has been, among other things, a story of their institutionalization, prompting many commentators — including the Supreme Court of Canada (*R v. Gladue* 1999) — to remark that prisons have become the new residential schools, the contemporary equivalent of what the schools represented for previous generations of Indigenous people (Jackson 1988–89; MacDonald 2016).

PRISON AS A HEALING PLACE?

The opening of the Women's Correctional Centre in February 2012 marked what many commentators had hoped would be a dramatic improvement in the treatment of incarcerated women in the province. There is no doubt that the physical structure of the WCC is an advance over the old Portage Correctional Institution. The planning that went into the design and the size of the building, however, underestimated the increasing number of women who would be held there. Similar to women's incarceration rates globally (Walmsley 2015), Manitoba has witnessed more and more women being taken into custody, especially women being held on remand awaiting their court dates. As a result, a facility designed to house 196 women is now regularly at 50 percent over its capacity.

Clearly, overcrowded conditions have had an impact on the women's experience of incarceration, including the ability of the prison management to provide access to counselling, programs, and other resources. It would be a mistake, however, to simply attribute the troublesome nature of the women's prison experience to overcrowding. While reducing the number of women being held at the WCC would probably improve upon that experience, the issue runs much deeper than just numbers.

Fundamentally, prison is about punishment. It is a space where "the mechanisms of power are being deployed" (Rabinow 2010: 18) and where time is the proverbial Groundhog Day, with its repetition of daily routines and the boredom that comes along with it. Under the terms of neo-liberal risk management, it is within this confluence of time and space that the women are expected to undertake their own self-governance, to manage their risk, to engage in self-improvement and self-examination; in short, to be empowered — which requires having control over one's life and the ability to make choices. Yet in practice the women in confinement have very little control in their day-to-day lives, including meeting basic needs such as food, exercise, and fresh air and negotiating their relationships with other prisoners and correctional officers. The paradox here is that so many of the women have histories of abuse. A key feature of abuse is the taking of control away from the person subject to it. In that sense, prisoning involves yet another manifestation or form of abuse.

To heal from their trauma the women need to gain control over their lives. How is this possible in an institution which, by its very nature, endeavours to control their lives in almost every detail, an institution in which punishment trumps empowerment? Pat Carlen (2004: 261) comments on the fundamental disconnect between prison as a healing place and prison as a site of punishment that has security as its primary concern:

> One of the commonly described characteristics of women prisoners is "low self-esteem." Is it possible to believe that any person's self-esteem would be enhanced by the regular strip-searching that women in prison undergo in the name of security? Similarly, with programmes designed to help women be more assertive or manage

their anger better. Prisoners are not expected to answer back or question rules. So much for self assertion! And as for anger? Is it not hypocritical to offer anger management techniques in a situation where strip searching and innumerable petty rules are such that they would be likely to try the patience of a saint?

Complicating the matter further is that the sources of the women's trauma are not strictly individual or psychological but *social*. Those sources reside in the social conditions and systemic processes that have contoured the women's lives on the outside. That some of the women understand their prisoning as a form of refuge or salvation tells us something about the difficulties and challenges of their lives on the outside. That some of the women have managed to engage in their healing process while they are incarcerated speaks volumes about their own resilience in the face of incredible adversity.

CHAPTER SEVEN

MAKING CHANGE

C learly, individuals need to be held accountable for their actions, especially when they do harm to others. The women at the Women's Correctional Centre *are* being held to account. They have been made subject to one of the most severe penalties available in our society: the loss of their freedom. At the same time, the women's narratives clearly indicate that they have ended up in this space of punishment and confinement as a result of the trauma experienced in their lives. Unless we attend to the social sources of that trauma, the cycle will only continue, with women coming back again and again to jail.

Although some of the women did manage to engage in their healing process while in confinement, the sources of their troubles ultimately remain outside the prison, promulgated by the processes and practices of the settler colonial, capitalist, patriarchal society in which they reside. The myriad dimensions of historical colonialism that involve systemic and individualized racism towards Indigenous peoples—the residential schools, the flawed treaty process, the Indian Act, the child welfare system—are the necessary backdrop for situating present-day conditions. In contemporary times, disparities in educational achievement, Indigenous child poverty, substandard living conditions, and chronic health problems stand as markers of the individual and collective trauma generated in First Nations communities. But these often remote and isolated communities are not the only sites in which trauma is being generated. The processes of capitalist globalization, deindustrialization, and suburbanization have concentrated a complex, racialized poverty in inner-city communities across North America. Winnipeg's inner city has been no exception. Indigenous people make up over one-fifth of the population of Winnipeg's inner-city communities, and the majority are living in poverty. The disruption caused by these impoverished social conditions takes its toll on families, reflected in the inordinately high percentage of Indigenous children being taken into the care of the child welfare system. This complex, racialized poverty also generates the conditions for violence to flourish, especially in relation to the trade in sex and drugs and the street-gang activity that prevail in inner-city communities, creating the conditions for further trauma.

The narratives of the women at the WCC reveal the numerous ways in which trauma has invaded their lives. Economic hardship, broken families, drugging and drinking, and violence became part of their "normal" as children. The trauma trail or "ripple effect" of the residential schools was also evident in their accounts. Grandparents, parents, and siblings had to deal with the flow of that experience; it spilled over into the women's lives in the form of physical, sexual, and emotional abuse. As the women entered their teen and adults years, their childhood trauma trails continued to have an impact. Exposure to the drug and sex trades and street-gang activity — with all the accompanying violence — led the women along a path of further trauma. So too did their sexual vulnerability and personal relationships stained by abuse. Many of the troubles that the women faced — violence in their intimate relationships, pregnancy and the demands of mothering, exploitation in the sex trade — they encountered *as* women and *because* they were women living in a patriarchal society. The trauma of grief and loss added to their troubles — marked by the untimely and often violent deaths of family members, friends, and other loved ones, and the loss of their children to the child welfare system.

As coping strategies, drugging and drinking were readily available options to deal with this trauma and the intense problems generated — strategies that nonetheless exacerbated the women's troubles and drew them into the criminal justice net, and into custody. Those same troubles and coping strategies are waiting for the women on their return to the community.

WHAT CAN BE DONE?

In his book *Firewater*, Harold Johnson (2016), a Cree lawyer with over twenty years' experience working in the Northern criminal court circuit, addresses the devastation brought about through the effects of alcohol in First Nation communities. Johnson maintains that the criminal justice system is woefully inadequate in dealing with the issue of alcohol. In a way similar to the point that Carol Smart (1989) makes about how law translates everyday experiences into legal relevances and then forms a judgment based on the tailored or scripted account, Johnson notes that the adversarial legal system produces an answer that "might be correct in law, but it rarely ever solves the problem" of alcohol — and that is because "law cannot look at the problem and all its relations" (pp. 53, 54). Johnson criticizes models that cast Indigenous people as victims of colonization or as lacking in any agency over their use of alcohol. His way forward is to question the "alcohol story" that predominates in colonial society, a story that represents alcohol as a "natural, normal, and necessary" product that can be used as "medicine to dissolve grief, or as a way to cope" (p. 105). Instead, Johnson suggests that a new story be created. He looks for a narrative premised on a life of sobriety and abstention from alcohol.

Johnston is skeptical about drawing connections between colonial trauma and the use of alcohol: "It attempts to explain the reasons but ends up creating excuses and continuing the problem" (p. 35). One difficulty with his analysis is that he treats colonialism as a historical artefact, as something of the past as opposed to a continuing process. While it would be a mistake to engage in a "culture of victimhood" that casts Indigenous people as being simply at the mercy of colonial powers, it is also the case that the trauma confronting Indigenous communities is a product of ongoing colonial relations. Sobriety may well constitute one tactic for dealing with those colonial relations, but finding a way forward requires also addressing the social conditions that produce the trauma and prompt Indigenous people to turn to alcohol as a coping mechanism. As Gabor Maté (2008) observes, addictions always originate in pain. The question to be addressed is not "why the addiction?" but "why the pain?" In short, without addressing the sources of the pain, the urge to resort to drugging and drinking will continue.

The assimilationist project of colonialism is a key component of the social conditions producing trauma in Indigenous communities. Colonial policies and practices — including the outlawing of spiritual and cultural practices and the government's intention to "kill the Indian in the child" by means of the residential school system — made concerted efforts to destroy Indigenous cultures. These attempts at forced assimilation and cultural genocide took their toll, leaving many Indigenous people alienated from their own histories and cultures.

One of the ironies to emerge from the women's accounts at the Portage Correctional Institution was that only after they were caught up in the criminal justice system were they able to receive access to the resources they needed to begin resolving their troubles. The same irony holds true for some of the women at the Women's Correctional Centre, especially in terms of gaining an awareness of their Indigenous cultures through drumming, singing, smudging, and sharing circles run by the cultural facilitator. Many of the women only learned about these cultural practices while incarcerated. Doreen, who was a traditional singer, noted, "I've got a Creator prayer song that the girls love hearing me sing. 'Cause they're only familiar with the songs they hear here." Doris was one of those women. When asked whether she was in touch with her culture, she responded: "I'm just learning it now when I came to jail."

In another project I worked on with Lawrence Deane, Larry Morrissette, and Jim Silver (Comack et al. 2013), we met with Elders to learn their views on Aboriginal street gangs and what they saw as a way forward to resolve the issues of violence, crime, and the drug and sex trades that surround the gangs. One of those Elders shared a teaching about a young boy who was looking for answers to the troubles in his community. The boy travelled in one direction, then another and another and another. Wherever he sought answers he found only more questions, along with the advice to return home. The Elder also spent time describing the traditional clan systems, which designated roles and responsibilities to individuals and tied them into their community.

What we heard the Elder saying to us was that Indigenous people — including the young men we met who were involved in street gangs — had lost their way and that the way forward was to go back and reconnect with their traditional identities, values, and ceremonies. The story of the young boy's quest took him in four directions, consistent with the symbolism of the medicine wheel. His quest was to find a way to heal and to create a better life for his community. In every direction that he searched, the boy was told that the answers lie within his community — that he needed to go back to the traditional values of love, respect, courage, honesty, wisdom, humility, and truth — and take on the clan responsibilities based on those values.

In essence, the Elder was telling a story of hope, of reclaiming identity as an Indigenous person. One of the women at the WCC voiced a similar viewpoint. Referring to the younger women at the WCC, Helen commented:

> These girls need their tradition, they need their Aboriginal Elder, they need to be taught their religion. That soothes me so good. And you know what? When I'm in a circle with these girls here they're totally different, you know. It just mellows them right out when they hear the drum, when they hear the music.

The Elder's story also represents the pathway of decolonization, which entails "coming to understand that the pain and misery that so many Aboriginal people have experienced and continue to experience are not a function of individual failings, but rather are the product of a historical process that caused great damage by severing almost all Aboriginal people, often forcibly, from their ways of being" (Comack et al. 2013: 3). Decolonization also involves Indigenous people reclaiming their identity by learning about their cultures and ways of being and participating in traditional ceremonies. But it is more than that. Decolonization means attending to material circumstances, creating healthy communities in which Indigenous people can safely live and thrive.

Non-Indigenous people are implicated in this process of decolonization. While Indigenous people need to take the lead in determining their way forward in the making of a decolonized future, non-Indigenous people have a role to play as allies, walking beside and not in front of or behind Indigenous people in their quest for change (Silver et al. 2006: 156). As the Truth and Reconciliation Commission (2015: 316) noted, reconciliation for the harms caused by colonial policies and practices requires the engagement of "people from all walks of life and at all levels of society." It involves personal, group, and community action, as well as action and commitment on the part of governments at all levels.

Trauma work, too, needs to be decolonized. For Anishinaabe scholar Renee Linklater (2014), decolonizing trauma work has a dual meaning. On the one hand, it insists on "the need to challenge the mainstream disciplines of psychiatry and psychology and their influences on healing and wellness in our communities" (p. 158). While "most of the imbalance and disharmony experienced by Indigenous people is a result of external colonial forces," a psychiatric diagnosis (such as PTSD) "too often pathologizes the person rather than the process that they experienced" (p. 160). On the other hand, decolonizing trauma work means advancing "principles of self-determination and community control in regards to Indigenous health in the context of healing" (p. 158). Primarily, to move out of and beyond the trauma trails of colonialism, Indigenous people "require healing practices that reflect Indigenous experience, worldviews and knowledge" (p. 45).

While the Western medical model focuses on illness and tends to treat the mind and body as separate entities, models that stem from Indigenous philosophies focus more on wellness. They adopt a "wholistic" approach that considers the spiritual, emotional, mental, and physical aspects of the person (pp. 21, 50fn). Rather than focusing on pathology and dysfunction,

Indigenous wellness models highlight strengths and resiliency: "the ability to withstand trauma and turmoil and be able to proceed with living and engaging in a productive life" (p. 25). Practising wellness involves creating balance and harmony in an inclusive and interconnected way (spiritually, emotionally, mentally, physically), "being in Creation" or looking beyond the self to relations with others and all aspects of life to understand your place and purpose within the universe. It means exercising care and compassion not only for one's self but also for family and community relations (pp. 74–78).

Decolonization, however, is at odds with the neo-liberal rationality that has taken hold in recent times. Neo-liberalism, with its ideals of self-reliance, efficiency, and competition to bolster a market-oriented, capitalist society, runs counter to the collective ideals of social citizenship embedded in decolonization. Nonetheless, neo-liberalism — and the risk discourse that accompanies it — is not cemented in the social fabric, nor is it an inevitable feature of correctional policies and practices. As Pat O'Malley (2010: 41) suggests:

> The terrain of risk is a good deal less stable than would be supposed by some of the more pessimistic and totalizing readings. Rather than imagining risk as "hegemonic" or as capable of only one reading, we need to take more seriously the idea that risk itself is a domain of struggle and also that its implications are not fixed or always foreseeable…. Resistance takes many forms, its success is neither guaranteed nor its outcomes knowable in advance.

Countering the damage that colonialism has caused in Indigenous communities involves resistance, including resistance to the neo-liberal ideals of how citizens should live their lives. Significantly, Indigenous peoples have always resisted the colonial intrusions into their lives — from the uprising of Louis Riel and his followers and the efforts of parents to shield their children from being taken to the residential schools to the standoffs at Ipperwash and Kanehsatake to the more recent Idle No More movement and the mobilization to take action around the issue of missing and murdered Indigenous women and girls (Palmater 2015; Green 2014; NWAC 2010a; Amnesty International 2004). Indigenous peoples have demonstrated incredible resilience in the face of the colonial onslaught and the trauma it has produced in their lives. As Nahanni Fontaine (2014: 129) comments: "We were not supposed to be here. Indeed, that was the plan so methodically and strategically executed. But despite every imaginable assault, we are still here and, in some capacity or another, flourishing." Rupert Ross (2014: 180) makes a similar point:

> Despite the astounding assaults on the mental, physical, emotional and spiritual health of so many aboriginal people, the majority are *not* in jail, nor are their lives swamped by addictions, violence and despair. While the rates of suicide, incarceration and addictions are indeed higher than in the non-aboriginal population, and call for concerted attention from everyone, we must keep in mind the remarkable truth that a much higher proportion of aboriginal people have found ways to keep the colonial onslaught from overwhelming them.

Then too, intersecting with colonialism and capitalism are the discourses and practices of patriarchy. One of the manifestations of patriarchy or male domination is the perpetuation of violence against women. The feminist movement has made great strides over the past few decades in naming that violence and calling for concerted action to address patriarchy in all of its manifestations. Nevertheless, the experiences of the women at the WCC point to the pressing need to continue that struggle for change. The women regularly encountered gendered violence not only in their homes and intimate relationships but also on the streets in the form of sexual exploitation in the sex trade and the "patriarchal bargain" encountered in street gangs. Resistance, therefore, involves the continued efforts to address the harms — and the trauma — that women and girls experience in a patriarchal society.

In resisting colonialism, the dictates of the neo-liberal rationality that bolster a capitalist society, and patriarchal discourses and practices that perpetuate gendered violence, individuals, families, and communities require support and resources to heal from their lived experience of trauma. While the women I spoke to were able to gain access to some of those resources in custody — at considerable cost to their own well-being, not to mention the cost to the public purse in maintaining a prison industrial complex — change-making needs to occur in their communities.

Much of that work is already underway. In Winnipeg, the inner-city neighbourhoods are the site of a growing number of community-based organizations, many of them Indigenous-driven. Their mandate is to attend to the complex material, cultural, and emotional needs of the residents (see, for example, Silver 2006, 2011, 2013). Several of the women at the

WCC were aware of the supports available in the community to assist them. Yet many were not. Some of the women only learned about the work of community-based organizations from attending the Resource Fair held in the WCC, which brings in some seventy-five different organizations twice a year to inform the women of the work they do.

Carol attended the fair and said, "Oh, I got lots of pamphlets and that, yeah. That was very helpful. So, yeah, just being here I kind of learn about these resources for women." Corrine also commented:

> From my experience I noticed that I didn't know there was a lot of stuff like that out there till I came to jail…. Yeah, and I've noticed that when women come to jail that's when they find out all this stuff that's out there for them. But for women that haven't been to jail, how do they know what's out there for them? I don't know how they're supposed to know about stuff like that.

Another irony to emerge from the women's narratives, then, is that many of the women had to come to jail to learn about the supports available to them in the community.

But what of the prisoning of women? While trauma experiences brought the women to jail, once incarcerated they confronted more challenges as they endeavoured to "do time," including dealing with the monotony of the daily routines and their confinement in segregation or in crowded cells, and negotiating relationships with each other and with correctional officers while at the same time struggling to maintain relationships with those on the outside, especially their children. It is also within this carceral space that the women are expected to engage in their own rehabilitation so that they can be successfully reintegrated back into society. Nevertheless, the parlance of "rehabilitation" presupposes that the troubles the women confront are located primarily within *them*, in *their* thought processes and behaviours. According to the neo-liberal criminal justice system, by altering these thought processes and behaviours (through the appropriate therapy and programming), the women's troubles can be resolved and reintegration can occur. Left unquestioned are the social conditions — the complex poverty, systemic racism, and gendered violence — that impinge on the women's lives on their release, conditions that were instrumental in setting the stage for their troubles in the first place. For many of the women, therefore, "reintegration" means going back to those very same troublesome conditions.

One significant development in the past two decades has been the advent of gender-responsive programming as an antidote to correctional policies and practices premised on male prisoners. Women are now recognized as having different needs and experiences than men, and therefore require gender-based understandings and responses. Yet this women-centred approach has been advanced in a neo-liberal correctional climate in which risk-management strategies predominate. While the correctional system may recognize women's unique needs (they are more relational than men, they are more likely to have histories of abuse than men), those needs are interpreted in relation to their risk to reoffend. The empowerment of women is therefore absorbed into a carceral logic that gives priority to managing their "riskiness."

Also working against the effort of the correctional system to be "gender-responsive" is the carceral context: although women are expected to engage in their own healing, punishment trumps empowerment. While the Women's Correctional Centre is a marked improvement over the old Portage jail, its size and structure have meant a much more bureaucratic and militaristic setting (evidenced by the uniforms of the correctional officers and even the names given to the different units: Alpha, Bravo, Charlie, Fox Trot). The deployment of mechanisms of power within the prison belies its standing as a site in which women can be "empowered" and heal from their trauma.

Another significant development has been the move to incarcerate increasing numbers of women. Overcrowding has posed organizational challenges for the prison administration and limited access to resources for the women housed there. Reducing the number of incarcerated women, especially those being held on remand, would most likely alleviate the situation. Women would presumably no longer be held in overcrowded cells, and access to counselling and programming would be improved. But it would not, in and of itself, fix the problem. For one, the loneliness and isolation that come with confinement would no doubt continue to prevail; and so too would the disconnect between prison as a site of punishment and a site of empowerment. Prison is primarily about punishment, and the women experience it as such.

Making change, therefore, requires maintaining a critical stance on why we are sending women to prison, and in increasing numbers. The financial investment in building "new and improved" prisons and the turn to gender-responsive programming to fashion more women-friendly therapeutic prisons may well make the experience of imprisonment more tolerable, but it is unreasonable to expect that incarcerating women will resolve their troubles. At bottom, women are sent to prison for punishment. Calling it a "correctional centre" does not erase that fact. Moreover, as the Truth and Reconciliation Commission (2015: 170) notes, "It is assumed that locking up offenders makes communities safer, but there is no evidence to demonstrate that this is indeed the case." Among its many recommendations, the Commission calls for governments at all levels to commit to eliminating the overrepresentation of Indigenous people in custody through the next decade (p. 324).

In addition to curbing the growth of the prison industrial complex, governments have a responsibility to practise what Pat Carlen (2004) calls "penal probity," running prisons according to moral principles that aim to "limit the damage done to prisoners and the harm done to society" (p. 262). Acting with penal probity means not pretending that prison "is something else (for example, a hospital, an addictions rehabilitation centre, an education establishment, or a women's refuge where the powerless can be 'empowered' and the impoverished learn to take responsibility for their own impoverishment)" (p. 260). Carlen puts it even more bluntly: "Prison programming cannot provide the magic bullet which will reduce recidivism independently of a change in women's circumstances outside prison" (p. 260).

NOT COMING BACK TO JAIL

The future of some of the women I spoke to looks uncertain. Grace said, "I don't think about the future. I just take it day by day. 'Cause you never know what's going to happen." Other women were resolved never to come back to jail. As Alicia said, "I've come to the point in my life where I don't want to come back between these walls. I don't want to see these people ever again. I don't want to be here. I don't want to ever come back here and I don't ever want to get charged again." For Alicia, the future revolves around her children: "I just want to stay at home and be a mom."

Melody described what she hoped for:

> This is my fairy tale. If I were to work, have my kids, and go home, just do the daily routine thing, wake up, send my kids to school, and me wake up, go to work, and then they'll be home. And then I cook supper for them when they get off school. And I'd do the same thing every day. And the weekend, have a few little drinks and go to sleep and then wait for Sunday night. Calm down, take it easy, and the same thing over every day. That would, yeah, I would like that.

Melody's aspirations align with what many Canadians would consider a "normal" life. Sadly, for her it is but a fairy tale.

When I met Sarah, she was serving a two-year sentence for assaulting her common-law partner. The Crown was seeking another Section 810 (imposing restrictive conditions after her release from custody), even though Sarah had done her best to engage in her own "responsibilization" and risk management during her time in jail. "I have done good here. I've done my programs, this, and this. I've never caused any trouble. This was the perfect stay for me, you know, I've done whatever. And I haven't broken any rules or been caught with anything. But you know what, they want to do it again."

Despite the restrictions that would probably be placed on her after she completed her sentence, Sarah was looking forward to her release. She had a house she could live in and was determined to end the long-time relationship with her common-law partner.

> I see my future as being okay now, as long as he's out of my life. And he's not going to now. He's not. I'm tired of it. I'm not going there anymore. I know the abuse and everything like that. I'm tired of it. I mean, two years away from him gave me a lot of time to think about who I was and what I wanted, not always worried about him. 'Cause it was always about him, never about me, you know?

Sarah realized that her life going forward would be a challenge. She knew that it was always going to be "a struggle" and that her addiction problems would always be foremost. "I know that I'm going to get lonesome," she told me. "I know ... what I'm going to be doing, instead of running to be with the wrong crowd and things like that. I know all that.... I recognize all that. But it's one day at a time. I learned how to do that, you know, and I do it here." Still, she said, "I know I can succeed. It's up to me."

Sarah believed she had gained insights into how her past history influenced who she became — especially in terms of all of the anger that had built up over the years.

> I know when I'm angry. I think about, okay, this is what it's going to do, this is why I feel like I do. I've learned how to recognize my feelings too, which I never did before, you know what I mean, all my emotions. Things like that. And I know what makes me mad. I just don't get mad for nothing like I used to. "Don't look at me," you know what I mean? Like that, "don't look at me," and I'd be mad.

But, as she said, "It took me fifty years to hold this, all this behaviour. It's not going to take me a day to get rid of it, you know what I mean? It's going to take a learning process. And I am learning, you know."

Near the end of our conversation I asked if she was okay with me writing about "Sarah" and what happened to her.

Sarah: Through her journey

Elizabeth: Yeah.

Sarah: Well, there ain't an ending yet.

Elizabeth: No.

Sarah: You still got to do another one for me. [laughs] Yeah. After I'm out of this place.

Elizabeth: I'm not waiting another twenty years, though. [laughs]

Sarah: Yeah, I know. No, you won't. Just give me a few more years and see where I'm at.

Elizabeth: Yeah.

Sarah: But I think this is the end of the line for me. Fifty years old. It's got to break the cycle here.

Elizabeth: Yeah.

Sarah: You know, yeah, I think I've had it. I'm done.

THE RESEARCH PROCESS

Conducting prison research can be a challenging endeavour. The researcher first has to convince correctional officials that the project has merit and then navigate the protocols of the correctional system to gain access to an institution. My previous experience of doing research in correctional facilities probably put me in good stead when I approached Manitoba Corrections in March 2013 with a request to interview the women at the Women's Correctional Centre (see, for example, Comack 2008). With that initial approval in place, gaining access to the institution involved a few more bureaucratic negotiations: a Winnipeg Police Service criminal record search, a Child Abuse Registry check, and a security screening by Manitoba Corrections. The first two steps were relatively straightforward; the third was more complicated.

The security screening entailed filling out an application form and then sitting for an hour-long interview. The woman I met with explained that the interview was designed to flag any potential criminal involvements an applicant may have that would jeopardize her ability to work in a prison setting. The questions posed were wide-ranging, and aimed at uncovering any such possibilities. I left the interview feeling as though I had confessed to pretty much every deviant or disreputable thing I had done in my life, but I did manage to pass the security screening. A formal agreement was then signed with Manitoba Corrections to conduct the research.

With the official permission in place, a more significant challenge remained: connecting with women at the WCC. To recruit participants, staff posted a notice in each of the WCC units, describing the study and asking for volunteers. I also visited each of the units to introduce myself and explain to the women that I was doing a study that followed up on *Women and Trouble* and intended to write a similar book. I brought along several copies of *Women in Trouble* to be distributed on the units so that the women could gain a sense of the kind of work I do. Women interested in meeting with me were told to fill out a request form, which was passed along to the Program Coordinator. She then provided me with a list of women who had volunteered. The list grew longer as word got out, in part because once I began meeting with the women they would share that experience with other women in their unit. While I was initially hoping to interview twenty-four women (the same number as I interviewed for *Women in Trouble*), forty-two women ended up agreeing to an interview.

The interviews began at the end of May and continued into the first week of July 2014. I would arrive at the WCC in the morning and, after passing through security, was taken to one of the units. I was provided with a room (most often either the small meeting room or the classroom adjacent to the unit) where I could meet with a woman. At the start of each meeting I introduced myself and explained the purpose of the study, which was to determine whether some of the connections I had found in the *Women in Trouble* project between abuse histories and law violations were still present in the lives of the women at the WCC. We then went over the consent form, which spelled out issues of informed consent, confidentiality, and risk and benefits. I had an Interview Schedule that followed the same questions I had used in my earlier study (which asked about experiences of abuse a woman may have had over her life course, her conflicts with the law, and how she found being in jail). Each of the interviews, however, tended to have a flow of its own as a woman talked about her upbringing and other details of her life, as well as her thoughts and opinions about the things that had happened to her. Most of the time I would only interject in our conversation when I wanted clarification of or elaboration on something a woman was telling me. Near the end of an interview I would review the Interview Schedule to make sure that all of the questions had been covered. The shortest interview was thirty-six minutes long and the longest an hour and forty-five minutes; most interviews were over an hour in duration.

In terms of confidentiality, the WCC staff was aware of which women were participating in the study, but they were not privy to what was being said during the interviews. The one exception for breaching confidentiality (indicated on the consent form) was if there was a disclosure of abuse involving a child. During one of the interviews, a woman raised concerns that her child, who was in foster placement, had bruises on his body when she last visited with him. I reminded her at that point that I was legally obligated to report her concerns to the authorities. Following the protocol that had been laid down in my university ethics application, I informed the superintendent at the WCC of the woman's suspicion and was assured that they would investigate the matter.

Sharing intimate details of one's life is seldom an easy undertaking. That is especially so under conditions of confinement. As one example, the WCC's protocols required that the women I met with in the Secure or Step-Down Unit were handcuffed during our meeting. I was also asked whether I wanted a correctional officer present in the interview room when we met. I declined the offer because I had no concerns for my safety. However, a guard was stationed outside the door of the glassed-in room where our meeting took place. The women seemed to handle the situation in stride. When I commented to one woman that I had never interviewed anyone in handcuffs before, she responded with, "Yeah. I feel like a big criminal!" We managed a laugh at that point.

It has become common practice for qualitative researchers to situate ourselves in the context of the subject-matter of our research. This issue becomes especially important when the research centres on the experiences of marginalized groups with whom the researcher does not share a common social location. In that regard, while I share some commonalities with the women based on my gender, being a white university professor has afforded me privileges in life that have been denied to them. Some readers might argue that this disconnect between a non-Indigenous researcher and the (mostly) Indigenous participants in the study precludes a full understanding of their lives and the impinging colonial forces. I share this concern. An Indigenous researcher who has the benefit of a shared knowledge with the women may well produce a different accounting of their lives than I could.

Another significant difference was that I have not had the experience of being incarcerated. I do not know what it is like to be restrained with handcuffs, confined in an overcrowded cell, or held in segregation. Nor do I know what it is like to be separated from family and loved ones for an extended period of time. The best one can do, in that regard, is — as Maureen Cain (1993: 88) suggests — "to grasp a putting of oneself into another's shoes." Doing so involves listening closely as the women relay their prisoning experience and what it has meant for them.

The women were no doubt aware of our differences. But, to their credit, they were willing to place their trust in me and share their stories. During one interview, a woman read me a poignant letter that she had composed to her mother. The letter expressed her feelings about the pain she had experienced from their relationship, her efforts at forgiveness, and her resolve to remember only the good things about her mother. She wasn't certain that she would ever give the letter to her mother but found the process of writing it to be cathartic. In another interview, a woman shared a secret that she hadn't told anyone else. I have kept her trust in not revealing that secret.

The opportunity to tell their stories — in many cases for the first time — was a motivation for many of the women to participate. As an interview came to a close I would ask a woman if there was anything else she wanted to talk about. The intention was to leave it up to the woman to determine when we were done. One woman replied, "No. I think this is it. I covered mostly everything I wanted to talk about and I feel much lighter. Yeah. I finally got to tell my story and I like that." Another woman told me, "I was waiting for this. I wanted to do it." Many of the women were motivated by a desire to help other women who found themselves in similar situations. As one woman commented: "I just hope that I could help protect other girls one day and that I can share my story and try to prevent some things from happening to some people and they could turn the other way."

Given the trauma that the women had experienced in their lives, I was aware that the interviews might amount to a reliving of that trauma, potentially opening up old wounds and difficult memories. One woman actually began our meeting by saying, "Don't mind me. I might cry." I replied, "I might cry too. So we'll both cry. We have lots of Kleenex [both laugh]." So while many tears were shed, they were intermingled with laughter, which I take to be a sign of the women's enduring resilience. Alert to the emotional distress the interview might have produced, I would ask a woman at the end of our meeting how she was feeling and how she planned on spending the rest of her day. We also talked about whether she had anyone in the facility that she felt she could talk to if need be (many of the women named their cellmates as a source of support) as well as other strategies (such as doing a journal) that she might use. In addition, I gave each woman a list of counselling supports and resources that were available in the community that she could access on her release.

The spring following the interviews I was invited back to the WCC to attend their Resource Fair and talk about my study. Several of the women raised the fair in the interviews, commenting on how useful it was for them to find out about the various supports available in the community. It was also an opportunity for me to briefly connect with some of the women who were still in custody when they attended the fair. As a way of giving something back to the women, I also collected boxes of books for the WCC library. During the summer of 2015 I wrote a twenty-page report that outlined the main themes of the study and included quotes from the women. The report was mailed to all of the participants. Unfortunately, the only address I had for several of the women was the WCC and so several of the reports were returned unopened. I am hoping that when the book is published I will be able to reconnect with some of the women who contributed to it.

The accountability of a researcher, however, extends beyond an effort to share the main findings with the people who participate in the study. It is also embedded in what she does with the stories she has been given. I was mindful of this responsibility during the construction of the book manuscript. I equate my role with that of a midwife: to use my position of privilege as an academic to give the women a voice, to make their knowledge visible. Giving the women a voice therefore means taking care in relaying their standpoints, communicating their thoughts and their experiences "as they see it." It also means sharing authority with them on the written page, making it clear when they are speaking, and giving their words space alongside mine. In this sense, to give space to the women's standpoints my own voice is sometimes more muted in the text.

Giving the women a voice is complicated when confidentiality is at issue. To ensure confidentiality when relaying what the women had to say, I have edited out any information about a woman's life that I thought might identify who she is. In some cases that meant not giving her specific age; in others it meant not naming a street gang she had been affiliated with. I also used pseudonyms in place of the women's real names, but with two exceptions: Cyndi and Jennifer requested that their real names be used, which I have done. In some cases the women indicated the pseudonym they preferred; at other times I used the names of women in my own life. This seemed an appropriate decision because these women could just as easily be the women with whom I share a close relationship (my daughter, friends, co-workers) were it not for the systemic conditions they have encountered in their lives.

Another complication was working with the interview transcripts. It is often difficult to turn oral speech into written text, especially in terms of inserting appropriate punctuation, as the result often reads like a long, run-on sentence. As well, oral speech (my own included) is often littered with a lot of "uhs," "likes," and "you knows," and the speaker may unintentionally repeat a word more than once in the process of getting her thoughts out. While an author has the opportunity to edit her own text (and can also rely on the skills of a professional copy editor), the research participants are not afforded such an opportunity. For these reasons, I made the decision to edit the women's words so that their narratives flowed more easily — without, of course, altering the substance of what was being said (for a further discussion of "translating" transcriptions, see Bourdieu 1993: 621–26).

In addition to midwifing the women's standpoints, I have also been engaged in theorizing or making sense of these women's lives. In the course of listening to the women's accounts, it became clear to me that focusing solely on "abuse" as a way of making sense was inadequate. Rather, "trauma" seemed a more complete notion for capturing the full range of experiences that the women had encountered, including their experiences of loss and grief. It also became evident that those experiences needed to be understood — not simply in psychological terms (as in PTSD) — but through a sociological lens that would attend to the social conditions of our settler colonial, patriarchal, capitalist society that produce the trauma. As such, while the heart of the work is the standpoints of the women, the structure and design of the work represent my own standpoint, my attempt to come to know and to make sense of the lives of these forty-two women.

As with all forms of knowledge production, however, my knowledge of these women's lives is partial. While I indicated at the end of each interview that I was quite willing to meet with the woman again if she had more that she wanted to share, none of the women took up that offer. As such, all of the interviews were a one-time event. If we have difficulty fully knowing even those with whom we spend a lifetime, how much can we expect to know from just one encounter with a person? (Even so, the depth of the knowledge that the women shared was remarkable.) The knowledge is also partial in the sense that it is each woman's perspective that I was listening to, her telling of her life. Moreover, it is partial in that what was told depended very much upon what a woman was willing or able to disclose to me at the time of our meeting. While the women were forthcoming in sharing many of the intimate details of their lives, they also made it clear when there were certain issues that they did not want to talk about. One woman who was on remand, for instance, declined to talk about her charges (a point on which lawyers will often advise their clients). Further, the knowledge is partial in that what was told was also contoured by the sort of information about a woman's life that I chose to elicit from her. In that regard, the issue of abuse figured prominently in the interviews because I was intent on learning about that aspect of a woman's life and the impact it has had on her. As I noted in *Women in Trouble*, in focusing on the women's abuse experiences there is a danger of imposing an artificial uni-dimensionality to their lives, constructing them as "embodying victimization." There is clearly much more going on in a woman's life than can be captured in a master status as a "victim" or "survivor" of trauma. Yet trauma has had a profound effect on who these women are and what they are trying to become.

Despite these limitations, I firmly believe there is much to be learned from these women. In the same way that I have engaged in the hard work of listening to — and hearing — what they have to say, so too does the reader of this book need to similarly engage. In a talk she gave in Winnipeg, Amy Goodman of *Democracy Now!* noted, "When you hear someone describing their own experience it changes you." I have been changed by hearing from these women. My hope is that you will be too.

REFERENCES

Adams, H. 1975. *Prison of Grass: Canada from a Native Point of View*. Toronto: New Press.

Adelberg, E., and C. Currie (eds.). *Too Few to Count: Canadian Women in Conflict with the Law*. Vancouver: Press Gang.

AJIC (Aboriginal Justice Implementation Commission). 2001. *Final Report*. Winnipeg: Manitoba Justice. <ajic.mb.ca/reports/final_summary.html>.

Alberta Council of Women's Shelters. 2009. *ACWS Orientation Manual*. Edmonton: ACWS. <acws.ca/sites/default/files/documents/1Introduction.pdf>.

Amnesty International. 2004. *Stolen Sisters: A Human Rights Response to Discrimination and Violence against Indigenous Women in Canada*. (October). Ottawa: Amnesty International Canada. <amnesty.ca/sites/default/files/amr200032004enstolensisters.pdf>.

Anderson, B., and J. Richards. 2016. "Students in Jeopardy: An Agenda for Improving Results in Band-Operated Schools." C.D. Howe Institute (Commentary No. 444). <cdhowe. org/sites/default/files/attachments/research_papers/mixed/Commentary_444_0. pdf>.

Andrews, D., and J. Bonta. 2006. "The Recent Past and Near Future of Risk/Need Assessment." *Crime and Delinquency*, 52.

Andrews, D., J. Bonta, and R.D. Hoge. 1990. "Classification for Effective Rehabilitation: Rediscovering Psychology." *Criminal Justice and Behavior*, 17.

APA (American Psychiatric Association). 2013. *Diagnostic and Statistical Manual of Mental Disorders* (fifth edition). Arlington VA: American Psychiatric Publishing.

____. 2000. *Diagnostic and Statistical Manual of Mental Disorders* (fourth edition, Text Revision). Arlington VA: American Psychiatric Publishing.

____. 1995. *Diagnostic and Statistical Manual of Mental Disorders* (fourth edition). Arlington VA: American Psychiatric Publishing.

____. 1987. *Diagnostic and Statistical Manual of Mental Disorders* (third edition, Text Revision). Arlington VA: American Psychiatric Publishing.

____. 1980. *Diagnostic and Statistical Manual of Mental Disorders* (third edition). Arlington VA: American Psychiatric Publishing.

Arnold, R. 1995. "The Processes of Victimization and Criminalization of Black Women." In B.R. Price and N. Sokoloff (eds.), *The Criminal Justice System and Women*. New York: McGraw Hill.

Assembly of First Nations. 1994. *Breaking the Silence: An Interpretive Study of Residential School Impact and Healing as Illustrated by the Stories of First Nations Individuals*. Ottawa: Assembly of First Nations.

Atkinson, J. 2002. *Trauma Trails: Recreating Song Lines, The Transgenerational Effects of Trauma in Indigenous Australia*. North Melbourne: Spinifex.

Ballard, M. 2012. *Flooding Hope: The Lake St. Martin First Nation Story*. <youtube.com/watch?v=SQStePF5jeg>.

Ballard, M., and S. Thompson. 2013. "Flooding Hope and Livelihoods: Lake St. Martin First Nation." *ANSERJ*, 4, 1.

Barrett. S. R. 1987. *Is God a Racist? The Right Wing in Canada*. Toronto: University of Toronto Press.

Belknap, J. 2010. "'Offending Women': A Double Entendre." *The Journal of Criminal Law and Criminology*, 100, 3.

Blackstock, C. 2003. "First Nations Child and Family Services Restoring Peace and Harmony in First Nations Communities." In K. Kufeldt and B. McKenzie (eds.), *Child Welfare: Connecting Research, Policy, and Practice*. Waterloo: Wilfred Laurier University Press.

Blackstock, C., and N. Trocmé. 2004. "Community Based Child Welfare for Aboriginal Children: Supporting Resilience through Structural Change." <cecw-cepb.ca/sites/default/files/publications/en/communityBasedCWAboriginalChildren.pdf>.

Block, S., and G-E. Galabuzi. 2011. *Canada's Colour Coded Labour Market: The Gap for Racialized Workers*. Ottawa and Toronto: Canadian Centre for Policy Alternatives and The Wellsley Institute.

Bloom, B. 1999. "Gender Responsive Programming for Women Offenders: Guiding Principles and Practices." *Let's Talk/Entre Nous*. Correctional Service Canada.

Bloom, B., and S. Covington. 2008. "Addressing the Mental Health Needs of Women Offenders." In R. Gido and L. Dalley (eds.), *Women's Mental Health Issues Across the Criminal Justice System*. Columbus, Ohio: Prentice Hall.

____. 2006. "Gender Responsive Treatment Services in Correctional Settings." *Inside and Out: Women, Prison and Therapy*, 29, 3.

Bloom, B., B. Owen, and S. Covington. 2003. *Gender Responsive: Research, Practice and Guiding Principles for Women Offenders*. Washington, DC: National Institute of Corrections, US Department of Justice.

Bombay, A., K. Matheson, and H. Anisman. 2014. "The Impact of Stressors on Second Generation Indian Residential School Survivors." *Transcultural Psychiatry*, 48, 4.

____. 2009. "Intergenerational Trauma: Convergence of Multiple Processes among First Nations Peoples in Canada." *Journal of Aboriginal Health* (November).

Bonta, J., and D. Andrews. 2007. "Risk–Need-Responsivity Model for Offender Assessment and Rehabilitation 2007–06." Ottawa: Public Safety Canada. <publicsafety.gc.ca/cnt/rsrcs/pblctns/rsk-nd-rspnsvty/rsk-nd-rspnsvty-eng.pdf>.

Bourdieu, P. (ed.). 1993. *The Weight of the World: Social Suffering in Contemporary Society*. Stanford: Stanford University Press.

Bourgois, P. 2003. *In Search of Respect: Selling Crack in El Barrio* (second edition). New York: Cambridge University Press.

Boyce, J. 2015. "Police-Reported Crime Statistics in Canada, 2014." *Juristat*. <statcan.gc.ca/pub/85-002-x/2015001/article/14211-eng.pdf>.

Brandon, J., and E. Peters. 2014. *Moving to the City: Housing and Aboriginal Migration to Winnipeg*. (November.) Winnipeg: Canadian Centre for Policy Alternatives–Manitoba.

Brennan, J. 2012. *A Shrinking Universe: How Concentrated Corporate Power Is Shaping Income Inequality in Canada*. Ottawa: Canadian Centre for Policy Alternatives.

Brennan, T., M. Breitenbach, W. Dieterich, E. Salisbury, and P. Van Hooris. 2012. "Women's Pathways to Serious and Habitual Crime: A Person-Centered Analysis Incorporating Gender Responsive Factors." *Criminal Justice and Behavior*, 39, 11.

Brewer, R.M. 1997. "Theorizing Race, Class, and Gender: The New Scholarship of Black Feminist Intellectuals and Black Women's Labour." In R. Hennessy and C. Ingraham (eds.), *Materialist Feminism*. London: Routledge.

Broad, D. 2000. *Hollow Work, Hollow Society? Globalization and the Casual Labour Problem in Canada*. Halifax: Fernwood Publishing.

Broad, D., J. Cruikshank, and J. Mulvale. 2006. "Where's the Work? Labour Market Trends in the New Economy." In D. Broad and W. Antony (eds.), *Capitalism Rebooted? Work and Welfare in the New Economy*. Winnipeg and Halifax: Fernwood Publishing.

Brodie, J. 1995. *Politics on the Margins: Restructuring and the Canadian Women's Movement*. Halifax: Fernwood Publishing.

Brodsky, G. 2014. "McIvor v. Canada: Legislated Patriarchy Meets Aboriginal Women's Equality Rights." In J. Green (ed.), *Indivisible: Indigenous Human Rights*. Winnipeg and Halifax: Fernwood Publishing.

Brown, J., N. Higgit, C. Miller, S. Wingert, M. Williams, and L. Morrissette. 2006. "Challenges Faced by Women Working in the Inner City Sex Trade." *Canadian Journal of Urban Research*, 15, 1.

Brownell, M., M. Chartier, R. Santos, O. Ekuma, W. Au, J. Sarkar, L. MacWilliam, E. Burland, I. Koseva, and W. Gurnette. 2012. *How Are Manitoba's Children Doing?* Winnipeg: Manitoba Centre for Health Policy.

Brownell, M., C. De Coster, R. Penfold, S. Derksen, W. Au, J. Schultz, and M. Dahl. 2008. *Manitoba Child Health Atlas Update*. Winnipeg: Manitoba Centre for Health Policy.

Brownell, M., R. Fransoo, and P. Martens. 2015. "Social Determinants of Health and the Distribution of Health Outcomes in Manitoba." In L. Fernandez, S. MacKinnon, and J. Silver (eds.), *The Social Determinants of Health in Manitoba* (second edition). Winnipeg: Canadian Centre for Policy Alternatives–Manitoba.

Brownell, M., L. Lix, S. Derksen, S. De Haney, R. Bond, R. Fransoo, L. MacWilliam, and J. Bodnarchuk. 2003. *Why Is the Health Status of Some Manitobans Not Improving? The Widening Gap in the Health Status of Manitobans*. Winnipeg: Manitoba Centre for Health Policy.

Brownmiller, S. 1975. *Against Our Will: Men, Women and Rape*. New York: Simon and Schuster.

Burstow, B. 2005. "A Critique of Post-Traumatic Stress Disorder and the DSM." *Journal of Humanistic Psychology*, 45, 4.

____. 2003. "Toward a Radical Understanding of Trauma." *Violence Against Women*, 9, 11.

Cain, M. 1993. "Foucault, Feminist and Feeling: What Foucault Can and Cannot Contribute to Feminist Epistemology." In C. Ramazangolu (ed.), *Up Against Foucault: Explorations of Some Tensions between Foucault and Feminism*. London: Routledge.

Campaign 2000. 2010. *Report Card on Child and Family Poverty in Canada: 1989–2010*.

<campaign2000.ca/reportCards/national/2010EnglishC2000NationalReportCard. pdf>.

Canadian Centre for Policy Alternatives, MB and John Howard Society of Manitoba, Inc. 2012. *Bill C-10: The Truth about Consequences.* Winnipeg: Canadian Centre for Policy Alternatives–Manitoba.

Carlen, P. 2004. "Risk and Responsibility in Women's Prisons." *Current Issues in Criminal Justice,* 15, 1.

Carlen, P. 1988. *Women, Crime and Poverty.* Milton Keynes: Open University Press.

CBC News. 2016a. "More Details Emerge about Suicide Crisis at Pimicikamak Cree Nation." (March 10). <cbc.ca/news/canada/manitoba/more-details-emerge-about-suicide-crisis-at-pimicikamak-cree-nation-1.3485074>.

____. 2016b. "Poverty, Inequality Fuelling Suicide Crisis, First Nations Leader Says." (March 13). <cbc.ca/news/indigenous/poverty-inequality-fueling-suicide-crisis-1.3487028>.

____. 2015. "Lake St. Martin Relocation Plans 1 Step Closer to Becoming a Reality." (June 22). <cbc.ca/news/canada/manitoba/lake-st-martin-relocation-plans-1-step-closer-to-becoming-a-reality-1.3123327>.

____. 2012. "Lake St. Martin Flood Evacuees' School Shut Down." (November 6). <cbc.ca/news/canada/manitoba/lake-st-martin-flood-evacuees-school-shut-down-1.1176704>.

Chan, W., and K. Mirchandani. 2002. "From Race and Crime to Racialization and Criminalization." In W. Chan and K. Mirchandani (eds.), *Crimes of Colour: Racialization and the Criminal Justice System in Canada.* Peterborough: Broadview Press.

Chan, W., and G. Rigakos. 2002. "Risk, Crime and Gender." *British Journal of Criminology,* 42.

Chesnay, C. 2015. "Doing Health, Undoing Prison: A Study of Women Who Have Experienced Incarceration in a Provincial Prison." Ph.D. dissertation, Faculty of Health Studies, University of Ottawa.

Chesney-Lind, M., and N. Rodriguez. 1983. "Women under Lock and Key." *The Prison Journal,* 63.

Chesney-Lind, M., and R. Sheldon. 1998. *Girls, Delinquency and Juvenile Justice.* California: Wadsworth.

Cheung, L. 2005. *Racial Status and Employment Outcomes.* Research Paper #34. Ottawa: Canadian Labour Congress.

Chunn, D., and S. Gavigan. 2014. "From Welfare Fraud to Welfare as Fraud: The Criminalization of Poverty." In G. Balfour and E. Comack (eds.), *Criminalizing Women: Gender and (In)justice in Neoliberal Times* (second edition). Winnipeg and Halifax: Fernwood Publishing.

Comack, E. 2014. "The Feminist Engagement with Criminology." In G. Balfour and E. Comack (eds.), *Criminalizing Women: Gender and (In)justice in Neo-Liberal Times* (second edition). Halifax and Winnipeg: Fernwood Publishing.

____. 2012. *Racialized Policing: Aboriginal People's Encounters with the Police.* Winnipeg and Halifax: Fernwood Publishing.

____. 2008. *Out There/In Here: Masculinity, Violence, and Prisoning.* Winnipeg and Halifax: Fernwood Publishing.

____. 1996. *Women in Trouble: Connecting Women's Law Violations to Their Histories of Abuse.* Halifax: Fernwood Publishing.

____. 1993a. *Women Offenders' Experiences with Physical and Sexual Abuse: A Preliminary*

Report. Winnipeg: Criminology Research Centre, University of Manitoba.

____. 1993b. *The Feminist Engagement with the Law: The Legal Recognition of the "Battered Woman Syndrome."* Ottawa: Canadian Research Institute for the Advancement of Women.

Comack, E., and G. Balfour. 2004. *The Power to Criminalize: Violence, Inequality and the Law*. Winnipeg and Halifax: Fernwood Publishing.

Comack, E., L. Deane, L. Morrissette, and J. Silver. 2013. *"Indians Wear Red": Colonialism, Resistance, and Aboriginal Street Gangs*. Halifax and Winnipeg: Fernwood Publishing.

Comack, E., C. Fabre, and S. Burgher. 2015. *The Impact of the Harper Government's "Tough on Crime" Strategy: Hearing from Frontline Workers*. (September) Winnipeg: Canadian Centre for Policy Alternatives–Manitoba.

Comack, E., and M. Seshia. 2010. "Bad Dates and Street Hassles: Violence in the Winnipeg Street Sex Trade." *Canadian Journal of Criminology and Criminal Justice*, 52, 2.

Community Legal Education Association. 2013. *Criminal Law & Procedure*. Winnipeg: CLEA. <communitylegal.mb.ca/wp-content/uploads/Full-Document-Criminal-Law-Procedure-amended.pdf>.

Connell, R.W. 2000. *The Men and the Boys*. Berkley: University of California Press.

____. 1995. *Masculinities*. Cambridge: Polity Press.

____. 1987. *Gender and Power*. Cambridge: Polity Press.

Connell, R.W., and J. Messerschmidt. 2005. "Hegemonic Masculinity: Rethinking the Concept." *Gender & Society*, 19, 6.

Cooper, S. 2011. "Housing for People, Not Markets: Neoliberalism and Housing in Winnipeg's Inner City." *State of the Inner City Report. Neoliberalism: What a Difference a Theory Makes*. Winnipeg: Canadian Centre for Policy Alternatives–Manitoba.

Correctional Services Program. 2017. *Trends in the Use of Remand in Canada, 2004/2005 to 2014/2015*. Ottawa: Statistics Canada. <statcan.gc.ca/pub/85-002-x/2017001/article/14691-eng.pdf>.

____. 2015. *Adult Correctional Statistics in Canada, 2013/2014*. Statistics Canada. <statcan.gc.ca/pub/85-002-x/2015001/article/14163-eng.htm>.

Cosgrove, L., S. Krimsky, M. Vijayaraghavan, and L. Schneider. 2006. "Financial Ties between DSM-IV Panel Members and the Pharmaceutical Industry." *Psychotherapy and Psychosomatics*, 75.

Covington, S., and B. Bloom. 2006. "Gender Responsive Treatment and Services in Correctional Settings." *Women & Therapy*, 29, 3/4.

Crenshaw, K. 1989. "Demarginalizing the Intersection of Race and Sex: A Black Feminist Critique of Antidiscrimination Doctrine, Feminist Theory and Antiracist Politics." *The University of Chicago Legal Forum*.

Criminal Code (R.S.C.). 1985. C. C-46.

CSC (Correctional Service Canada). n.d. *Deficit Reduction Action Plan by Program Activity*. <csc-scc.gc.ca/reporting/007005-1500-eng.shtml>.

CTV News. 2015. "Illness, Despair Plague Manitoba First Nation Displaced by Flood 4 Years Ago." (March 18.) <ctvnews.ca/canada/illness-despair-plague-manitoba-first-nation-displaced-by-flood-4-years-ago-1.2287106>

Daly, K. 1998. "Women's Pathways to Felony Court: Feminist Theories of Lawbreaking and Problems of Representation." In K. Daly and L. Maher (eds.), *Criminology at the*

Crossroads: Feminist Readings in Crime and Justice. New York: Oxford.

Daly, K., and L. Maher. 1998. "Crossroads and Intersections: Building from Feminist Critique." In K. Daly and L. Maher (eds.), *Criminology at the Crossroads: Feminist Readings in Crime and Justice.* New York: Oxford University Press.

Das Gupta, T. 2009. *Real Nurses and Others: Racism in Nursing.* Winnipeg and Halifax: Fernwood Publishing.

Deane, L. 2006. *Under One Roof: Community Economic Development and Housing in the Inner City.* Winnipeg and Halifax: Fernwood Publishing.

DeHart, D., S. Lynch, J. Belknap, P. Dass-Brailsford, and B. Green. 2013. "Life History Models of Female Offending: The Roles of Serious Mental Illness and Trauma in Women's Pathways to Jail." *Psychology of Women Quarterly,* 38, 1.

Denham, A.R. 2008. "Rethinking Historical Trauma: Narratives of Resilience." *Transcultural Psychiatry* (September).

Derksen, D., L. Booth, A. McConnell, and K. Taylor. 2012. *Mental Health Needs of Federal Women Offenders.* Research Report R-267. Ottawa: Correctional Service Canada.

Deshman, A., and N. Myers. 2014. *Set Up to Fail: Bail and the Revolving Door of Pre-Trial Detention* (July). Canadian Civil Liberties Association and Education Trust. <ccla.org/dev/v5/_doc/CCLA_set_up_to_fail.pdf>.

Dobash, R.E., and R. Dobash. 1992. *Women, Violence and Social Change.* London: Routledge.

Downe, P. 2002. "'I Don't Know What the Hell it Is but it Sounds Nasty': Health Issues for Girls Working the Streets." In K. Gorkoff and J. Rule (eds.), *Being Heard: The Experiences of Young Women in Prostitution.* Winnipeg and Halifax: Fernwood Publishing.

Drummond, D., and E.K. Rosenbluth. 2013. "The Debate on First Nations Education Funding: Minding the Gap." *Policy Studies* Working Paper 49 (December). Kingston: School of Policy Studies, Queen's University.

Duran, E., and B. Duran. 1995. *Native American Postcolonial Psychology.* Albany, NY: SUNY Press.

_____. 1990. *Transforming the Soul Wound: A Theoretical/Clinical Approach to American Indian Psychology.* Berkeley: Folklore Institute.

Duran, B., E. Duran, and M. Yellow Horse Brave Heart. 1999. "Native Americans and the Trauma of History." In R. Thornton (ed.), *Studying Native Americans: Problems and Prospects.* Wisconsin: University of Wisconsin Press.

Erikson, K. 1995. "Notes on Trauma and Community." In C. Caruth (ed.), *Trauma: Explorations in Memory.* Baltimore: John Hopkins University Press.

_____. 1976. *Everything in its Path: Destruction of Community in the Buffalo Creek Flood.* New York: Simon and Shuster.

Essed, P. 2002. "Everyday Racism: A New Approach to the Study of Racism." In P. Essed and D.T. Goldberg (eds.), *Race Critical Theories.* Oxford: Blackwell.

Evans-Campbell, T. 2008. "Historical Trauma in American Indian/Native Alaska Communities: A Multilevel Framework for Exploring Impacts on Individuals, Families, and Communities." *Journal of Interpersonal Violence,* 23, 3.

Faith, K. 1993. *Unruly Women: The Politics of Confinement and Resistance.* Vancouver: Press Gang.

Farley, M., J. Lynne, and A.J. Cotton. 2005. "Prostitution in Vancouver: Violence and the Colonization of First Nations Women." *Transcultural Psychiatry,* 42, 2.

Flynn, L.-L. 2011. "Plains Indian Ways to Inter-Tribal Cultural Healing in Vancouver." In H.A. Howard and C. Proulx (eds.), *Aboriginal Peoples in Canadian Cities*. Waterloo: Wilfred Laurier University Press.

Fontaine, N. 2014. "Surviving Colonialism: Anishinaabe Ikwe Street Gang Participation." In G. Balfour and E. Comack (eds.), *Criminalizing Women: Gender and (In)justice in Neoliberal Times*. Winnipeg and Halifax: Fernwood Publishing.

Food Banks Canada. 2016. *Hunger Count 2016: A Comprehensive Report on Hunger and Food Banks Use in Canada, and Recommendations for Change*. Mississauga: Food Banks Canada. <foodbankscanada.ca/getmedia/6173994f-8a25-40d9-acdf-660a28e40f37/HungerCount_2016_final_singlepage.pdf>.

Foucault, M. 2010. *The Foucault Reader* (Paul Rabinow, editor). New York: Vintage Books.

____. 1978. *The History of Sexuality*, Volume I (Robert Hurley, translator). New York: Pantheon Books.

Friedman, M.J. 2016. "PTSD History and Overview." PTSD: National Center for PTSD. U.S. Department of Veterans Affairs. <ptsd.va.gov/professional/PTSD-overview/ptsd-overview.asp>.

Galloway, G. 2012. "Flooded Out to Save Winnipeg, Lake St. Martin Residents Now Feel Forgotten." *Globe and Mail* (November 24). <theglobeandmail.com/news/national/flooded-out-to-save-winnipeg-lake-st-martin-residents-now-feel-forgotten/article5621936/>.

Galtung, J. 1969. "Violence, Peace, and Peace Research." *Journal of Peace Research*, 6.

Garland, D. 2001. *The Culture of Control*. New York: Oxford University Press.

Gibbins, R., and R. Ponting. 1986. "Historical Background and Overview." In R. Ponting (ed.), *Arduous Journey*. Toronto: McLelland and Stewart.

Gilfus, M. 1992. "From Victims to Survivors to Offenders: Women's Routes of Entry and Immersion into Street Crime." *Women and Criminal Justice*, 4, 1.

Gilligan, C. 1982. *In a Different Voice: Psychological Theory and Women's Development*. Cambridge: Harvard University Press.

Gobeil, R., and M. Barrett. 2007. *Rates of Recidivism for Women Offenders*. Research Report R-192. Ottawa: Correctional Service Canada.

Goodhand, M. 2017. *Runaway Wives and Rogue Feminists: The Origins of the Women's Shelter Movement in Canada*. Winnipeg and Halifax: Fernwood Publishing.

Government of Manitoba. 2012. "Province Prepares to Open New Women's Correctional Centre" (January 26). <news.gov.mb.ca/news/index.html?item=13063>.

____. 2006. "Province Accepts Recommendations to Reform Women's Corrections." News Release (April 3). <news.gov.mb.ca/news/index.html?item=28415&posted=2006-04-03>.

Gradus, J. 2016. "Epidemiology of PTSD." PTSD: National Center for PTSD. <ptsd.va.gov/professional/PTSD-overview/epidemiological-facts-ptsd.asp>

Green, J. 2014. "From Colonialism to Reconciliation through Indigenous Human Rights." In J. Green (ed.), *Indivisible: Indigenous Human Rights*. Winnipeg and Halifax: Fernwood Publishing.

Grekul, J., and P. LaRocque. 2011. "Hope is Absolute: Gang-Involved Women—Perceptions from the Front Line." *Aboriginal Policy Studies*, 1, 2.

Guina, J., R. Welton, P. Broderick, T. Correll, and R. Peirson. 2016. "DSM–5 Criteria and Its

Implications for Diagnosing PTSD in Military Service Members and Veterans." *Current Psychiatry Report*, 18.

Hagedorn, J. M. 2008. *A World of Gangs: Armed Young Men and Gangsta Culture*. Minneapolis and London: University of Minnesota Press.

Hall, S. 1997. "The Spectacle of the 'Other.'" In S. Hall (ed.), *Representation: Cultural Representations and Signifying Practices*. Milton Keynes: The Open University.

Hall, S., C. Critcher, T. Jefferson, J. Clarke, and B. Roberts. 1978. *Policing the Crisis: Mugging, the State, and Law and Order*. London: MacMillan Press.

Hamilton, A.C., and C.M. Sinclair. 1991. *The Justice System and Aboriginal People: Report of the Aboriginal Justice Inquiry of Manitoba*. Vol. 1. Winnipeg: Queen's Printer.

Hancock, P., and Y. Jewkes. 2011. "Architectures of Incarceration: The Spatial Pains of Imprisonment." *Punishment & Society*, 13, 5.

Hannah-Moffat, K. 2009. "Gridlock or Mutability: Reconsidering 'Gender' and Risk Assessment." *Criminology & Public Policy*, 8, 1.

_____. 2008. "Re-Imagining Gendered Penalities: The Myth of Gender Responsivity." In P. Carlen (ed.), *Imaginary Penalities*. Collumpton, Devon: Willan.

_____. 2000a. "Prisons that Empower: Neo-Liberal Governance in Canadian Women's Prisons." *British Journal of Criminology*, 40.

_____. 2000b. "Re-forming the Prison—Rethinking Our Ideals." In K. Hannah-Moffat and M. Shaw (eds.), *An Ideal Prison? Critical Essays on Women's Imprisonment in Canada*. Halifax: Fernwood Publishing.

_____. 1999. "Moral Agent or Actuarial Subject: Risk and Canadian Women's Imprisonment." *Theoretical Criminology*, 3, 1.

Hannah-Moffat, K., and M. Shaw. 2001. *Taking Risks: Incorporating Gender and Culture into the Classification and Assessment of Federally Sentenced Women in Canada*. Ottawa: Status of Women Canada.

Harper, S. 2008. "Statement of Apology—to Former Students of Indian Residential Schools." <aadnc-aandc.gc.ca/eng/1100100015644/1100100015649>.

Hart, M.A. 2010. "Colonization, Social Exclusion and Indigenous Health." In L. Fernandez, S. MacKinnon, and J. Silver (eds.), *The Social Determinants of Health in Manitoba*. Winnipeg: Canadian Centre for Policy Alternatives–Manitoba.

_____. 2002. *Seeking Mino-Pimatisiwin: An Aboriginal Approach to Helping*. Halifax: Fernwood Publishing.

Haskell, L., and M. Randall. 2009. "Disrupted Attachments: A Social Context Complex Trauma Framework and the Lives of Aboriginal Peoples in Canada." *Journal of Aboriginal Health* (November).

Hayward, C.R. 2000. *De-Facing Power*. Cambridge: Cambridge University Press.

Heimer, K. 1995. "Gender, Race and Pathways to Delinquency." In J. Hagan and R. Peterson (eds.), *Crime and Inequality*. Stanford: Stanford University Press.

Henry, F., C. Tator, W. Mattis, and T. Rees. 2009. "The Ideology of Racism." In M. Wallis and A. Feras (eds.), *The Politics of Race in Canada*. Toronto: Oxford University Press.

Herman, J.L. 2012. "CPTSD is a Distinct Entity: Comment on Resick et al. (2012)." *Journal of Traumatic Stress*, 25 (June).

_____. 1992a. *Trauma and Recovery: The Aftermath of Violence—From Domestic Abuse to Political Terror*. New York: Basic Books.

____. 1992b. "Complex PTSD: A Syndrome in Survivors of Prolonged and Repeated Trauma." *Journal of Traumatic Stress,* 5, 3.

Hudson, P., and B. McKenzie. 2003. "Extending Aboriginal Control over Child Welfare Services." *Canadian Review of Social Policy/Revue Canadienne de politique sociale,* 51 (Spring/Summer).

Jackson, M. 1988–89. "Locking Up Natives in Canada." *University of British Columbia Law Review,* 23.

James, D.J., and L.E. Glaze. 2006. "Mental Health Problems of Prison and Jail Inmates." *Bureau of Justice Statistics Special Report.* U.S. Department of Justice.

John Howard Society of Ontario. 2013. *Reasonable Bail?* Toronto: John Howard Society of Ontario. <johnhoward.on.ca/wp-content/uploads/2014/07/JHSO-Reasonable-Bail-report-final.pdf>.

Johnson, H. 2016. *Firewater: How Alcohol Is Killing My People (and Yours).* Regina: University of Regina Press.

Johnson, P. 1983. *Native Children and the Child Welfare System.* Ottawa: Canada Council on Social Development.

Juristat. 2016. *Family Violence in Canada: A Statistical Profile, 2014.* Ottawa: Statistics Canada.

Kaiser-Derrick, E. 2012. "Listening to What the Criminal Justice System Hears and the Stories It Tells: Judicial Sentencing Discourses about the Victimization and Criminalization of Aboriginal Women." Master of Laws thesis, University of British Columbia.

Kari, S. 2016. "Provincial Court Snakes & Ladders – Page 2: Scope of Provincial Court Jurisdiction." *Canadian Lawyer Magazine* (July 4). <canadianlawyermag.com/6083/Provincial-court-snakes-ladders/Page-2.html?showall=1>.

Kazemipur, A., and S. Halli. 2000. *The New Poverty in Canada: Ethnic Groups and Ghetto Neighbourhoods.* Toronto: Thompson.

Kelly, L. 1988. *Surviving Sexual Violence.* Minneapolis: University of Minnesota Press.

Kendall, K. 2002. "Time to Think Again About Cognitive Behavioural Programmes." In P. Carlen (ed.), *Women and Punishment: The Struggle for Justice.* Cullompton: Willan Publishing.

Kilty, J. 2012. "'It's Like They Don't Want You to Get Better': Psy Control of Women in the Carceral Context." *Feminism & Psychology,* 22, 2.

Kimelman, Associate Chief Judge E.C. 1985. *No Quiet Place.* Report of the Review Committee on Indian and Métis Adoptions and Placements (Final Report). Winnipeg: Manitoba Community Services.

Kirmayer, L., J. Gone, and J. Moses. 2014. "Rethinking Historical Trauma." *Transcultural Psychiatry,* 51, 3.

Kline, M. 1994. "The Colour of Law: Ideological Representations of First Nations in Legal Discourse." *Social & Legal Studies,* 3.

Knockwood, I. 2015. *Out of the Depths: The Experiences of Mi'kmaw Children at the Indian Residential School at Shubenacadie, Nova Scotia* (fourth edition). Halifax: Rosewood.

Kulchyski, P. 2007. "The Town that Lost Its Name: The Impact of Hydroelectric Development on Grand Rapids, Manitoba." In J. Loxley (ed.), *Doing Community Economic Development.* Halifax and Winnipeg: Fernwood Publishing.

Kusch, L. 2012. "Intimate Spaces Highlight New Headingley Women's Jail." *Winnipeg Free Press* (January 27). <winnipegfreepress.com/local/intimate-spaces-highlight-new-headingley-womens-jail-138186304.html>.

Laberge, D. 1991. "Women's Criminality, Criminal Women, Criminalized Women? Questions in and for a Feminist Perspective." *Journal of Human Justice*, 2, 2.

Lafreniere, C., N. Fontaine, and E. Comack. 2005. *The Challenge for Change: Realizing the Legacy of the Aboriginal Justice Inquiry Report*. Winnipeg: Canadian Centre for Policy Alternatives – Manitoba. <policyalternatives.ca/publications/reports/challenge-change>.

Langner, N., J. Barton, and D. McDonagh. 2002. "Rates of Prescribed Medication Use by Women in Prison." *Forum on Corrections Research*, 14, 2.

Larocque, E. 2002. "Violence in Aboriginal Communities." In K. McKenna and J. Larkin (eds.), *Violence against Women: New Canadian Perspectives*. Toronto: Inanna.

Lezubski, D., and J. Silver. 2015. "High and Rising Revisited: Changes in Poverty and Related Inner City Characteristics 1996 to 2011." *State of the Inner City: Drawing on Our Strengths*. Winnipeg: Canadian Centre for Policy Alternatives–Manitoba.

Linklater, R. 2014. *Decolonizing Trauma Work: Indigenous Stories and Strategies*. Halifax and Winnipeg: Fernwood Publishing.

Lowman, J., and L. Fraser. 1996. *Violence against Persons Who Prostitute: The Experience of British Columbia*. Ottawa: Department of Justice.

Loxley, J. 2010. *Aboriginal, Northern, and Community Economic Development: Papers and Retrospectives*. Winnipeg: Arbeiter Ring.

Luxenberg, T., J. Spinazzola, and B. van der Kolk. 2001. "Complex Trauma and Disorders of Extreme Stress (DESNON) Diagnosis, Part One: Assessment." *Directions in Psychiatry*, vol. 21 lesson 25.

Lynch, S., A. Fritch, and N. Heath. 2012. "Looking Beneath the Surface: The Nature of Incarcerated Women's Experiences of Interpersonal Violence, Treatment Needs, and Mental Health." *Feminist Criminology*, 7.

MacDonald, D., and D. Wilson. 2016. *Shameful Neglect: Indigenous Child Poverty in Canada*. Ottawa: Canadian Centre for Policy Alternatives. <policyalternatives.ca/sites/default/files/uploads/publications/National%20Office/2016/05/Indigenous_Child%20_Poverty.pdf>.

MacDonald, N. 2016. "Canada's Prisons Are the 'New Residential Schools.'" *MacLean's* (February 18). <macleans.ca/news/canada/canadas-prisons-are-the-new-residential-schools/>.

Mackenzie, H. 2016. *Staying Power: CEO Pay in Canada*. Ottawa: Canadian Centre for Policy Alternatives.

_____. 2012. *Canada's Elite 100: The 0.01%*. Ottawa: Canadian Centre for Policy Alternatives.

MacKinnon, C. 1983. "Feminism, Marxism, Method, and the State: Toward Feminist Jurisprudence." *Signs*, 8, 4.

MacKinnon, S. 2009. "Tracking Poverty in Winnipeg's Inner City: 1996–2006." *State of the Inner City Report 2009*. Winnipeg: Canadian Centre for Policy Alternatives–Manitoba.

MacKinnon, S., Z. Salah, and S. Stephens. 2006. *Inner-City Refugee Women: Stories of Hope and Survival, Lessons for Public Policy*. Winnipeg: Canadian Centre for Policy Alternatives-Manitoba.

Maher, L., E. Dunlap, and B.D. Johnson. 2006. "Black Women's Pathways to Involvement in

Illicit Drug Distribution and Sales." In Leanne Alarid and Paul Cromwell (eds.), *In Her Own Words: Women Offenders' Views on Crime and Victimization.* Los Angeles: Roxbury.

Mahony, T. 2011. *Women in Canada: A Gender-Based Statistical Report Women and the Criminal Justice System.* Ottawa: Statistics Canada. <statcan.gc.ca/pub/89-503-x/2010001/article/11416-eng.pdf>.

Mallea, P. 2012. *Fearmonger: Stephen Harper's Tough on Crime Agenda.* Toronto: Lorimer.

Manitoba Family Services. 2015. *Manitoba Family Services Annual Report 2014–2015.* Winnipeg: Community Engagement and Corporate Services.

Martel, J. 2006. "To Be One Has to Be Somewhere: Spatio-Temporality in Prison Segregation." *British Journal of Criminology,* 46.

____. 2000. "Women in the 'Hole': The Unquestioned Practice of Segregation." In K. Hannah-Moffat and M. Shaw (eds.), *An Ideal Prison? Critical Essays on Women's Imprisonment in Canada.* Halifax: Fernwood Publishing.

Maté, G. 2008. *In the Realm of Hungry Ghosts: Close Encounters with Addiction.* Toronto: Vintage.

Maxwell, A. 2017. *Adult Criminal Court Statistics in Canada, 2014/2015.* (February 21.) Ottawa: Statistics Canada. <statcan.gc.ca/pub/85-002-x/2017001/article/14699-eng.pdf>.

Maxwell, K. 2014. "Historicizing Historical Trauma Theory: Troubling the Trans-Generational Transmission Paradigm." *Transcultural Psychiatry,* 51, 3.

McCalla, A., and V. Satzewich. 2002. "Settler Capitalism and the Construction of Immigrants and 'Indians' as Racialized Others." In W. Chan and K. Mirchandani (eds.), *Crimes of Colour: Racialization and the Criminal Justice System in Canada.* Peterborough: Broadview Press.

McCaskill, D. 2012. *Discrimination and Public Perceptions of Aboriginal People in Canadian Cities.* Ottawa: Urban Aboriginal Knowledge Network.

McGibbon, E. 2017. "Embodied Oppression: The Social Determinants of Health." In W. Antony, J. Antony, and L. Samuelson (eds.), *Power and Resistance: Critical Thinking about Canadian Social Issues* (sixth edition). Winnipeg and Halifax: Fernwood Publishing.

McKenzie, B., and C. Shangreaux. 2015. "Indigenous Child Welfare and Health Outcomes in Manitoba." In L. Fernandez, S. MacKinnon, and J. Silver (eds.), *The Social Determinants of Health in Manitoba* (second edition). Winnipeg: Canadian Centre for Policy Alternatives–Manitoba.

McLeod, J. 2000. *Beginning Postcolonialism.* New York: Palgrave.

Messerschmidt, James. 2015. *Masculinities in the Making: From the Local to the Global.* Maryland: Rowman and Littlefield.

____. 2013. *Crime as Structured Action: Gender, Race, Class, and Crime in the Making* (second edition). Thousand Oaks, CA: Sage.

____. 2005. "Men, Masculinities, and Crime." In M. Kimmel, J. Hearn and R.W. Connell (eds.), *Handbook of Studies on Men and Masculinities.* Thousand Oaks, CA: Sage.

____. 2004. *Flesh and Blood: Adolescent Gender Diversity and Violence.* Maryland: Rowman and Littlefield.

____. 1993. *Masculinities and Crime: Critique and Reconceptualization of Theory.* Maryland: Rowman and Littlefield.

Miles, R. 1989. *Racism.* Milton Keynes: Open University Press.

Miller, E. 1986. *Street Woman*. Philadelphia: Temple University Press.

Miller, J. 2001. *One of the Guys: Girls, Gangs, and Gender*. New York: Oxford University Press.

Miller, J.R. 1996. *Shingwauk's Vision: A History of Native Residential Schools*. Toronto: University of Toronto Press.

Million, D. 2013. *Therapeutic Nations: Healing in an Age of Indigenous Human Rights*. Tucson: University of Arizona Press.

Milloy, J. 1999. *A National Crime: The Canadian Government and the Residential School System, 1879 to 1986*. Winnipeg: University of Manitoba Press.

Mills, C.W. 1959. *The Sociological Imagination*. London: Oxford University Press.

Milward, D., and D. Parkes. 2014. "Colonialism, Systemic Discrimination, and the Crisis of Indigenous Over-Incarceration." In E. Comack (ed.), *Locating Law: Race/Class/Gender/ Sexuality Connections* (third edition). Winnipeg and Halifax: Fernwood Publishing.

Monture, P. 2014. "Standing Against Canadian Law: Naming Omissions of Race, Culture, and Gender." In E. Comack (ed.), *Locating Law: Race/Class/Gender/Sexuality Connections* (third edition). Winnipeg and Halifax: Fernwood Publishing.

____. 2007. "Racing and Erasing: Law and Gender in White Settler Societies." In S. Hier and S. Bolaria (eds.), *Race & Racism in 21st-Century Canada*. Peterborough: Broadview Press.

Monture-Angus, P. 1999. "Women and Risk: Aboriginal Women, Colonialism." *Canadian Woman Studies/Les Cahiers de la Femme*, 19, 2.

____. 1995. *Thunder in My Soul: A Mohawk Woman Speaks*. Halifax: Fernwood Publishing.

Moran, D. 2015. *Carceral Geography: Spaces and Practices of Incarceration*. London: Ashgate.

____. 2012. "'Doing Time' in Carceral Space: Timespace and Carceral Geography." *Geografiska Annaler: Series B, Human Geography*, 94, 4.

Moran, D., and Y. Jewkes. 2015. "Linking the Carceral and the Punitive State: A Review of Research on Prison Architecture, Design, Technology and the Lived Experience of Carceral Space." *Annales de Geographie*, 702–3.

Mosher, J. 2014. "The Construction of 'Welfare Fraud' and the Wielding of the State's Iron Fist." In E. Comack (ed.), *Locating Law: Race/Class/Gender/Sexuality Connections* (third edition). Winnipeg and Halifax: Fernwood Publishing.

Motiuk, L. 1997. "Classification for Correctional Programming: The Offender Intake Assessment (OIA) Process." *Forum on Corrections Research*, 9, 1.

Moyer, S., and M. Basic. 2004. *Pre-Trial Detention Under the Young Offenders Act: A Study of Urban Courts*. Ottawa: Department of Justice. <justice.gc.ca/eng/rp-pr/cj-jp/yj-jj/ rr04_yj1-rr04_jj1/rr04_yj1.pdf>.

Myers, N., and S. Dhillon. 2013. "The Criminal Offence of Entering Any Shoppers Drug Mart in Ontario: Criminalizing Ordinary Behaviour with Youth Bail Conditions." *Canadian Journal of Criminology and Criminal Justice*, 55, 2.

Nepinak, D. 2012. "Flood Damages about Much More than Dollars and Cents." *First Nations Voice* (May 2). <firstnationsvoice.com/index.php?action=article_details&title=Flood +damages+about+much+more+than+dollars+and+cents&id=235>.

New York Times Health Guide. 2016. "Post-Traumatic Stress Disorder." (April 18.) <nytimes. com/health/guides/disease/post-traumatic-stress-disorder/risk-factors.html>.

Ng, R. 1989. "Sexism, Racism, Nationalism." In Jesse Vorst (ed.), *Race, Class, Gender: Bonds and Barriers*. Socialist Studies/Etudes Socialistes: A Canadian Annual 5. Toronto: University of Toronto Press.

Nolan, A., and L. Stewart. 2017. "Chronic Health Conditions among Incoming Canadian Federally Sentenced Women." *Journal of Correctional Health Care*, 23, 1.

NWAC (Native Women's Association of Canada). 2010a. *What Their Stories Tell Us: Research Findings from the Sisters in Spirit Initiative*. Ottawa: NWAC. <nwac.ca/sites/default/files/imce/2010_NWAC_SIS_Report_EN.pdf>.

____. 2010b. "Fact Sheet: Missing and Murdered Aboriginal Women and Girls." Ottawa: Native Women's Association of Canada. <nwac.ca/wp-content/uploads/2015/05/Fact_Sheet_Missing_and_Murdered_Aboriginal_Women_and_Girls.pdf>.

____. 2010c. "Fact Sheet: Missing and Murdered Aboriginal Women and Girls in Manitoba." Ottawa: Native Women's Association of Canada. <nwac.ca/wp-content/uploads/2015/05/2010-Fact-Sheet-Manitoba-MMAWG.pdf>.

O'Donnell, V., and S. Wallace. 2011. "First Nations, Métis and Inuit Women." *Women in Canada: A Gender-Based Statistical Report* (sixth edition). Ottawa: Statistics Canada.

O'Keefe, Derrick. 2009. "Harper in Denial at G20: Canada Has 'No History of Colonialism.'" <rabble.ca/blogs/bloggers/derrick/2009/09/harper-denial-g20-canada-has-no-history-colonialism>.

O'Malley, P. 2010. *Crime and Risk*. London: Sage.

____. 1992. "Risk, Power and Crime Prevention." *Economy and Society*, 21, 3.

OCI (Office of the Correctional Investigator). 2015. *Administrative Segregation in Federal Corrections: 10 Year Trends*. Ottawa: The Correctional Investigator Canada. <oci-bec.gc.ca/cnt/rpt/pdf/oth-aut/oth-aut20150528-eng.pdf>.

____. 2014. *Annual Report of the Office of the Correctional Investigator, 2013–2014*. Ottawa: The Correctional Investigator Canada. <oci-bec.gc.ca/cnt/rpt/pdf/annrpt/annrpt20132014-eng.pdf>.

____. 2013. *Annual Report of the Office of the Correctional Investigator, 2012–2013*. Ottawa: The Correctional Investigator Canada. <oci-bec.gc.ca/cnt/rpt/pdf/annrpt/annrpt20122013-eng.pdf>.

Office of the Auditor General Canada. 2015. *Preparing Male Offenders for Release – Correctional Service Canada*. Ottawa: Reports of the Auditor General of Canada. Report 6. <oag-bvg.gc.ca/internet/English/parl_oag_201504_06_e_40352.html>.

Office of the Auditor General Manitoba. 2014. *Managing the Province's Adult Offenders*. (March.) <oag.mb.ca/wp-content/uploads/2014/03/Chapter-6-Managing-the-Provinces-Adult-Offenders-Web.pdf>

Ontario Ministry of Community Safety and Correctional Services. 2017. "Rates of Recidivism (Re-conviction) in Ontario." <mcscs.jus.gov.on.ca/english/Corrections/RatesRecidivism.html>.

Palmater, P. 2015. *Indigenous Nationhood: Empowering Grassroots Citizens*. Winnipeg and Halifax: Fernwood Publishing.

Paperny, A.M. 2011. "Manitoba Unveils $200-Million Relief Plan for Victims of Deliberate Flood." *Globe and Mail* (May 24). <theglobeandmail.com/news/national/manitoba-unveils-200-million-relief-plan-for-victims-of-deliberate-flood/article580852/>.

Parkes, D. 2015. "Ending the Isolation: An Introduction to the Special Volume on Human Rights and Solitary Confinement." *Canadian Journal of Human Rights*, 4, 1.

Parkes, D., and E. Cunliffe. 2015. "Women and Wrongful Convictions: Concepts and

Challenges." *International Journal of Law in Context,* 11, 3.

Parole Board of Canada. n.d. *Fact Sheet: Types of Release.* <pbc-clcc.gc.ca/infocntr/factsh/rls-eng.shtml>.

Paul, A. 2013. "'Not Fit for Human Habitation.'" *Winnipeg Free Press* (July 3). <winnipegfreepress.com/local/not-fit-for-human-habitation-214108921.html>.

Paul, D. 2006. *We Were Not the Savages.* Halifax and Winnipeg: Fernwood Publishing.

Perrault, S. 2009. "The Incarceration of Aboriginal People in Adult Correctional Services." *Juristat,* 29, 3.

Perry, A. 2016. *Aqueduct: Colonialism, Resources and the Histories We Remember.* Winnipeg: ARP Books.

Petersen, A. R. 1996. "Risk and the Regulated Self: The Discourse of Health Promotion as Politics of Uncertainty." *Australian New Zealand Journal of Sociology,* 32, 1.

Pollack, S. 2014. "Rattling Assumptions and Building Bridges: Community Engaged Education and Action in a Women's Prison." In G. Balfour and E. Comack (eds.), *Criminalizing Women: Gender and (In)justice in Neoliberal Times* (second edition). Winnipeg and Halifax: Fernwood Publishing.

____. 2010. "Labelling Clients 'Risky': Social Work and the Neo-lLiberal Welfare State." *British Journal of Social Work,* 40.

____. 2009. "'You Can't Have It Both Ways;" Punishment and Treatment of Imprisoned Women." *Journal of Progressive Human Services,* 20.

____. 2004. "Anti-Oppressive Practice with Women in Prison: Discursive Reconstructions and Alternative Practices." *British Journal of Social Work,* 34, 5.

Price, L. 2005. *Feminist Frameworks: Building Theory of Violence Against Women.* Halifax: Fernwood Publishing.

PTSD Checklist – Civilian Version (PCL – C). 1994. National Centre for PTSD, Behavioral Science Division. <mirecc.va.gov/docs/visn6/3_PTSD_CheckList_and_Scoring.pdf>.

Public Safety Canada. 2016. *Corrections and Conditional Release Statistical Overview 2015.* Ottawa. <publicsafety.gc.ca/cnt/rsrcs/pblctns/ccrso-2015/ccrso-2015-en.pdf>.

____. 2015. *Corrections and Conditional Release Statistical Overview 2014.* Ottawa. <s3.amazonaws.com/s3.documentcloud.org/documents/2110762/ps-sp-1483284-v1-corrections-and-conditional.pdf>.

Puxley, C. 2011. "Native Flood Evacuees in Constant Turmoil, Suffer 'Deep Trauma': National Chief." Canadian Press. <huffingtonpost.ca/2011/10/17/native-flood-evacuees-in-_n_1015787.html>.

R v. Gladue. 1999. 1 S.C.R. 688.

R v. Tatton. 2015. SCC 33 [2015] 2 S.C.R. 544.

Rabinow, P. 2010. "Introduction." In M. Foucault, *The Foucault Reader* (P. Rabinow, Editor). New York: Vintage Books.

Rabson, M. 2016. "Flood Plan Lacking: Audit." *Winnipeg Free Press* (May 19).

Raphael, D. 2010. *About Canada: Health and Illness.* Winnipeg and Halifax: Fernwood Publishing.

Razack, S. 2007. "When Place Becomes Race." In T. Das Gupta, C.E. James, R. Maaka, G-E. Galabuzi, and C. Andersen (eds.), *Race and Racialization: Essential Readings.* Toronto: Canadian Scholars' Press.

____ (ed.). 2002. *Race, Space and the Law: Unmapping the White Settler Society.* Toronto:

Between the Lines.

RCAP (Royal Commission on Aboriginal Peoples). 1996. *Report of the Royal Commission on Aboriginal Peoples*. Ottawa: Indian and Northern Affairs Canada. <ainc-inac.gc.ca/ch/rcap/sg/sgmm_e.html>.

RCMP (Royal Canadian Mounted Police). 2015. *Missing and Murdered Aboriginal Women: 2015 Update to the National Operational Overview*. Ottawa: Royal Canadian Mounted Police. <rcmp-grc.gc.ca/wam/media/455/original/c3561a284cfbb9c244bef57750941439.pdf>.

____ 2014. *Missing and Murdered Aboriginal Women: A National Operational Overview*. Ottawa: Royal Canadian Mounted Police. <rcmp-grc.gc.ca/wam/media/460/original/0cbd8968a049aa0b44d343e76b4a9478.pdf>.

Reiman, J., and P. Leighton. 2016. *The Rich Get Richer and the Poor Get Prison: Ideology, Class and Criminal Justice*. New York: Routledge.

Renaud, Judge G. 2016. "The Decision to Detain or Release: The Nuts and Bolts of Bail." In J.V. Roberts and M.G. Grossman (eds.), *Criminal Justice in Canada: A Reader* (fifth edition). Toronto: Nelson Education.

Resick, P., M. Bovin, A. Calloway, A. Dick, M. King, K. Mitchell, M. Suwak, S. Wells, S. Stirman, and E. Wolf. 2012. "A Critical Evaluation of the Complex PTSD Literature: Implications for DSM–5." *Journal of Traumatic Stress*, 25.

Resig, M., K. Holtfreter, and M. Morash. 2006. "Assessing Recidivism Risk across Female Pathways to Crime." *Justice Quarterly*, 32, 3.

Richie, B. 1996. *Compelled to Crime: The Gender Entrapment of Battered Black Women*. New York: Routledge.

Rios, V.M. 2011. *Punished: Policing the Lives of Black and Latino Boys*. New York and London: New York University Press.

Ristock, J. 2002. *No More Secrets: Violence in Lesbian Relationships*. London: Routledge.

Ross, R. 2014. *Indigenous Healing: Exploring Traditional Paths*. Toronto: Penguin.

Salisbury, E., and P. Van Voorhis. 2009. "Gendered Pathways: A Quantitative Investigation of Women Probationers' Paths to Incarceration." *Criminal Justice and Behavior*, 36, 6.

Schnittiker, J., M. Massoglia, and C. Uggen. 2012. "Out and Down: Incarceration and Psychiatric Disorders." *Journal of Health and Social Behavior*, 53.

Seligman, M.E.P., and S.F. Maier. 1967. "Failure to Escape Traumatic Shock." Journal of Experimental Psychology, 74, 1.

Seshia, Maya. 2005. *The Unheard Speak Out*. Winnipeg: Canadian Centre for Policy Alternatives–Manitoba.

Shantz, L., J. Kilty, and S. Frigon. 2009. "Echoes of Imprisonment: Women's Experiences of 'Successful (Re)integration.'" *Canadian Journal of Law and Society*, 24, 1.

Shaw, M., K. Rodgers, J. Blanchette, T. Hattem, L.S. Thomas, and L.Tamarack. 1991. *Survey of Federally Sentenced Women: Report of the Task Force on Federally Sentenced Women*. User Report 1991–4. Ottawa: Corrections Branch, Ministry of Solicitor General of Canada.

Shearing, C., and R. Ericson. 1991. "Culture as Figurative Action." *British Journal of Sociology*, 42, 4.

Sheehy, E. 2014. *Defending Battered Women on Trial: Lessons from the Transcripts*. Vancouver: UBC Press.

Short, J., and L. Hughes (eds.). 2006. *Studying Youth Gangs*. Walnut Creek: Alta Mira Press.

Silver, J. 2017. "Persistent Poverty: A Matter of Political Will." In W. Antony, J. Antony, and L. Samuelson (eds.), *Power and Resistance: Critical Thinking about Canadian Social Issues* (sixth edition). Winnipeg and Halifax: Fernwood Publishing.

____. 2016. *Solving Poverty: Innovative Strategies from Winnipeg's Inner City.* Winnipeg and Halifax: Fernwood Publishing.

____. 2015. "Spatially Concentrated, Racialized Poverty as a Social Determinant of Health: The Case of Winnipeg's Inner City." In L. Fernandez, S. MacKinnon, and J. Silver (eds.), *The Social Determinants of Health in Manitoba* (second edition). Winnipeg: Canadian Centre for Policy Alternatives–Manitoba.

____. 2013. *Moving Forward, Giving Back: Transformative Adult Education.* Winnipeg and Halifax: Fernwood Publishing.

____. 2011. *Good Places to Live: Poverty and Public Housing in Winnipeg.* Winnipeg and Halifax: Fernwood Publishing.

____. 2010. "Segregated City: A Century of Poverty in Winnipeg." In P. Thomas and C. Brown (eds.), *Manitoba Politics and Government.* Winnipeg: University of Manitoba Press.

____. 2006. "Building a Path to a Better Future: Urban Aboriginal People." In J. Silver (ed.), *In Their Own Voices: Building Urban Aboriginal Communities.* Halifax and Winnipeg: Fernwood Publishing.

Silver, J., P. Ghorayshi, J. Hay, and D. Klyne. 2006. "Sharing, Community and Decolonization." In J. Silver (ed.), *In Their Own Voices: Building Urban Aboriginal Communities.* Halifax and Winnipeg: Fernwood Publishing.

Sim, J. 2005. "At the Centre of the New Professional Gaze: Women, Medicine and Confinement." In W. Chan, D. Chunn, and R. Menzies (eds.), *Women, Madness and the Law: A Feminist Reader.* London: Glasshouse Press.

Skelton, I., C. Selig, and L. Deane. 2007. "CED and Social Housing Initiatives in Inner-City Winnipeg." In J. Loxley, J. Silver, and K. Sexsmith (eds.), *Doing Community Economic Development.* Halifax and Winnipeg: Fernwood Publishing.

Sleeth, P., and J. Barnsley. 1989. *Recollecting Our Lives: Women's Experience of Childhood Sexual Abuse.* Vancouver: Press Gang.

Smart, C. 1989. *Feminism and the Power of Law.* London: Routledge.

Smith, C. 2000. "'Healthy Prisons': A Contradiction in Terms?" *The Howard Journal,* 39, 4.

Snider, L. 2015. *About Canada: Corporate Crime.* Winnipeg and Halifax: Fernwood Publishing.

____. 2014. "Making Change in Neoliberal Times." In G. Balfour and E. Comack (eds.), *Criminalizing Women: Gender and (In)justice in Neoliberal Times (second edition).* Winnipeg and Halifax: Fernwood Publishing.

____. 2006. "Relocating Law: Making Corporate Crime Disappear." In E. Comack (ed.), *Locating Law: Race/Class/Gender/Sexuality Connections* (second edition). Winnipeg and Halifax: Fernwood Publishing.

Sniderman, A. S. 2012. "Aboriginal Students: An Education Underclass." *MacLean's Magazine* (August 8). <macleans.ca/news/canada/an-education-underclass/>.

Spitzer, S. 1975. "Toward a Marxian Theory of Deviance." *Social Problems,* 22, 5.

Stanko, E. 1990. *Everyday Violence: How Women and Men Experience Sexual and Physical Danger.* London: Pandora Press.

Statistics Canada. 2017. "Study: Women in Canada: Women and the Criminal Justice System." *The Daily* (June 6). <statcan.gc.ca/daily-quotidien/170606/dq170606a-eng. htm>.

____. 2011. "National Household Survey, Aboriginal Persons Based on Identity." Accessed from *Aboriginal Persons Highlights – City of Winnipeg*. <winnipeg.ca/cao/ pdfs/2011Aboriginal_Persons_Highlights_National_Household_Survey.pdf>.

____. 2008. *Aboriginal Peoples in Canada in 2006: Inuit, Métis and First Nations, 2006 Census*. <12.statcan.ca/census-recensement/2006/as-sa/97-558/pdf/97-558-XIE2006001. pdf>.

____. 1993. "The Violence Against Women Survey." *The Daily* (November 18).

Sudbury, J. 2005. "Introduction: Feminist Critiques, Transnational Landscapes, Abolitionist Visions." In J. Sudbury (ed.), *Global Lockdown: Race, Gender, and the Prison-Industrial Complex*. New York: Routledge.

Sudnow, D. 1968. "Normal Crimes: Sociological Aspects of the Penal Code." In E. Rubington and M. Weinberg (eds.), *Deviance: The Interactionist Perspective*. London: Macmillan.

Sugar, F., and L. Fox. 1989. "Nistem Peyako Seht'wawin Iskwewak: Breaking the Chains." *Canadian Journal of Women and the Law*, 3, 2.

Task Force on Federally Sentenced Women. 1990. *Creating Choices: The Task Force Report on Federally Sentenced Women*. Ottawa: Correctional Service Canada.

Taylor, L. 2011. "Teen Pregnancy Matters: Lives Are Likely to Be 'Poorer' in Every Way for Young Mothers." *Winnipeg Free Press* (March 3).

Thompson, S., M. Ballard, and D. Martin. 2014. "Lake St. Martin First Nation Community Members' Experiences of Induced Displacement: "We're like Refugees." *Refuge*, 29, 2.

TRC (Truth and Reconciliation Commission of Canada). 2015. *Final Report of the Truth and Reconciliation Commission of Canada. Volume One: Summary Honouring the Truth, Reconciling the Future*. Toronto: Lorimer.

Trestman, R.L., J. Ford, W. Zhan, and V. Westbrock. 2007. "Current and Lifetime Psychiatric Illness among Inmates Not Identified as Acutely Mentally Ill at Intake in Connecticut's Jails." *Journal of the American Academy of Psychiatry and the Law*, 35.

Ursel, J., L. Tutty, and J. Lemaistre (eds.). 2008. *What's Law Got to Do with It? The Law, Specialized Courts, and Domestic Violence in Canada*. Toronto: Cormorant Books

Van Ameringen, M., C. Mancini, B. Patterson, and M.H. Boyle. 2008. "Post-Traumatic Stress Disorder in Canada." *CNS Neuroscience & Therapeutics*, 14.

van der Kolk, B., S. Roth, D. Pelcovitz, S. Sunday, and J. Spinazzola. 2005. "Disorders of Extreme Stress: The Empirical Foundation of a Complex Adaptation to Trauma." *Journal of Traumatic Stress*, 18, 5.

van Gemert, F., D. Peterson, and I.-L. Lien (eds.). 2008. *Youth Gangs, Migration, and Ethnicity*. Devon: Willan Publishing.

Viggiani, N. 2007. "Unhealthy Prisons: Exploring Structural Determinants of Prison Health." *Sociology of Health & Illness*, 29, 1.

Wacquant, L. 2008. *Urban Outcasts: A Comparative Sociology of Advanced Marginality*. Cambridge: Polity Press.

Walby, S. 1989. "Theorizing Patriarchy." *Sociology*, 23, 2.

Waldram, J.B. 2004. *Revenge of the Windigo: The Construction of the Mind and Mental Health of North American Aboriginal Peoples*. Toronto: University of Toronto Press.

____. 1997. *The Way of the Pipe: Aboriginal Spirituality and Symbolic Healing in Canadian Prisons*. Peterborough: Broadview Press.

____. 1988. *As Long as the Rivers Run: Hydroelectric Development and Native Communities*. Winnipeg: University of Manitoba Press.

Walker, L. 1989. *Terrifying Love: Why Battered Women Kill and How Society Responds*. New York: Harper Collins.

____. 1977–78. "Battered Women and Learned Helplessness." *Victimology*, 2, 3 and 4.

Walmsley, Roy. 2015. "World Female Imprisonment List." <prisonstudies.org/sites/default/files/resources/downloads/world_female_imprisonment_list_third_edition_0.pdf>.

War Against Women. 1991. "Report of the Standing Committee on Health and Welfare, Social Affairs, Seniors and the Status of Women." (June.) Ottawa.

Webster, C., A. Doob, and N. Myers. 2009. "The Parable of Ms Baker: Understanding Pre-Trial Detention in Canada." *Current Issues in Criminal Justice*, 21, 1.

Wesley-Esquimaux, C.C., and M. Smolewski. 2004. *Historic Trauma and Aboriginal Healing*. Ottawa: Aboriginal Healing Foundation.

White, R. 2009. "Indigenous Youth and Gangs as Family." *Youth Studies Australia*, 28, 3.

Wolfe, P. 2006. "Settler Colonialism and the Elimination of the Native." *Journal of Genocide Research*, 8, 4.

Woolford, A. 2015. *This Benevolent Experiment: Indigenous Boarding Schools, Genocide, and Redress in Canada and the United States*. Winnipeg: University of Manitoba Press.

Worrall, A. 1990. *Offending Women: Female Lawbreakers and the Criminal Justice System*. New York: Routledge and Keagan Paul.

Wright, L. 2011. *The Rise of the Therapeutic Society: Psychological Knowledge and the Contradictions of Cultural Change*. Washington, DC: New Academia Publishing.

York, G. 1990. *The Dispossessed: Life and Death in Native Canada*. London: Vintage.

Zendo, S. 2015. "The Experiences of Criminalized Women when Accessing Health Care Services during Incarceration within Provincial Jails: A Critical Narrative Study." Master of Science thesis, University of Western Ontario.

INDEX